Calculus

Test Masters

Second Edition

Calculus
Second Edition

Test Masters

Copyright © 2002 by Saxon Publishers, Inc.

Printed in the United States of America.

ISBN: 1-56577-147-8

Manufacturing Code: 01S0501

Reaching us via the Internet

WWW: www.saxonpub.com

E-mail: info@saxonpub.com

Saxon Publishers, Inc.
2450 John Saxon Blvd.
Norman, OK 73071

Calculus
Test Masters

Test Solutions

About the Solutions

These solutions are designed to be representative of a student's work. Please keep in mind that many test problems will have more than one correct solution. We have attempted to stay as close as possible to the methods and procedures outlined in the textbook. The final answers have been set in bold type so that they can be easily seen for grading purposes. Below each problem number we have included a Lesson Reference Number. This number refers to the lesson in which the concepts for that problem type were taught.

TEST 1, FORM A

1. $(\cos^2 \theta)(\sec \theta)(\tan^2 \theta)(\csc \theta)$
(4)

$$= (\cos^2 \theta)\left(\frac{1}{\cos \theta}\right)\left(\frac{\sin^2 \theta}{\cos^2 \theta}\right)\left(\frac{1}{\sin \theta}\right)$$

$$= \frac{\sin \theta}{\cos \theta} = \tan \theta$$

The correct choice is **C**.

2. $27a^3 - 8b^6 = (3a)^3 - (2b^2)^3$
(1)
$$= (3a - 2b^2)(9a^2 + 6ab^2 + 4b^4)$$

The correct choice is **D**.

3. $y - 2 = 7[x - (-3)]$
(2)

$y - 2 = 7(x + 3)$

$y - 2 = 7x + 21$

$\quad y = 7x + 23$

The correct choice is **D**.

4. $\sin^2 \dfrac{\pi}{3} + \tan \dfrac{\pi}{4} = \left(\dfrac{\sqrt{3}}{2}\right)^2 + 1 = \dfrac{3}{4} + 1$
(4)

$$= \frac{7}{4}$$

5. $\displaystyle\sum_{n=0}^{5} n^2 = 0^2 + 1^2 + 2^2 + 3^2 + 4^2 + 5^2$
(1)

$$= 0 + 1 + 4 + 9 + 16 + 25$$

$$= 55$$

6. $\begin{cases} x^2 + y^2 = 4 \\ x + y = 1 \end{cases}$
(2)

Solve the second equation for y: $y = 1 - x$

Substitute into the first equation.

$$x^2 + (1 - x)^2 = 4$$
$$x^2 + 1 - 2x + x^2 = 4$$
$$2x^2 - 2x - 3 = 0$$
$$x = \frac{2 \pm \sqrt{28}}{4}$$

$x = \dfrac{1}{2} + \dfrac{\sqrt{7}}{2}$ or $x = \dfrac{1}{2} - \dfrac{\sqrt{7}}{2}$

$y = \dfrac{1}{2} - \dfrac{\sqrt{7}}{2}$ $y = \dfrac{1}{2} + \dfrac{\sqrt{7}}{2}$

$\left(\dfrac{1}{2} + \dfrac{\sqrt{7}}{2}, \dfrac{1}{2} - \dfrac{\sqrt{7}}{2}\right)$ and $\left(\dfrac{1}{2} - \dfrac{\sqrt{7}}{2}, \dfrac{1}{2} + \dfrac{\sqrt{7}}{2}\right)$

7. $\dfrac{50!}{46!\,4!} = \dfrac{50(49)(48)(47)(\cancel{46!})}{\cancel{46!}\,(4!)} = \dfrac{50(49)(48)(47)}{4(3)(2)(1)}$
(1)

$= 50(49)(2)(47) = 100(49)(47) = 100(2303)$

$= \mathbf{230,300}$

8. Contrapositive: **If $ab \neq 4$, then $a + b \neq 5$.**
(3)

Converse: **If $ab = 4$, then $a + b = 5$.**

Inverse: **If $a + b \neq 5$, then $ab \neq 4$.**

9. $\dfrac{1}{1 + \dfrac{1}{1 + \dfrac{1}{2}}} = \dfrac{1}{1 + \dfrac{1}{\dfrac{3}{2}}} = \dfrac{1}{1 + \dfrac{2}{3}} = \dfrac{1}{\dfrac{5}{3}} = \dfrac{3}{5}$
(1)

10. $3y = 2x - 3$
(2)
$$y = \frac{2}{3}x - 1$$

The slope of a line parallel to this one is $\dfrac{2}{3}$.

$y - 3 = \dfrac{2}{3}(x - 5)$

$y - 3 = \dfrac{2}{3}x - \dfrac{10}{3}$

$\quad y = \dfrac{2}{3}x - \dfrac{1}{3}$

11. The roots of $ax^2 + bx + c = 0$ are
(2)
$$x = \frac{-b \pm \sqrt{b^2 - 4ac}}{2a}.$$

12. (a) $\begin{cases} y = x^2 - 4x + 1 \\ y = x - 3 \end{cases}$
(2)

Substitute for y in the first equation.

$$x - 3 = x^2 - 4x + 1$$
$$0 = x^2 - 5x + 4$$
$$0 = (x - 4)(x - 1)$$

$x = 4$ or $x = 1$

$y = 1$ $y = -2$

The intersection points are **(4, 1)** and **(1, –2)**.

(b) The distance between $(4, 1)$ and $(1, -2)$ is

$$D = \sqrt{(4 - 1)^2 + (1 + 2)^2}$$
$$= \sqrt{9 + 9} = \sqrt{18} = \mathbf{3\sqrt{2}}$$

TEST 1, FORM B

1.
(4)
$(\sin^2 \theta)(\sec \theta)(\cot^2 \theta)(\csc \theta)$

$= (\sin^2 \theta)\left(\dfrac{1}{\cos \theta}\right)\left(\dfrac{\cos^2 \theta}{\sin^2 \theta}\right)\left(\dfrac{1}{\sin \theta}\right)$

$= \dfrac{\cos \theta}{\sin \theta} = \cot \theta$

The correct choice is **D**.

2.
(1)
$m^6 x^3 + n^3 y^9$

$= (m^2 x)^3 + (n y^3)^3$

$= (\boldsymbol{m^2 x + n y^3})(\boldsymbol{m^4 x^2 - m^2 x n y^3 + n^2 y^6})$

The correct choice is **B**.

3.
(2)
$y - 2 = 5(x - 3)$

$y - 2 = 5x - 15$

$\boldsymbol{y = 5x - 13}$

The correct choice is **B**.

4.
(4)
$\cos^2 \dfrac{\pi}{3} + \tan \dfrac{\pi}{4} = \left(\dfrac{1}{2}\right)^2 + 1 = \dfrac{1}{4} + 1 = \dfrac{5}{4}$

5.
(1)
$\displaystyle\sum_{n=0}^{5} n^3 = 0^3 + 1^3 + 2^3 + 3^3 + 4^3 + 5^3$

$= 0 + 1 + 8 + 27 + 64 + 125$

$= 225$

6.
(2)
$\begin{cases} x^2 + y^2 = 9 \\ x - y = 1 \end{cases}$

Solve the second equation for y: $y = x - 1$
Substitute into the first equation.

$x^2 + (x - 1)^2 = 9$

$x^2 + x^2 - 2x + 1 = 9$

$2x^2 - 2x - 8 = 0$

$x^2 - x - 4 = 0$

$x = \dfrac{1 \pm \sqrt{17}}{2}$

$x = \dfrac{1}{2} + \dfrac{\sqrt{17}}{2} \qquad \text{or} \qquad x = \dfrac{1}{2} - \dfrac{\sqrt{17}}{2}$

$y = -\dfrac{1}{2} + \dfrac{\sqrt{17}}{2} \qquad\qquad y = -\dfrac{1}{2} - \dfrac{\sqrt{17}}{2}$

$\left(\dfrac{1}{2} + \dfrac{\sqrt{17}}{2}, -\dfrac{1}{2} + \dfrac{\sqrt{17}}{2}\right)$ and

$\left(\dfrac{1}{2} - \dfrac{\sqrt{17}}{2}, -\dfrac{1}{2} - \dfrac{\sqrt{17}}{2}\right)$

7.
(1)
$\dfrac{106!}{104! \, 2!} = \dfrac{106(105)(\cancel{104!})}{\cancel{104!} \, 2!} = \dfrac{106(105)}{2(1)} = 5565$

8.
(3)
Contrapositive: If $a + b \neq 5$, then $ab \neq 4$.

Converse: If $a + b = 5$, then $ab = 4$.

Inverse: If $ab \neq 4$, then $a + b \neq 5$.

9.
(1)
$\dfrac{1}{1 + \dfrac{1}{1 + \dfrac{1}{1 + \dfrac{1}{3}}}} = \dfrac{1}{1 + \dfrac{1}{1 + \dfrac{1}{\dfrac{4}{3}}}} = \dfrac{1}{1 + \dfrac{1}{1 + \dfrac{3}{4}}} = \dfrac{1}{\dfrac{7}{4}} = \dfrac{4}{7}$

10.
(2)
$3y = 2x - 3$

$y = \dfrac{2}{3}x - 1$

The slope of a line perpendicular to this one is $-\dfrac{3}{2}$.

$y - 3 = -\dfrac{3}{2}(x + 1)$

$y - 3 = -\dfrac{3}{2}x - \dfrac{3}{2}$

$y = -\dfrac{3}{2}x + \dfrac{3}{2}$

11.
(2)
The roots of $ax^2 + bx + c = 0$ are

$x = \dfrac{-b \pm \sqrt{b^2 - 4ac}}{2a}.$

12.
(2)
(a)

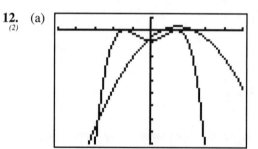

There are two intersection points,
(−0.146, −3.916) and **(−2.828, −35.960)**.

(b) The distance between the two points is:

$\sqrt{(-0.146 + 2.828)^2 + (-3.916 + 35.960)^2}$

$\approx \boldsymbol{32.156}$

TEST 2, FORM A

1.
(7)
The graph is $y = 2^x$ reflected in both the x-axis and the y-axis, so $y = -2^{-x}$.

The correct choice is **B**.

2.
(6) The points $(0, 1)$, $(0, 2)$, and $(0, 3)$ lie on a vertical line and thus cannot be points on the graph of a function.

The correct choice is **D.**

3.
(7) $P = (x, y) = \left(\cos \dfrac{3\pi}{4}, \sin \dfrac{3\pi}{4} \right) = \left(-\dfrac{\sqrt{2}}{2}, \dfrac{\sqrt{2}}{2} \right)$

The correct choice is **B.**

4.
(4) $\cot \dfrac{7\pi}{6} \sin -\dfrac{4\pi}{3} = \left(\dfrac{\sqrt{3}}{1} \right)\left(\dfrac{\sqrt{3}}{2} \right) = \dfrac{3}{2}$

5.
(8)
$$\dfrac{4}{L} = \dfrac{5}{x + L}$$
$$4(x + L) = 5L$$
$$4x + 4L = 5L$$
$$4x = L$$
$$x = \dfrac{L}{4}$$

6.
(5)

$$2x + s = 300$$
$$2x = 300 - s$$
$$x = 150 - \dfrac{s}{2}$$

$$A = sx$$
$$A = s\left(150 - \dfrac{s}{2} \right)$$
$$A = 150s - \dfrac{s^2}{2}$$

7.
(5) $R = an + b$, where R = revenue,

$\qquad\qquad\qquad\qquad\quad n$ = number of bikes sold

$\quad 850 = a(10) + b$

$1180 = a(16) + b$

Subtraction yields $-330 = -6a$, or $a = 55$.

Then $850 = 55(10) + b$, or $b = 300$.

So $R = 55n + 300$.

To find the number of bikes that must be sold for a revenue of \$2060, solve

$$2060 = 55n + 300$$
$$1760 = 55n$$
$$n = \textbf{32 bikes}$$

8.
(6) $\dfrac{f(x + h) - f(x)}{h} = \dfrac{-2(x + h) + 3 - (-2x + 3)}{h}$

$\qquad = \dfrac{-2x - 2h + 3 + 2x - 3}{h} = \dfrac{-2h}{h} = \textbf{-2}$

9.
(2)
$$x^2 + 2x - 1 = x^2 - 5$$
$$2x - 1 = -5$$
$$2x = -4$$
$$x = -2$$

The point of intersection is **$(-2, -1)$.**

10.
(6)
$$x + 3 \geq 0$$
$$x \geq -3$$

Domain: $\{x \in \mathbb{R} \mid x \geq -3\}$

Range: $\{y \in \mathbb{R} \mid y \geq 0\}$

11.
(7) $y = 7 + 4 \cos\left(x - \dfrac{\pi}{4} \right)$

Amplitude: **4**

Period: **2π**

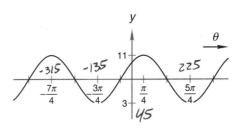

12.
(8)
$$\sin^2 \theta + \cos^2 \theta = 1$$
$$\dfrac{\sin^2 \theta + \cos^2 \theta}{\cos^2 \theta} = \dfrac{1}{\cos^2 \theta}$$
$$\dfrac{\sin^2 \theta}{\cos^2 \theta} + \dfrac{\cos^2 \theta}{\cos^2 \theta} = \dfrac{1}{\cos^2 \theta}$$
$$\textbf{tan}^2\, \boldsymbol{\theta} + \textbf{1} = \textbf{sec}^2\, \boldsymbol{\theta}$$

TEST 2, FORM B

1.
(7) The graph is $y = 2^x$ reflected in the x-axis, so $\boldsymbol{y = -2^x}$.

The correct choice is **D.**

2.
(6) The points $(0, 1)$ and $(0, 3)$ lie on a vertical line and thus cannot both be points on the graph of a function.

The correct choice is **B.**

3.
(7)
$$P = (x, y) = \left(\cos -\frac{3\pi}{4}, \sin -\frac{3\pi}{4} \right)$$

$$= \left(-\frac{\sqrt{2}}{2}, -\frac{\sqrt{2}}{2} \right)$$

The correct choice is **C.**

4.
(4)
$$\cos -\frac{2\pi}{3} \cot \frac{2\pi}{3} = \left(-\frac{1}{2} \right)\left(-\frac{1}{\sqrt{3}} \right) = \frac{1}{2\sqrt{3}}$$

$$= \frac{\sqrt{3}}{6}$$

5.
(8)
$$\frac{x}{L} = \frac{5}{L + 2}$$

$$x = \frac{5L}{L + 2}$$

6.
(5)

$$2x + s = 450$$

$$2x = 450 - s$$

$$x = 225 - \frac{s}{2}$$

$$A = sx$$

$$A = s\left(225 - \frac{s}{2} \right)$$

$$A = 225s - \frac{s^2}{2}$$

7.
(5)
$R = an + b$, where $R =$ revenue,

$\qquad\qquad\qquad n =$ number of bikes sold

$$810 = a(9) + b$$

$$1655 = a(22) + b$$

Subtraction yields $-845 = -13a$, or $a = 65$.

Then $810 = 65(9) + b$, or $b = 225$.

So $R = 65n + 225$.

To find the number of bikes that must be sold for a revenue of $2500, solve

$$2500 = 65n + 225$$

$$2275 = 65n$$

$$n = \textbf{35 bikes}$$

8.
(6)
$$\frac{f(x + h) - f(x)}{h} = \frac{\dfrac{2}{x + h} - \dfrac{2}{x}}{h}$$

$$= \frac{\dfrac{2x - 2(x + h)}{x(x + h)}}{h} = \frac{2x - 2x - 2h}{x(x + h)h}$$

$$= \frac{-2\cancel{h}}{x(x + h)\cancel{h}} = \frac{-2}{x(x + h)}$$

9.
(2)

10.
(6)

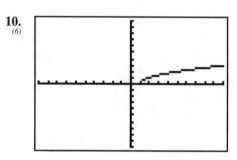

$$x - 1 \geq 0$$

$$x \geq 1$$

Domain: $\{x \in \mathbb{R} \mid x \geq 1\}$

Range: $\{y \in \mathbb{R} \mid y \geq 0\}$

11.
(7)
$$y = 3 + 5 \sin\left(x - \frac{\pi}{4} \right)$$

Amplitude: **5**

Period: $\mathbf{2\pi}$

12.
(8)

$$\sin^2 \theta + \cos^2 \theta = 1$$

$$\frac{\sin^2 \theta + \cos^2 \theta}{\sin^2 \theta} = \frac{1}{\sin^2 \theta}$$

$$\frac{\sin^2 \theta}{\sin^2 \theta} + \frac{\cos^2 \theta}{\sin^2 \theta} = \frac{1}{\sin^2 \theta}$$

$$1 + \cot^2 \theta = \csc^2 \theta$$

TEST 3, FORM A

1.
(6)

$$x^2 - 1 \geq 0$$

$$x^2 \geq 1$$

$$x \leq -1 \text{ or } x \geq 1$$

Domain: $\{x \in \mathbb{R} \mid x \leq -1 \text{ or } x \geq 1\}$

The correct choice is **C**.

2.
(11)

As x approaches 3 from the right, the value of $f(x)$ approaches 5, so $\lim\limits_{x \to 3^+} f(x) = \mathbf{5}$.

The correct choice is **C**.

3.
(10)

Possible rational roots of $x^3 - 7x - 6 = 0$:

$$\frac{\text{Factors of } -6}{\text{Factors of } 1} = \frac{\pm 1, \pm 2, \pm 3, \pm 6}{\pm 1}$$

$$= \pm 1, \pm 2, \pm 3, \pm 6$$

The correct choice is **D**.

4.
(9)

5.
(9)

6.
(5)

Let l = length of the rectangle, w = width of the rectangle, and s = length of a side of the square. The three facts given lead to three equations.

$$\begin{cases} lw = 12s^2 \\ w = 3s \\ 2l + 2w = 30 + 4s \end{cases}$$

Use the first two equations to find l in terms of s.

$$l(3s) = 12s^2$$

$$l = 4s$$

Substitute for l and w in the third equation.

$$2(4s) + 2(3s) = 30 + 4s$$

$$8s + 6s = 30 + 4s$$

$$10s = 30$$

$$s = \mathbf{3 \text{ units}}$$

$$l = 4(3) = \mathbf{12 \text{ units}}$$

$$w = 3(3) = \mathbf{9 \text{ units}}$$

7.
(10)

The value of $f(c)$ is equal to the remainder when a polynomial $f(x)$ is divided by $x - c$.

(a)

$-2\rfloor$	1	-1	0	2	-4	3
		-2	6	-12	20	-32
	1	-3	6	-10	16	$\boxed{-29}$

$$f(-2) = \mathbf{-29}$$

(b)

$1\rfloor$	1	-1	0	2	-4	3
		1	0	0	2	-2
	1	0	0	2	-2	$\boxed{1}$

$$f(1) = \mathbf{1}$$

(c)

$-1\rfloor$	1	-1	0	2	-4	3
		-1	2	-2	0	4
	1	-2	2	0	-4	$\boxed{7}$

$$f(-1) = \mathbf{7}$$

8.
(9)

$$\log_x (8 - 2x) = 2$$

$$8 - 2x = x^2$$

$$x^2 + 2x - 8 = 0$$

$$(x - 2)(x + 4) = 0$$

$$x = 2 \text{ or } -4$$

Logarithms are not defined for negative bases, so the only solution is $x = \mathbf{2}$.

9.
(10)

$$f(x) = k(x - 3)(x + 4)$$

$$6 = k(0 - 3)(0 + 4)$$

$$6 = k(-12)$$

$$-\frac{1}{2} = k$$

$$f(x) = -\frac{1}{2}(x - 3)(x + 4)$$

$$f(x) = -\frac{1}{2}(x^2 + x - 12)$$

$$f(x) = -\frac{1}{2}x^2 - \frac{1}{2}x + 6$$

10. $\tan 15° = \tan(45° - 30°)$
(12)

$$= \frac{\tan(45°) - \tan(30°)}{1 + \tan(45°)\tan(30°)} = \frac{1 - \dfrac{1}{\sqrt{3}}}{1 + 1\left(\dfrac{1}{\sqrt{3}}\right)}$$

$$= \frac{\sqrt{3} - 1}{\sqrt{3} + 1}\left(\frac{\sqrt{3} - 1}{\sqrt{3} - 1}\right) = \frac{3 - 2\sqrt{3} + 1}{3 - 1}$$

$$= \mathbf{2 - \sqrt{3}}$$

11. $f(x) = x^3 + x^2 - x + 1$
(10)
$f(2) = 2^3 + 2^2 - 2 + 1 = 11$

The remainder when $x^3 + x^2 - x + 1$ is divided by $x - 2$ is **11**.

12. $\sin(A + B) = \sin A \cos B + \cos A \sin B$
(12)
$\qquad \sin(2t) = \sin t \cos t + \cos t \sin t$

$\qquad \mathbf{\sin(2t) = 2 \sin t \cos t}$

TEST 3, FORM B

1. $x^2 - 2x + 1 \geq 0$
(6)
$\qquad (x - 1)^2 \geq 0$

This is true for any real number x.

Domain: $\mathbb{R}$

The correct choice is **D**.

2. As x approaches 3 from the left, the value of $f(x)$
(11) approaches -1, so $\lim\limits_{x \to 3^-} f(x) = \mathbf{-1}$.

The correct choice is **B**.

3. Possible rational roots of $x^4 - 5x^3 + 8 = 0$:
(10)
$$\frac{\text{Factors of 8}}{\text{Factors of 1}} = \frac{\pm 1, \pm 2, \pm 4, \pm 8}{\pm 1}$$

$$= \mathbf{\pm 1, \pm 2, \pm 4, \pm 8}$$

The correct choice is **B**.

4.
(9)

5.
(9)

6. Let l = length of the rectangle, w = width of the
(5) rectangle, and s = length of a side of the square. The three facts given lead to three equations.

$$\begin{cases} lw = 10s^2 \\ w = 2s \\ 2l + 2w = 50 + 4s \end{cases}$$

Use the first two equations to find l in terms of s.

$$l(2s) = 10s^2$$
$$l = 5s$$

Substitute for l and w in the third equation.

$$2(5s) + 2(2s) = 50 + 4s$$
$$10s + 4s = 50 + 4s$$
$$10s = 50$$
$$s = \mathbf{5 \text{ units}}$$

$l = 5(5) = \mathbf{25 \text{ units}}$

$w = 2(5) = \mathbf{10 \text{ units}}$

7. Define $\texttt{Y1=0.1X\^{}5-}\pi\texttt{X3+(1/2)X2}$
(10) $\texttt{-}\sqrt{\texttt{(2)X+1}}$ and use the $\texttt{value}$ feature from the $\texttt{CALCULATE}$ menu.

(a) $f(\sqrt{31}) \approx \mathbf{1.447}$

(b) $f\left(-\dfrac{\pi}{4}\right) \approx \mathbf{3.911}$

(c) $f(e) \approx \mathbf{-47.409}$

8. $\log_x(x + 9) = 2$
(9)
$\qquad x + 9 = x^2$

$x^2 - x - 9 = 0$

Using the TI-83 to find the zeros, $x \approx 3.5414$ or $x \approx -2.5414$.

Logarithms are not defined for negative bases, so the only solution is $x \approx \mathbf{3.5414}$.

9. $f(x) = k(x - 5)(x + 1)$
(10)
$\quad -8 = k(0 - 5)(0 + 1)$

$\quad -8 = k(-5)$

$\quad \dfrac{8}{5} = k$

$f(x) = \dfrac{8}{5}(x - 5)(x + 1)$

$f(x) = \dfrac{8}{5}(x^2 - 4x - 5)$

$f(x) = \dfrac{8}{5}x^2 - \dfrac{32}{5}x - 8$

10. $\tan 75° = \tan (45° + 30°)$
(12)

$$= \frac{\tan (45°) + \tan (30°)}{1 - \tan (45°) \tan (30°)} = \frac{1 + \dfrac{1}{\sqrt{3}}}{1 - 1\left(\dfrac{1}{\sqrt{3}}\right)}$$

$$= \frac{\sqrt{3} + 1}{\sqrt{3} - 1}\left(\frac{\sqrt{3} + 1}{\sqrt{3} + 1}\right) = \frac{3 + 2\sqrt{3} + 1}{3 - 1}$$

$$= \mathbf{2 + \sqrt{3}}$$

11. $f(x) = x^3 - x^2 + x + 1$
(10)

$f(-2) = (-2)^3 - (-2)^2 + (-2) + 1 = -13$

The remainder when $x^3 - x^2 + x + 1$ is divided by $x + 2$ is **–13.**

12. $\cos (A + B) = \cos A \cos B - \sin A \sin B$
(12)

$\cos (2t) = \cos t \cos t - \sin t \sin t$

$\mathbf{\cos (2t) = \cos^2 t - \sin^2 t}$

Other possible formulas are $\mathbf{\cos (2t) = 1 - 2\sin^2 t}$ and $\mathbf{\cos (2t) = 2\cos^2 t - 1.}$

TEST 4, FORM A

1. $\displaystyle\lim_{x \to 3} \frac{x - 3}{x^2 - x - 6} = \lim_{x \to 3} \frac{x - 3}{(x - 3)(x + 2)}$
(14)

$$= \lim_{x \to 3} \frac{1}{x + 2} = \frac{1}{5}$$

The correct choice is **A.**

2. $x + 2 > 0$
(6)

$x > -2$

Domain: $\{x \in \mathbb{R} \mid x > -2\}$

The correct choice is **B.**

3. $\sin^2 \theta + \cos^2 \theta = 1$
(12)

$\sin^2 \theta + \left(\dfrac{1}{4}\right)^2 = 1$

$\sin^2 \theta = 1 - \dfrac{1}{16}$

$\sin^2 \theta = \dfrac{15}{16}$

$\cos (2\theta) = \cos^2 \theta - \sin^2 \theta$

$= \left(\dfrac{1}{4}\right)^2 - \dfrac{15}{16}$

$= -\dfrac{14}{16} = -\dfrac{7}{8}$

The correct choice is **D.**

4.
(15)

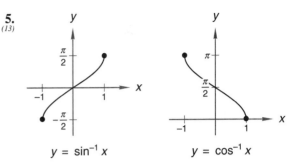

The correct choice is **D.**

5.
(13)

$y = \sin^{-1} x$ $y = \cos^{-1} x$

$y = \tan^{-1} x$

6. $\begin{cases} L + M = 503 \\ L = 2M - 19 \end{cases}$
(5)

$(2M - 19) + M = 503$

$3M = 522$

$M = \mathbf{174}$

$L = 2(174) - 19 = \mathbf{329}$

7. $\displaystyle\lim_{h \to 0} \frac{f(x + h) - f(x)}{h}$
(14)

$$= \lim_{h \to 0} \frac{[5(x + h)^2 + 7] - (5x^2 + 7)}{h}$$

$$= \lim_{h \to 0} \frac{5(x^2 + 2xh + h^2) + 7 - 5x^2 - 7}{h}$$

$$= \lim_{h \to 0} \frac{5x^2 + 10xh + 5h^2 + 7 - 5x^2 - 7}{h}$$

$$= \lim_{h \to 0} \frac{10xh + 5h^2}{h} = \lim_{h \to 0} (10x + 5h) = \mathbf{10x}$$

8. $25^{3x - 2} = 5^{2x}$
(16)

$25^{3x - 2} = 25^x$

$3x - 2 = x$

$2x = 2$

$x = 1$

9.
(16)

(a) $\log (2^3 7^5) = \log (2^3) + \log (7^5)$

$= 3 \log 2 + 5 \log 7$

(b) $\ln \dfrac{x^4}{y^8} = \ln (x^4) - \ln (y^8) = 4 \ln x - 8 \ln y$

10.
(9)

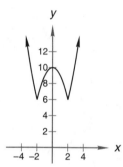

11.
(13)

$\sin^2 x + 2 \cos x - 2 = 0$

$(1 - \cos^2 x) + 2 \cos x - 2 = 0$

$-\cos^2 x + 2 \cos x - 1 = 0$

$\cos^2 x - 2 \cos x + 1 = 0$

$(\cos x - 1)^2 = 0$

$\cos x - 1 = 0$

$\cos x = 1$

$x = \mathbf{0}$

12. Shift the graph of $y = |x^2 - 4|$ up 6 units.
(9)

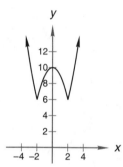

TEST 4, FORM B

1.
(14)

$\lim\limits_{x \to 5} \dfrac{x + 6}{x^2 - 4x + 7} = \dfrac{5 + 6}{25 - 20 + 7} = \dfrac{11}{12}$

$\approx \mathbf{0.917}$

The correct choice is **C**.

2.
(6)

$x - 3 > 0$

$x > 3$

Domain: $\{x \in \mathbb{R} \mid x > 3\}$

The correct choice is **D**.

3.
(12)

$\sin^2 \theta + \cos^2 \theta = 1$

$\left(\dfrac{1}{3}\right)^2 + \cos^2 \theta = 1$

$\cos^2 \theta = \dfrac{8}{9}$

$\cos \theta = \dfrac{2\sqrt{2}}{3}$

$\sin (2\theta) = 2 \sin \theta \cos \theta$

$= 2\left(\dfrac{1}{3}\right)\left(\dfrac{2\sqrt{2}}{3}\right)$

$= \dfrac{4\sqrt{2}}{9}$

The correct choice is **C**.

4.
(15)

The correct choice is **C**.

5.
(13)

$y = \sin^{-1} x$

$y = \cos^{-1} x$

$y = \tan^{-1} x$

6.
(5)

$\begin{cases} L + M = 643 \\ L = 4M + 8 \end{cases}$

$(4M + 8) + M = 643$

$5M = 635$

$M = \mathbf{127}$

$L = 4(127) + 8 = \mathbf{516}$

7. $f(x) = 4x^2 - 9$
(14)

$\lim\limits_{h \to 0} \dfrac{f(x + h) - f(x)}{h}$

$= \lim\limits_{h \to 0} \dfrac{[4(x + h)^2 - 9] - (4x^2 - 9)}{h}$

$= \lim\limits_{h \to 0} \dfrac{4(x^2 + 2xh + h^2) - 9 - 4x^2 + 9}{h}$

$= \lim\limits_{h \to 0} \dfrac{4x^2 + 8xh + 4h^2 - 9 - 4x^2 + 9}{h}$

$= \lim\limits_{h \to 0} \dfrac{8xh + 4h^2}{h} = \lim\limits_{h \to 0} (8x + 4h) = \mathbf{8x}$

8. Graph $Y_1=7^\wedge(3X-2)$ and $Y_2=13^\wedge(X+1)$
(16) with $Xmin=0$, $Xmax=3$, $Xscl=1$, $Ymin=-800$, $Ymax=300$, and $Yscl=100$. Then use `intersect` in the CALCULATE menu.

Intersection
X=1.9728694 Y=2049.3121

$x \approx \mathbf{1.973}$

9. (a) $\ln(x^5 y^6) = \ln(x^5) + \ln(y^6)$
(16) $\qquad = \mathbf{5\ln x + 6\ln y}$

    (b) $\log \dfrac{3^2}{5^7} = \log(3^2) - \log(5^7)$
$\qquad = \mathbf{2\log 3 - 7\log 5}$

10.
(9)
2.0   2.5   3.0   3.5   4.0

11. $\qquad \cos^2 x + 2\sin x - 2 = 0$
(13) $\qquad (1 - \sin^2 x) + 2\sin x - 2 = 0$
$\qquad -\sin^2 x + 2\sin x - 1 = 0$
$\qquad \sin^2 x - 2\sin x + 1 = 0$
$\qquad (\sin x - 1)^2 = 0$
$\qquad \sin x - 1 = 0$
$\qquad \sin x = 1$
$\qquad x = \dfrac{\pi}{2}$

12. Shift the graph of $y = |x^2 - 5|$ up 3 units.
(9)

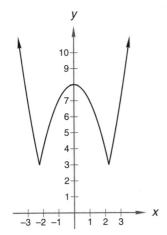

1. $\displaystyle\lim_{x\to 2} \frac{x+7}{x^2+5x-14} = \lim_{x\to 2} \frac{x+7}{(x+7)(x-2)}$
(17)
$$= \lim_{x\to 2} \frac{1}{x-2}$$

The left-hand limit is $-\infty$ and the right-hand limit is $+\infty$, so **the limit does not exist.**

The correct choice is **D.**

2. $\qquad \sin x = \cos x$
(13)
$\qquad \dfrac{\sin x}{\cos x} = 1$

$\qquad \tan x = 1$

$\qquad x = \dfrac{\pi}{4}, \dfrac{5\pi}{4}$

The correct choice is **C.**

3. One double-angle identity for the cosine function is
(12) $\cos(2x) = \cos^2 x - \sin^2 x$, so choice A is eliminated. This can be rewritten $\cos(2x) = \cos^2 x - (1 - \cos^2 x) = 2\cos^2 x - 1$, so choice B is eliminated. Similarly, $\cos(2x) = (1 - \sin^2 x) - \sin^2 x = 1 - 2\sin^2 x$, which is the negative of choice C. Checking choice D, $\cot(2x)\sin(2x) = \frac{\cos(2x)}{\sin(2x)}\sin(2x) = \cos(2x)$.

The correct choice is **C.**

4. $\displaystyle\lim_{x\to\infty} \frac{-x^5 + 14x^3 - 2}{6x^4 + 10x^2 - 1} = \lim_{x\to\infty} \frac{-x + \dfrac{14}{x} - \dfrac{2}{x^4}}{6 + \dfrac{10}{x^2} - \dfrac{1}{x^4}}$
(17)
$$= -\infty$$

The correct choice is **D.**

5. By the change-of-base formula, $\log_7 20 = \frac{\log_{10} 20}{\log_{10} 7}$.
(20)
The correct choice is **C.**

6. $I = \dfrac{k}{d^2}$, where $I =$ intensity, $d =$ distance
(5)

$15 = \dfrac{k}{5^2}$

$k = 25(15) = 375$

$I = \dfrac{375}{d^2} = \dfrac{375}{10^2} = \dfrac{375}{100} = \mathbf{3.75}$

7.
(16)
$$-3 \log 2 - \log (x + 1) = -\log \left(\frac{1}{3} \right)$$

$$\log (2^{-3}) - \log (x + 1) = \log \left(\frac{1}{3} \right)^{-1}$$

$$\log \left(\frac{2^{-3}}{x + 1} \right) = \log 3$$

$$\frac{2^{-3}}{x + 1} = 3$$

$$\frac{2^{-3}}{3} = x + 1$$

$$\frac{1}{24} = x + 1$$

$$-\frac{23}{24} = x$$

8.
(18)
$$(f \circ g)(x) = f(g(x)) = f(x - 1)$$
$$= (x - 1)^2 + 2(x - 1)$$
$$= x^2 - 2x + 1 + 2x - 2 = \mathbf{x^2 - 1}$$

$$(g \circ f)(x) = g(f(x)) = g(x^2 + 2x)$$
$$= \mathbf{x^2 + 2x - 1}$$

9.
(15)
$$y = x^2 + 7x - 30$$
$$y = \left(x + \frac{7}{2} \right)^2 - \frac{169}{4}$$

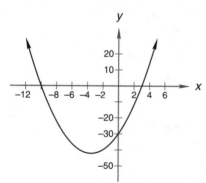

The vertex occurs at $x = -\frac{7}{2}$, so the function is decreasing over the interval $\left(-\infty, -\frac{7}{2} \right)$.

10.
(13)

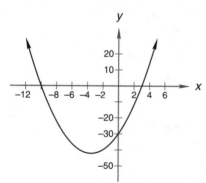

$$\cos^{-1} -\frac{1}{2} = \frac{2\pi}{3}$$

11.
(18)
$$\frac{f}{g}(x) = \frac{x^3 + 1}{\sqrt{x^2 - 16}}$$

$$x^2 - 16 > 0$$
$$x^2 > 16$$
$$x < -4 \text{ or } x > 4$$

Domain: $\{x \in \mathbb{R} \mid x < -4 \text{ or } x > 4\}$

12.
(19)
$$\frac{dy}{dx} = \lim_{\Delta x \to 0} \frac{3(x + \Delta x)^2 - 3x^2}{\Delta x}$$

$$= \lim_{\Delta x \to 0} \frac{3(x^2 + 2x(\Delta x) + (\Delta x)^2) - 3x^2}{\Delta x}$$

$$= \lim_{\Delta x \to 0} \frac{3x^2 + 6x(\Delta x) + 3(\Delta x)^2 - 3x^2}{\Delta x}$$

$$= \lim_{\Delta x \to 0} \frac{6x(\Delta x) + 3(\Delta x)^2}{\Delta x}$$

$$= \lim_{\Delta x \to 0} (6x + 3\Delta x)$$

$$= \mathbf{6x}$$

TEST 5, FORM B

1.
(17)
$$\lim_{x \to 3} \frac{2}{2x^2 - 12x + 18} = \lim_{x \to 3} \frac{1}{x^2 - 6x + 9}$$
$$= \lim_{x \to 3} \frac{1}{(x - 3)^2}$$

Since the denominator is squared, the left-hand and the right-hand limits are both $+\infty$, so the limit is $+\infty$.

The correct choice is **C**.

2.
(13)
$$\sin x = -\cos x$$

$$\frac{\sin x}{\cos x} = -1$$

$$\tan x = -1$$

$$x = \frac{3\pi}{4}, \frac{7\pi}{4}$$

The correct choice is **B**.

3.
(19)
Entering `nDeriv(2^X,X,1.75)` gives the result `2.331460104`.

The correct choice is **C**.

4.
(17)
$$\lim_{x \to \infty} \frac{x^5 - 14x^3 + 2}{6x^4 + 10x^2 - 1} = \lim_{x \to \infty} \frac{x - \frac{14}{x} + \frac{2}{x^4}}{6 + \frac{10}{x^2} - \frac{1}{x^4}}$$

$$= \infty$$

The correct choice is **C**.

5. By the change-of-base formula,
(20)

$$\log_3 17 = \frac{\log 17}{\log 3} \approx 2.5789$$

The correct choice is **D.**

6. $I = \dfrac{k}{d^2}$, where $I =$ intensity, $d =$ distance.
(5)

$$27 = \frac{k}{4^2}$$

$$k = 27(16)$$

$$k = 432$$

$$I = \frac{432}{d^2} = \frac{432}{11^2} = \frac{432}{121} \approx 3.57$$

7. $\dfrac{x^2}{16} + \dfrac{y^2}{25} = 1$
(20)

$$\frac{y^2}{25} = 1 - \frac{x^2}{16}$$

$$y^2 = 25\left(1 - \frac{x^2}{16}\right)$$

$$y = \pm\sqrt{25\left(1 - \frac{x^2}{16}\right)}$$

The two functions to graph are
Y₁=√(25(1−(X²/16))) and
Y₂=−√(25(1−(X²/16))) or Y₂=⁻Y₁.

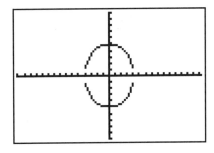

8. $(f \circ g)(x) = f(g(x))$
(18)
$$= f(x + 4) = (x + 4)^2 - 3(x + 4)$$
$$= x^2 + 8x + 16 - 3x - 12$$
$$= x^2 + 5x + 4$$
$$(g \circ f)(x) = g(f(x)) = g(x^2 - 3x)$$
$$= x^2 - 3x + 4$$

9. $y = |x^2 - 16|$
(15)

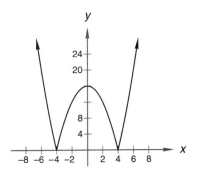

The function is decreasing over the intervals
$(-\infty, -4)$ and $(0, 4)$.

10.
(13)

sin$^{-1} - \dfrac{1}{2} = -\dfrac{\pi}{6}$

11. $\dfrac{g}{f}(x) = \dfrac{x^3 - 27}{\sqrt{x^2 - 4}}$
(18)

$$x^2 - 4 > 0$$
$$x^2 > 4$$
$$x < -2 \text{ or } x > 2$$

Domain: $\{x \in \mathbb{R} \mid x < -2 \text{ or } x > 2\}$

12. $\dfrac{dy}{dx} = \lim\limits_{\Delta x \to 0} \dfrac{\dfrac{3}{x + \Delta x} - \dfrac{3}{x}}{\Delta x}$
(19)

$$= \lim_{\Delta x \to 0} \frac{3x - 3x - 3\Delta x}{x(x + \Delta x)\Delta x}$$

$$= \lim_{\Delta x \to 0} \frac{-3\Delta x}{x(x + \Delta x)\Delta x}$$

$$= \lim_{\Delta x \to 0} \frac{-3}{x(x + \Delta x)}$$

$$= -\frac{3}{x^2}$$

TEST 6, FORM A

1.
(22) The coefficient of x^5y^3 in the expansion of $(x + 4y)^8$ is

$$\frac{8!}{5!\,3!}(1)^5(4)^3 = \frac{8 \cdot 7 \cdot 6}{3 \cdot 2 \cdot 1}(64) = (56)(64) = \mathbf{3584}$$

The correct choice is **C**.

2.
(21)
$$y = (x - 5)^2 - 3$$
$$y = x^2 - 10x + 22$$

The correct choice is **B**.

3.
(21) The graph of $y = \frac{1}{(x + 3)^2}$ is a "volcano" at $x = -3$.

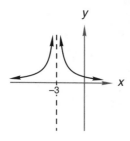

The correct choice is **B**.

4.
(17)
$$\lim_{x \to \infty} \frac{3x^2}{5x^3 - 4x + 1} = \lim_{x \to \infty} \frac{\dfrac{3}{x}}{5 - \dfrac{4}{x^2} + \dfrac{1}{x^3}}$$

$$= \frac{0}{5 - 0 + 0} = \mathbf{0}$$

The correct choice is **C**.

5.
(2)
$$x^2 - 20x + 14 = 0$$

By the quadratic formula,

$$x = \frac{+20 \pm \sqrt{400 - 56}}{2}$$

$$x = \frac{20 \pm \sqrt{344}}{2}$$

$$x = 10 \pm \sqrt{86}$$

The x-intercepts are $\mathbf{10 - \sqrt{86}}$ and $\mathbf{10 + \sqrt{86}}$.

6.
(23) Since θ is between 0 and 2π, 3θ is between 0 and 6π.

$$\sin(3\theta) = -\frac{1}{2}$$

$$3\theta = \frac{7\pi}{6}, \frac{11\pi}{6}, \frac{19\pi}{6}, \frac{23\pi}{6}, \frac{31\pi}{6}, \frac{35\pi}{6}$$

$$\theta = \frac{7\pi}{18}, \frac{11\pi}{18}, \frac{19\pi}{18}, \frac{23\pi}{18}, \frac{31\pi}{18}, \frac{35\pi}{18}$$

7.
(2) Solve for the distance between $(5, 6)$ and (x, x^3).

$$d = \sqrt{(x - 5)^2 + (x^3 - 6)^2}$$

8.
(8)
$$(1 - \sin^2 x)\sec^2 x - \cos^2 x$$

$$= (\cos^2 x)\frac{1}{\cos^2 x} - \cos^2 x = 1 - \cos^2 x$$

$$= \sin^2 x$$

9.
(24)
$$f(x) = \frac{1}{\sqrt[4]{x^3}} = x^{-3/4}$$

$$f'(x) = -\frac{3}{4}x^{-7/4}$$

10.
(22)
$$4x^2 + 9y^2 + 16x - 54y + 61 = 0$$
$$4(x^2 + 4x + 4) + 9(y^2 - 6y + 9)$$
$$= -61 + 16 + 81$$
$$4(x + 2)^2 + 9(y - 3)^2 = 36$$
$$\frac{(x + 2)^2}{9} + \frac{(y - 3)^2}{4} = 1$$

This is the equation of an **ellipse**.

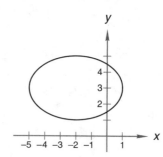

11.
(18) (a) $(f \circ g)(x) = (\sqrt{x})^2 = x$

The domain of $f \circ g$ is $\{x \in \mathbb{R} \mid x \geq 0\}$ since the inputs of g must be positive or zero.

(b) $(g \circ f)(x) = \sqrt{x^2} = |x|$

The domain of $g \circ f$ is $\mathbb{R}$, since the inputs of f can be any real number and the outputs of f will always be positive or zero.

12.
(19)
$$f'(x) = \lim_{\Delta x \to 0} \frac{f(x + \Delta x) - f(x)}{\Delta x}$$

$$= \lim_{\Delta x \to 0} \frac{8(x + \Delta x) - 5 - (8x - 5)}{\Delta x}$$

$$= \lim_{\Delta x \to 0} \frac{8x + 8\Delta x - 5 - 8x + 5}{\Delta x}$$

$$= \lim_{\Delta x \to 0} \frac{8\Delta x}{\Delta x} = \mathbf{8}$$

TEST 6, FORM B

1. The coefficient of $x^{10}y^5$ in the expansion of
(22)
$(2x - y)^{15}$ is

$$\tfrac{15!}{10!\,5!}(2)^{10}(-1)^5 = 3003(1024)(-1) = -3,075,072.$$

The correct choice is **D.**

2. $y = (x + 5)^2 + 3$
(21)
$y = x^2 + 10x + 28$

The correct choice is **D.**

3. The graph of $y = \frac{-1}{(x-3)^2}$ is an "upside-down
(21) volcano" at $x = 3$.

The correct choice is **D.**

4. $\displaystyle\lim_{x\to\infty} \frac{-3x^4}{5x^3 + 4x + 1} = \lim_{x\to\infty} \frac{-3x}{5 + \dfrac{4}{x^2} + \dfrac{1}{x^3}}$
(17)

$= -\infty$

The correct choice is **A.**

5.
(2)

The only real zero is $x \approx$ **19.2959.**

6. Since θ is between 0 and 2π, 3θ is between 0 and 6π.
(23)

$\tan(3\theta) = -1$

$$3\theta = \frac{3\pi}{4}, \frac{7\pi}{4}, \frac{11\pi}{4}, \frac{15\pi}{4}, \frac{19\pi}{4}, \frac{23\pi}{4}$$

$$\theta = \frac{3\pi}{12}, \frac{7\pi}{12}, \frac{11\pi}{12}, \frac{15\pi}{12}, \frac{19\pi}{12}, \frac{23\pi}{12}$$

7. Solve for the distance between $(1, 4)$ and (x, x^4).
(2)

$$d = \sqrt{(x - 1)^2 + (x^4 - 4)^2}$$

8. $(1 - \cos^2 x)\csc^2 x - \sin^2 x$
(8)

$= (\sin^2 x)\dfrac{1}{\sin^2 x} - \sin^2 x = 1 - \sin^2 x = \cos^2 x$

9. $f(x) = \dfrac{1}{\sqrt[3]{x^2}} = x^{-2/3}$
(24)

$f'(x) = -\dfrac{2}{3}x^{-5/3}$

10. $4x^2 - 9y^2 + 16x + 54y - 101 = 0$
(23)
$4(x^2 + 4x + 4) - 9(y^2 - 6y + 9)$
$= 101 + 16 - 81$

$4(x + 2)^2 - 9(y - 3)^2 = 36$

$$\frac{(x + 2)^2}{9} - \frac{(y - 3)^2}{4} = 1$$

This is the equation of a **hyperbola.**

$$\frac{(y - 3)^2}{4} = \frac{(x + 2)^2}{9} - 1$$

$$(y - 3) = \pm\sqrt{\frac{4}{9}(x + 2)^2 - 4}$$

$$y_1 = 3 + \sqrt{\frac{4}{9}(x + 2)^2 - 4}$$

$$y_2 = 3 - \sqrt{\frac{4}{9}(x + 2)^2 - 4}$$

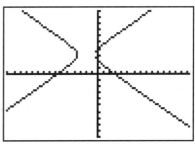

11. (a) $(f \circ g)(x) = e^{\ln x} = x$
(18)
The domain of $f \circ g$ is $\{x \in \mathbb{R} \mid x > 0\}$
since the inputs of g must be positive.

(b) The domain of $g \circ f$ is $\mathbb{R},$ since the inputs of
f can be any real number and the outputs of f
will always be positive.

12. $f'(x) = \displaystyle\lim_{\Delta x\to0} \dfrac{f(x + \Delta x) - f(x)}{\Delta x}$
(19)

$= \displaystyle\lim_{\Delta x\to0} \dfrac{16(x + \Delta x) + 7 - (16x + 7)}{\Delta x}$

$= \displaystyle\lim_{\Delta x\to0} \dfrac{16x + 16\Delta x + 7 - 16x - 7}{\Delta x}$

$= \displaystyle\lim_{\Delta x\to0} \dfrac{16\Delta x}{\Delta x} = \mathbf{16}$

TEST 7, FORM A

1.
(27)
$$y = x^{1/3}$$

$$\frac{dy}{dx} = \frac{1}{3}x^{-2/3} = \frac{1}{3x^{2/3}}$$

$$\left.\frac{dy}{dx}\right|_8 = \frac{1}{3(8)^{2/3}} = \frac{1}{3(4)} = \frac{1}{12}$$

The correct choice is **B.**

2.
(28)
$$\lim_{h \to 0} \frac{\ln(2+h) - \ln 2}{h} = f'(2) \text{ for } f(x) = \ln x$$

Since $f'(x) = \frac{1}{x},\ f'(2) = \frac{1}{2}.$

The correct choice is **B.**

3.
(27)
$$f(x) = \cos x$$
$$f'(x) = -\sin x$$
$$f''(x) = -\cos x$$
$$f'''(x) = -(-\sin x) = \sin x$$
$$f'''\left(\frac{\pi}{6}\right) = \sin\frac{\pi}{6} = \frac{1}{2}$$

The correct choice is **D.**

4.
(26)
$$y = 2x^{-3} + 3e^x + 4\cos x$$

$$\frac{dy}{dx} = -6x^{-4} + 3e^x - 4\sin x$$

The correct choice is **C.**

5.
(11)
$$\lim_{x \to -3^+} \frac{x^2 + x - 6}{x^3 + 3x^2}$$

$$= \lim_{x \to -3^+} \frac{(x+3)(x-2)}{x^2(x+3)}$$

$$= \lim_{x \to -3^+} \frac{x-2}{x^2} = -\frac{5}{9}$$

The correct choice is **A.**

6. $A(t) = 2000e^{kt}$
(26)
On the first, $t = 0$, so on the twenty-first, $t = 20$, and on the thirty-first, $t = 30$.

$$A(20) = 2000e^{k(20)}$$
$$500 = 2000e^{20k}$$
$$\frac{1}{4} = e^{20k}$$
$$\ln\frac{1}{4} = 20k$$
$$k = -\frac{\ln 4}{20}$$

$$A(t) = 2000e^{-(\ln 4)t/20}$$
$$A(30) = 2000e^{-(\ln 4)(30)/20}$$
$$A(30) = 2000e^{\ln\left(4^{-3/2}\right)}$$
$$A(30) = 2000\left(\frac{1}{8}\right)$$
$$A(30) = \mathbf{\$250}$$

7.
(21)
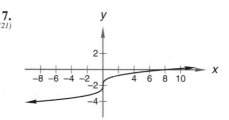

8. $\cos(2x) = 1 - 2\sin^2 x$
(12)
$$\frac{1}{4} = 1 - 2\sin^2 x$$
$$2\sin^2 x = \frac{3}{4}$$
$$\sin^2 x = \frac{3}{8}$$

9.
(28)

Not to scale

10.
(16)
$$\log(x-4) = 2\log 2 + \log(x-3) - \log x$$
$$\log(x-4) = \log(2^2) + \log\frac{x-3}{x}$$
$$\log(x-4) = \log\frac{4(x-3)}{x}$$
$$x - 4 = \frac{4x - 12}{x}$$
$$x^2 - 4x = 4x - 12$$
$$x^2 - 8x + 12 = 0$$
$$(x-2)(x-6) = 0$$
$$x = 2, 6$$

But $x = 2$ is not in the domain of $\log(x-2)$. Thus $x = \mathbf{6}.$

11.
(10)

$$f(7) = q(7)(7 - 7) - 17$$
$$= q(7)(0) - 17$$
$$= 0 - 17$$
$$= \mathbf{-17}$$

12.
(19)

$$\frac{d}{dx}\sqrt{x} = \lim_{\Delta x \to 0} \frac{\sqrt{x + \Delta x} - \sqrt{x}}{\Delta x}$$

$$= \lim_{\Delta x \to 0} \frac{x + \Delta x - x}{\Delta x(\sqrt{x + \Delta x} + \sqrt{x})}$$

$$= \lim_{\Delta x \to 0} \frac{1}{(\sqrt{x + \Delta x} + \sqrt{x})} = \frac{1}{\sqrt{x + 0} + \sqrt{x}}$$

$$= \frac{1}{\mathbf{2\sqrt{x}}}$$

TEST 7, FORM B

1.
(27)
Entering `nDeriv(4sin(X),X,11π/32)` yields **1.885586633.**

The correct choice is **C.**

2.
(28)
$$\lim_{h \to 0} \frac{e^{2+h} - e^2}{h} = f'(2) \text{ for } f(x) = e^x$$

Since $f'(x) = e^x$, $f'(2) = e^2$.

The correct choice is **A.**

3.
(27)
$$f(x) = \sin x$$
$$f'(x) = \cos x$$
$$f''(x) = -\sin x$$
$$f'''(x) = -\cos x$$
$$f'''\left(\frac{\pi}{6}\right) = -\cos \frac{\pi}{6} = -\frac{\sqrt{3}}{2}$$

The correct choice is **B.**

4.
(26)
$$y = -2x^{-4} + 6e^x - 5 \sin x$$
$$\frac{dy}{dx} = \mathbf{8x^{-5} + 6e^x - 5 \cos x}$$

The correct choice is **B.**

5.
(11)
$$\lim_{x \to -5^-} \frac{x^2 + 4x - 5}{x^4 + 5x^3}$$

$$= \lim_{x \to -5^-} \frac{(x + 5)(x - 1)}{x^3(x + 5)}$$

$$= \lim_{x \to -5^-} \frac{x - 1}{x^3} = \frac{6}{125} = \mathbf{0.048}$$

The correct choice is **C.**

6.
(26)
$$A(t) = 3000e^{kt}$$

On the first, $t = 0$, so on the eighteenth, $t = 17$, and on the thirtieth, $t = 29$.

$$A(17) = 3000e^{k(17)}$$
$$200 = 3000e^{17k}$$
$$\frac{1}{15} = e^{17k}$$
$$\ln \frac{1}{15} = 17k$$
$$k = -\frac{\ln 15}{17}$$
$$A(t) = 3000e^{-(\ln 15)t/17}$$
$$A(29) = 3000e^{-(\ln 15)(29)/17}$$
$$A(29) \approx \mathbf{\$29.57}$$

7.
(21)

8.
(12)
$$\cos(2x) = 2\cos^2 x - 1$$
$$-\frac{1}{6} = 2\cos^2 x - 1$$
$$\frac{5}{6} = 2\cos^2 x$$
$$\frac{5}{12} = \cos^2 x$$

9.
(28)

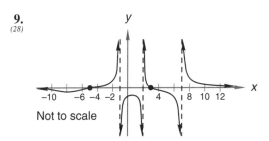

Not to scale

10.
(16)
$$2 \ln 2 - 2 \ln (x + 2) = \ln (x - 5)$$
$$\ln (2^2) - \ln (x + 2)^2 = \ln (x - 5)$$
$$\ln \frac{4}{(x + 2)^2} = \ln (x - 5)$$
$$\frac{4}{(x + 2)^2} = x - 5$$
$$(x + 2)^2(x - 5) - 4 = 0$$

Using a TI-83 to find the zeros, $x \approx \mathbf{5.0798.}$

11. $f(4) = q(4)(4 - 4) + 29$
(10)
$\qquad = q(4)(0) + 29$
$\qquad = 0 + 29$
$\qquad = \mathbf{29}$

12. $\dfrac{d}{dx}(x^{-2}) = \lim\limits_{h \to 0} \dfrac{(x + h)^{-2} - x^{-2}}{h}$
(24)

$\qquad = \lim\limits_{h \to 0} \dfrac{\dfrac{1}{(x + h)^2} - \dfrac{1}{x^2}}{h} = \lim\limits_{h \to 0} \dfrac{x^2 - (x + h)^2}{hx^2(x + h)^2}$

$\qquad = \lim\limits_{h \to 0} \dfrac{x^2 - x^2 - 2hx - h^2}{hx^2(x + h)^2}$

$\qquad = \lim\limits_{h \to 0} \dfrac{-2x - h}{x^2(x + h)^2} = \dfrac{-2x}{x^4} = \mathbf{-2x^{-3}}$

TEST 8, FORM A

1. $y = x^4 + 7$
(27)
$y' = 4x^3$
$y' = 4(3)^3$
$y' = 108$

$y = x^4 + 7$
$y = 3^4 + 7$
$y = 88$

$y - 88 = 108(x - 3)$
$y - 88 = 108x - 324$
$\qquad \mathbf{y = 108x - 236}$

The correct choice is **B.**

2. $(f \circ g)(-4) = f(g(-4))$
(18)
$\qquad\qquad\quad = f(\sqrt{-4})$

Since $\sqrt{-4}$ is undefined, **the value does not exist.**

The correct choice is **D.**

3. $f(x) = \dfrac{x^3 - 3x^2 + 2x}{x^4 + x^3 - 6x^2} = \dfrac{x(x^2 - 3x + 2)}{x^2(x^2 + x - 6)}$
(28)

$\qquad = \dfrac{x(x - 2)(x - 1)}{x^2(x + 3)(x - 2)} = \dfrac{x - 1}{x(x + 3)}$

Vertical asymptotes occur at $x = 0$ and $x = -3$.

The correct choice is **B.**

4. $\displaystyle\int 7x^6 \, dx = x^7 + C$
(32)

The correct choice is **D.**

5. $y = x^3 \ln x$
(31)

$dy = x^3\left(\dfrac{1}{x}\right) dx + (\ln x)(3x^2) \, dx$

$dy = (x^2 + 3x^2 \ln x) \, dx$

The correct choice is **D.**

6.
(5)

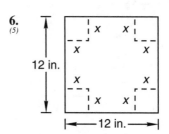

$V = $ (length)(width)(height)
$V = (12 - 2x)(12 - 2x)x$
$\mathbf{V = x(12 - 2x)^2}$

7. $\cos (A - B) = \cos A \cos B + \sin A \sin B$
(12)

$\qquad\qquad = \left(\dfrac{\sqrt{3}}{2}\right)\left(\dfrac{\sqrt{15}}{4}\right) + \left(\dfrac{1}{2}\right)\left(\dfrac{1}{4}\right)$

$\qquad\qquad = \dfrac{\sqrt{45}}{8} + \dfrac{1}{8} = \dfrac{3\sqrt{5} + 1}{8}$

8. $f(x) = e^x(x^3 + 7x^2 + 1)$
(31)
$f'(x) = e^x(3x^2 + 14x) + (x^3 + 7x^2 + 1)e^x$
$f'(x) = e^x(x^3 + 10x^2 + 14x + 1)$
$f''(x) = e^x(3x^2 + 20x + 14)$
$\qquad\qquad + (x^3 + 10x^2 + 14x + 1)e^x$
$\mathbf{f''(x) = e^x(x^3 + 13x^2 + 34x + 15)}$

9. Since the coefficients of x^2 and y^2 have opposite
(22) signs, the conic section is a **hyperbola.**

$x^2 - y^2 + 2y - 5 = 0$
$x^2 - (y^2 - 2y + 1) = 5 - 1$
$\dfrac{x^2}{4} - \dfrac{(y - 1)^2}{4} = 1$

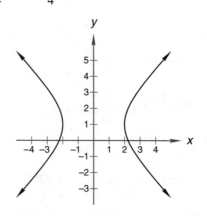

10. csc $x = 2$
(13)

$$\frac{1}{\sin x} = 2$$

$$\sin x = \frac{1}{2}$$

$$x = \frac{\pi}{6}, \frac{5\pi}{6}$$

11. (a) The zeros of f are $x = 3, 7$. There are **no**
(30)   **asymptotes** of f.

(b) The vertical asymptotes of $\frac{1}{f}$ occur at the zeros
of f, so they are $x = 3$ and $x = 7$.

The horizontal asymptote of $\frac{1}{f}$ is $y = 0$.

There are **no zeros** of $\frac{1}{f}$.

12.
(30)

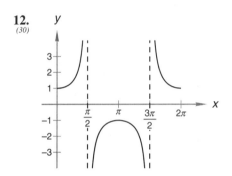

TEST 8, FORM B

1. $y = x^7 - 76$
(27)

$y' = 7x^6$

$y' = 7(2)^6$

$y' = 448$

$y = x^7 - 76$

$y = 2^7 - 76$

$y = 52$

$y - 52 = 448(x - 2)$

$y - 52 = 448x - 896$

$\mathbf{y = 448x - 844}$

The correct choice is **D.**

2. $(g \circ f)(-4) = g(f(-4)) = g((-4)^{10} + 2(-4))$
(18)
$$= g(1{,}048{,}568) = \sqrt{\mathbf{1{,}048{,}568}}$$

The correct choice is **B.**

3. $f(x) = \dfrac{x^3 - 3x^2 + 2x}{x^4 + x^3 - 6x^2} = \dfrac{x(x^2 - 3x + 2)}{x^2(x^2 + x - 6)}$
(28)
$$= \dfrac{x(x - 2)(x - 1)}{x^2(x + 3)(x - 2)} = \dfrac{x - 1}{x(x + 3)}$$

The only zero occurs at $x = \mathbf{1}$.

The correct choice is **A.**

4. $\displaystyle\int 5x^4 \, dx = x^5 + C$
(32)

The correct choice is **C.**

5. $y = x^2 e^x$
(31)
$dy = (x^2 e^x + 2xe^x) \, dx$

The correct choice is **A.**

6.
(5)

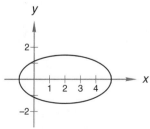

9 in.

14 in.

$V = (\text{length})(\text{width})(\text{height})$
$= (14 - 2x)(9 - 2x)x$

7. $\sin(A - B) = \sin A \cos B - \cos A \sin B$
(12)
$$= \left(\frac{4}{5}\right)\left(\frac{1}{2}\right) - \left(\frac{3}{5}\right)\left(\frac{\sqrt{3}}{2}\right)$$
$$= \frac{4}{10} - \frac{3\sqrt{3}}{10} = \frac{4 - 3\sqrt{3}}{10}$$

8. $f(x) = e^x(x^4 - 3x^3 + 4)$
(31)
$f'(x) = e^x(4x^3 - 9x^2) + (x^4 - 3x^3 + 4)e^x$
$f'(x) = e^x(x^4 + x^3 - 9x^2 + 4)$

$f''(x) = e^x(4x^3 + 3x^2 - 18x)$
$\qquad\quad + (x^4 + x^3 - 9x^2 + 4)e^x$
$f''(x) = e^x(x^4 + 5x^3 - 6x^2 - 18x + 4)$

9. Since the coefficients of x^2 and y^2 are unequal but
(23) both positive, the conic section is an **ellipse.**

$$x^2 - 4x + 4y^2 - 5 = 0$$
$$(x^2 - 4x + 4) + 4y^2 = 5 + 4$$
$$\frac{(x - 2)^2}{9} + \frac{y^2}{\frac{9}{4}} = 1$$

10. $\sec x = 2$
(13)

$$\frac{1}{\cos x} = 2$$

$$\cos x = \frac{1}{2}$$

$$x = \frac{\pi}{3}, \frac{5\pi}{3}$$

11. (a) The zeros of f are $x = $ **0, 2, and 6.** There is a
(30)   vertical asymptote of f at $x = $ **−4.**

(b) The vertical asymptotes of $\frac{1}{f}$ occur at the zeros
   of f, so they are $x = $ **0,** $x = $ **2,** and $x = $ **6.**

   There is a zero of $\frac{1}{f}$ at $x = $ **−4.**

12.
(30)

TEST 9, FORM A

1. $\int 3 \sin t \, dt = -3 \cos t + C$
(35)

The correct choice is **C.**

2. Since the leading term is $-2x^3$, the graph must go up
(33) on the left-hand end and down on the right-hand end.

The correct choice is **B.**

3. $\int 2x^3 \, dx = 2\left(\frac{x^4}{4}\right) + C = \frac{1}{2}x^4 + C$
(35)

The correct choice is **D.**

4. $y = \frac{1}{4}x^4 + 2x^3 + 4x^2$
(36)

$$y' = x^3 + 6x^2 + 8x$$

$$0 = x^3 + 6x^2 + 8x$$

$$0 = x(x^2 + 6x + 8)$$

$$0 = x(x + 4)(x + 2)$$

$$x = -4, -2, 0$$

The correct choice is **A.**

5. $\lim\limits_{t \to \infty} \dfrac{5t^2 + 8t + 1}{2 - 6t - 3t^2} = \lim\limits_{t \to \infty} \dfrac{5 + \dfrac{8}{t} + \dfrac{1}{t^2}}{\dfrac{2}{t^2} - \dfrac{6}{t} - 3} = -\dfrac{5}{3}$
(17)

The correct choice is **C.**

6. $y = x^4 + 4x^3 - 20x^2 + 21$
(36)

$$y' = 4x^3 + 12x^2 - 40x$$

$$0 = 4x^3 + 12x^2 - 40x$$

$$0 = 4x(x^2 + 3x - 10)$$

$$0 = x(x + 5)(x - 2)$$

$$x = -5, 0, 2$$

Since the leading term is x^4, the graph of y must go up at both ends. Since y has 3 critical numbers, its graph must have one of these shapes:

Whichever of these shapes is correct, $x = $ **−5 is a local minimum,** $x = $ **0 is a local maximum,** and $x = $ **2 is a local minimum.**

7. $y^3 + 7y = e^x$
(34)

$$3y^2 \, dy + 7 \, dy = e^x \, dx$$

$$3y^2 \frac{dy}{dx} + 7 \frac{dy}{dx} = e^x$$

$$\frac{dy}{dx}(3y^2 + 7) = e^x$$

$$\frac{dy}{dx} = \frac{e^x}{3y^2 + 7}$$

$$\frac{dy}{dx} = \frac{y^3 + 7y}{3y^2 + 7}$$

8.
(31)
$f(x) = x \cos x$
$f'(x) = x(-\sin x) + (\cos x)(1)$
$f'(x) = -x \sin x + \cos x$
$f'(0) = 0 + \cos 0$
$f'(0) = \mathbf{1}$

9. This is an **ellipse,** since the coefficients of x^2 and y^2
(22) have the same sign but are unequal.

$$x^2 + 4y^2 + 4x - 24y + 36 = 0$$
$$(x^2 + 4x + 4) + 4(y^2 - 6y + 9) = 4$$
$$\frac{(x + 2)^2}{4} + \frac{(y - 3)^2}{1} = 1$$

10. $\log_b 121 = 2$
(9)
$$b^2 = 121$$
$$b = \pm 11$$

The base of a logarithm must be positive, so $b = \mathbf{11}.$

11. The graph of $y = x(x - 1)(x + 1)(x - 2)^2$ must
(33) cross the x-axis at -1, 0, and 1, and must touch but not cross the x-axis at 2.

12. (a) Since the degree of the polynomial is odd, the
(33) "ends" of the graph must go in opposite directions. Since the coefficient of the x^3 term is positive, **the end on the left goes down to $-\infty$, while the end on the right goes up to $+\infty$.**

(b) The degree of this polynomial is even, so both ends must go in the same direction. Since the coefficient of the x^6 term is positive, **both ends go up to $+\infty$.**

TEST 9, FORM B

1. $\int 3 \cos t \, dt = \mathbf{3 \sin t + C}$
(35)
The correct choice is **B.**

2. Since the leading term is $5x^4$, the graph of y must go
(33) up on both ends.
The correct choice is **C.**

3. $\int 5\sqrt{t} \, dt = 5\left(\frac{2}{3}t^{3/2}\right) + C = \frac{10}{3}t^{3/2} + C$
(35)
The correct choice is **D.**

4. $y = 5x^{2/3} + x^{5/3}$
(36)
$$y' = \frac{10}{3}x^{-1/3} + \frac{5}{3}x^{2/3}$$
$$y' = \frac{5}{3}x^{-1/3}(2 + x)$$
$$y' = \frac{5(2 + x)}{x^{1/3}}$$
The value of y' is 0 when $x = -2$, and y' is undefined when $x = 0$. Thus the critical numbers are -2 **and 0.**
The correct choice is **A.**

5. $\lim_{t \to \infty} \frac{4t^3 - 7t^2 + 1}{8t^4 + 21} = \lim_{t \to \infty} \frac{\frac{4}{t} - \frac{7}{t^2} + \frac{1}{t^4}}{8 + \frac{21}{t^4}}$
(17)
$$= \frac{0}{8} = \mathbf{0}$$
The correct choice is **B.**

6. $y = x^4 + 4x^3 - 2x^2 - 12x + 4$
(36)
$$y' = 4x^3 + 12x^2 - 4x - 12$$
$$0 = 4x^3 + 12x^2 - 4x - 12$$
$$0 = x^3 + 3x^2 - x - 3$$
$$0 = x^2(x + 3) - (x + 3)$$
$$0 = (x^2 - 1)(x + 3)$$
$$x = -3, -1, +1$$

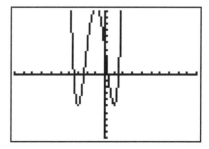

Thus $x = -3$ is a local minimum, $x = -1$ is a local maximum, and $x = 1$ is a local minimum.

7.
(34)
$$2xy + y^2 = \sin x$$
$$2x\,dy + 2y\,dx + 2y\,dy = \cos x\,dx$$
$$2x\frac{dy}{dx} + 2y + 2y\frac{dy}{dx} = \cos x$$
$$(2x + 2y)\frac{dy}{dx} = \cos x - 2y$$
$$\frac{dy}{dx} = \frac{\cos x - 2y}{2x + 2y}$$

8. nDeriv(Xcos(X),X,-1) yields **−0.3012**
(27) for the slope of the tangent line.

9. This is a **hyperbola,** since the coefficients of x^2 and
(23) y^2 have different signs.
$$x^2 + 4x - y^2 + 2y = 0$$
$$x^2 + 4x - (y^2 - 2y) = 0$$
$$x^2 + 4x + 4 - (y^2 - 2y + 1) = 4 - 1$$
$$(x + 2)^2 - (y - 1)^2 = 3$$
$$(x + 2)^2 - 3 = (y - 1)^2$$
$$\pm\sqrt{(x + 2)^2 - 3} = y - 1$$
$$1 \pm \sqrt{(x + 2)^2 - 3} = y$$

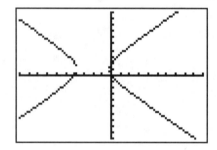

10. $\log_7 9 = \dfrac{\ln 9}{\ln 7} \approx \mathbf{1.129}$
(20)

11. zeros: $x = 0, -1$
(28)
asymptotes: $x = 1,\ x = 2,\ x = 3,\ y = 0$

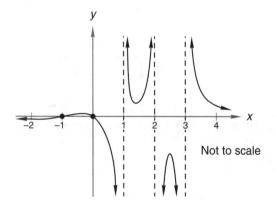

Not to scale

12. (a) Since the degree of the polynomial is even, the
(33) "ends" of the graph must go in the same direction.
Since the coefficient of the leading term is
negative, **both ends will go down to −∞.**

(b) The degree of this polynomial is odd, so the
ends of the graph go in opposite directions.
Since the coefficient of the leading term is
negative, **the end on the left-hand side goes
up to +∞, while the end on the right-hand
side goes down to −∞.**

TEST 10, FORM A

1. $\displaystyle\int (5\cos x - 6x - \sqrt{x} + 7)$
(38)
$$= 5\int \cos x\,dx - 3\int 2x\,dx - \int x^{1/2}\,dx + 7\int dx$$
$$= \mathbf{5\sin x - 3x^2 - \frac{2}{3}x^{3/2} + 7x + C}$$

The correct choice is **C.**

2. $y = \cos^3 x$
(37)
$\quad y = u^3,$ where $u = \cos x$
$$du = -\sin x\,dx$$
$$dy = 3u^2\,du$$
$$dy = 3\cos^2 x\,(-\sin x\,dx)$$
$$\frac{dy}{dx} = \mathbf{-3\cos^2 x \sin x}$$

The correct choice is **B.**

3. $s(t) = 8t^2 + \ln t$
(40)
$$v(t) = s'(t) = 16t + \frac{1}{t}$$
$$v(1) = 16(1) + \frac{1}{(1)} = \mathbf{17\ \frac{m}{s}}$$

The correct choice is **C.**

4. $f(x) = x^3 + 5\ln|x|$
(27)
$$f'(x) = 3x^2 + \frac{5}{x}$$
$$f''(x) = 6x - \frac{5}{x^2}$$
$$f''(2) = 6(2) - \frac{5}{2^2}$$
$$f''(2) = \mathbf{10.75}$$

The correct choice is **D.**

5.
(38)
$$\int f(x)\, dx = \int \frac{7}{x}\, dx = 7 \ln |x| + C$$

The correct choice is **B**.

6.
(40)
$$y = 3 \sin (2x)$$

$$\frac{dy}{dx} = 6 \cos (2x)$$

$$\left.\frac{dy}{dx}\right|_{\pi/8} = 6 \cos \frac{\pi}{4}$$

$$\left.\frac{dy}{dx}\right|_{\pi/8} = 3\sqrt{2}$$

The slope of the normal line is $-\dfrac{1}{3\sqrt{2}}$.

$$y = 3 \sin (2x)$$

$$y = 3 \sin\left[2\left(\frac{\pi}{4}\right)\right]$$

$$y = \frac{3\sqrt{2}}{2}$$

$$y - \frac{3\sqrt{2}}{2} = -\frac{1}{3\sqrt{2}}\left(x - \frac{\pi}{8}\right)$$

7.
(8)
$$(\tan^2 \theta + 1)(1 - \cos^2 \theta) = (\sec^2 \theta)(\sin^2 \theta)$$

$$= \frac{\sin^2 \theta}{\cos^2 \theta} = \tan^2 \theta$$

8.
(36)
$$f(x) = x^2 e^x$$
$$f'(x) = x^2 e^x + e^x(2x)$$
$$0 = (x^2 + 2x)e^x$$
$$0 = x(x + 2)e^x$$
$$x = 0, -2$$

9.
(34)
$$A = 4\pi r^2$$
$$dA = 4\pi(2r\, dr)$$
$$\frac{dA}{dt} = 8\pi r \frac{dr}{dt}$$

10.
(14)
$$\lim_{x \to 2} \frac{x^2 + 6x - 16}{x^2 - 2x} = \lim_{x \to 2} \frac{(x + 8)(x - 2)}{x(x - 2)}$$

$$= \lim_{x \to 2} \frac{x + 8}{x} = \frac{10}{2} = 5$$

11.
(39)

$$\Delta x = \frac{b - a}{n} = \frac{5 - 1}{4} = 1$$

$$\begin{aligned}
S_{Left} &= \Delta x(y_0 + y_1 + y_2 + y_3) \\
&= 1\big[(1^2 + 1) + (2^2 + 1) + (3^2 + 1) \\
&\quad + (4^2 + 1)\big] \\
&= (2 + 5 + 10 + 17) = \mathbf{34}
\end{aligned}$$

12.
(40)
$$s(t) = t^2 - 2t$$
$$v(t) = s'(t) = 2t - 2$$

$$v(0) = 2(0) - 2 = \mathbf{-2}\ \frac{\text{km}}{\text{min}}$$

$$v(1) = 2(1) - 2 = \mathbf{0}\ \frac{\text{km}}{\text{min}}$$

$$v(2) = 2(2) - 2 = \mathbf{2}\ \frac{\text{km}}{\text{min}}$$

TEST 10, FORM B

1.
(38)
$$\int \left(5 \sin x - 2x - \sqrt{x} + 7\right) dx$$

$$= -5 \int (-\sin x)\, dx - \int 2x\, dx - \int x^{1/2}\, dx + 7 \int dx$$

$$= -5 \cos x - x^2 - \frac{2}{3} x^{3/2} + 7x + C$$

The correct choice is **B**.

2.
(37)
$$y = \sin^3 x$$
$$y = u^3, \text{ where } u = \sin x$$
$$\qquad\qquad du = \cos x\, dx$$
$$dy = 3u^2\, du$$
$$dy = 3 \sin^2 x\, (\cos x\, dx)$$
$$\frac{dy}{dx} = 3 \sin^2 x \cos x$$

The correct choice is **C**.

3.
(40)

$s(t) = 8t^3 + \ln t$

$v(t) = s'(t) = 24t^2 + \dfrac{1}{t}$

$v(1) = 24(1)^2 + \dfrac{1}{(1)} = 25\ \dfrac{\text{m}}{\text{s}}$

The correct choice is **D.**

4.
(27)

$f(x) = x^3 + 7\ln|x|$

$f'(x) = 3x^2 + \dfrac{7}{x}$

$f''(x) = 6x - \dfrac{7}{x^2}$

$f''(2) = 6(2) - \dfrac{7}{2^2}$

$f''(2) = \mathbf{10.25}$

The correct choice is **B.**

5.
(38)

$\displaystyle \int f(x)\,dx = \int \dfrac{4}{x}\,dx = \mathbf{4\ln|x|} + C$

The correct choice is **A.**

6.
(40)

$y = 5\cos(2x)$

$\dfrac{dy}{dx} = -10\sin(2x)$

$\left.\dfrac{dy}{dx}\right|_{\pi/12} = -10\sin\left(\dfrac{\pi}{6}\right)$

$\left.\dfrac{dy}{dx}\right|_{\pi/12} = -5$

So the slope of the normal line is $\dfrac{1}{5}$.

$y = 5\cos(2x)$

$y = 5\cos\left(2\left(\dfrac{\pi}{12}\right)\right)$

$y = \dfrac{5\sqrt{3}}{2}$

$y - \dfrac{5\sqrt{3}}{2} = \dfrac{1}{5}\left(x - \dfrac{\pi}{12}\right)$

7.
(8)

$(\sec^2\theta - 1)(1 - \sin^2\theta) = (\tan^2\theta)(\cos^2\theta)$
$= \mathbf{\sin^2\theta}$

8.
(40)

Graphing $f(x) = x^3 e^{1-x^2}$

Maximum
X=1.2247464   Y=1.114268

Rounded to four decimal places, the maximum value of f is **1.1143,** occurring at $x \approx 1.2247$.

9.
(34)

$V = \dfrac{4}{3}\pi r^3$

$dV = \dfrac{4}{3}\pi(3r^2\,dr)$

$\dfrac{dV}{dt} = 4\pi r^2\,\dfrac{dr}{dt}$

10.
(14)

$\displaystyle \lim_{x\to-6}\dfrac{x^2 + 7x + 6}{x^2 + 4x - 12} = \lim_{x\to-6}\dfrac{(x+6)(x+1)}{(x-2)(x+6)}$

$= \displaystyle\lim_{x\to-6}\dfrac{x+1}{x-2} = \dfrac{-5}{-8} = \dfrac{5}{8}$

11.
(39)

$\Delta x = \dfrac{b-a}{n} = \dfrac{5-1}{4} = 1$

$\begin{aligned}
S_{Right} &= \Delta x(y_1 + y_2 + y_3 + y_4) \\
&= 1\big[(2^2 + 1) + (3^2 + 1) + (4^2 + 1) \\
&\quad + (5^2 + 1)\big] \\
&= (5 + 10 + 17 + 26) = \mathbf{58}
\end{aligned}$

12.
(40)

$v(t) = t^3 - 5t^2 + 6t + 165{,}000$
$a(t) = v'(t) = 3t^2 - 10t + 6$

$a(0) = 3(0) - 10(0) + 6 = \mathbf{6}\ \dfrac{\text{km}}{\text{s}^2}$

$a(0.5) = 3(0.5)^2 - 10(0.5) + 6 = \mathbf{1.75}\ \dfrac{\text{km}}{\text{s}^2}$

$a(2.75) = 3(2.75)^2 - 10(2.75) + 6$

$= \mathbf{1.1875}\ \dfrac{\text{km}}{\text{s}^2}$

TEST 11, FORM A

1.
(44)

$$y = \cos u \qquad\qquad u = 7x^2$$

$$\frac{dy}{du} = -\sin u \qquad\qquad \frac{du}{dx} = 14x$$

$$\frac{dy}{dx} = \frac{dy}{du} \cdot \frac{du}{dx}$$

$$= (-\sin u)(14x)$$

$$= -14x \sin (7x^2)$$

The correct choice is **D.**

2.
(42)

$$f(x) = \frac{x^2 + 1}{e^x + 2}$$

$$f'(x) = \frac{(e^x + 2)(2x) - (x^2 + 1)e^x}{(e^x + 2)^2}$$

The correct choice is **A.**

3.
(17)

$$\lim_{x \to 1} \frac{4x - 4}{x^2 - 2x + 1} = \lim_{x \to 1} \frac{4(x - 1)}{(x - 1)^2}$$

$$= \lim_{x \to 1} \frac{4}{x - 1}$$

$$\lim_{x \to 1^+} \frac{4}{x - 1} = +\infty$$

$$\lim_{x \to 1^-} \frac{4}{x - 1} = -\infty$$

Therefore $\displaystyle\lim_{x \to 1} \frac{4x - 4}{x^2 - 2x + 1}$ **does not exist.**

The correct choice is **D.**

4.
(13)

$$\sin^{-1} -\frac{\sqrt{3}}{2} = \mathbf{-60°}$$

The correct choice is **B.**

5.
(21)
The graph of g is the graph of f shifted 3 units to the right and 2 units up.

The correct choice is **A.**

6.
(44)

$$f'(4) = \lim_{x \to 4} \frac{f(x) - f(4)}{x - 4} = \lim_{x \to 4} \frac{7x^2 - 7(4)^2}{x - 4}$$

$$= \lim_{x \to 4} \frac{7(x^2 - 4^2)}{x - 4} = \lim_{x \to 4} \frac{7(x + 4)(x - 4)}{x - 4}$$

$$= \lim_{x \to 4} 7(x + 4) = 7(8) = \mathbf{56}$$

7.
(44)

$$s = 2 \ln v \qquad\qquad v = \frac{e^t}{t}$$

$$\frac{ds}{dv} = \frac{2}{v} \qquad\qquad \frac{dv}{dt} = \frac{te^t - e^t}{t^2}$$

$$\frac{ds}{dt} = \frac{ds}{dv} \cdot \frac{dv}{dt} = \frac{2}{v} \cdot \frac{te^t - e^t}{t^2}$$

$$= \frac{2t}{e^t} \cdot \frac{(t - 1)e^t}{t^2} = \frac{2(t - 1)}{t}$$

8.
(38)

$$\int \left(\frac{3}{x} + e^x \right) dx = 3 \int \frac{1}{x} dx + \int e^x dx$$

$$= \mathbf{3 \ln |x| + e^x + C}$$

9.
(31)

$$f(x) = (x^3 + 2x) \ln x$$

$$f'(x) = (x^3 + 2x)\left(\frac{1}{x} \right) + (\ln x)(3x^2 + 2)$$

$$f'(1) = (1^3 + 2)\left(\frac{1}{1} \right) + (0)(3 + 2) = \mathbf{3}$$

10.
(41)

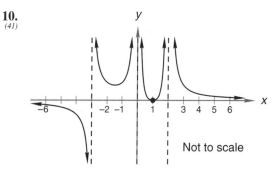

Not to scale

11.
(30)

12.
(43)

$$\Delta x = \frac{2 - 0}{n} = \frac{2}{n}$$

$$x_1 = \tfrac{2}{n}, \; x_2 = 2(\tfrac{2}{n}), \; x_3 = 3(\tfrac{2}{n}), \; ..., \; x_n = n(\tfrac{2}{n})$$

$$f(x_1) = (\tfrac{2}{n})^2, \; f(x_2) = 2^2(\tfrac{2}{n})^2, \; f(x_3) = 3^2(\tfrac{2}{n})^2,$$
$$..., \; f(x_n) = n^2(\tfrac{2}{n})^2$$

$$S_U = \Delta x\big[f(x_1) + f(x_2) + f(x_3) + \cdots + f(x_n)\big]$$

$$= \frac{2}{n}\left[\left(\frac{2}{n}\right)^2 + 2^2\left(\frac{2}{n}\right)^2 + 3^2\left(\frac{2}{n}\right)^2 + \cdots \right.$$
$$\left. + \; n^2\left(\frac{2}{n}\right)^2\right]$$

$$= \frac{2}{n}\left(\frac{2}{n}\right)^2\big[1^2 + 2^2 + 3^2 + \cdots + n^2\big]$$

$$= \frac{8}{n^3}\left[\frac{n(n + 1)(2n + 1)}{6}\right]$$

$$= \frac{4}{3}\left(\frac{2n^3 + 3n^2 + n}{n^3}\right)$$

$$A = \lim_{n \to \infty} S_U = \lim_{n \to \infty} \frac{4}{3}\left(\frac{2n^3 + 3n^2 + n}{n^3}\right)$$

$$= \lim_{n \to \infty} \frac{4}{3}\left(2 + \frac{3}{n} + \frac{1}{n^2}\right) = \frac{8}{3}$$

TEST 11, FORM B

1.
(44)
    $y = \sin u$ $u = 5x^2$

$$\frac{dy}{du} = \cos u \qquad\qquad \frac{du}{dx} = 10x$$

$$\frac{dy}{dx} = \frac{dy}{du} \cdot \frac{du}{dx}$$

$$= (\cos u)(10x)$$

$$= 10x \cos (5x^2)$$

The correct choice is **C.**

2.
(42)
   $f(x) = \dfrac{\sin x + 1}{e^x + 2}$

$$f'(x) = \frac{(e^x + 2)\cos x - (\sin x + 1)e^x}{(e^x + 2)^2}$$

The correct choice is **B.**

3.
(17)
$$\lim_{x \to 2} \frac{4x - 8}{x^2 - 4x + 4} = \lim_{x \to 2} \frac{4(x - 2)}{(x - 2)^2}$$
$$= \lim_{x \to 2} \frac{4}{x - 2}$$

$$\lim_{x \to 2^+} \frac{4}{x - 2} = +\infty$$

$$\lim_{x \to 2^-} \frac{4}{x - 2} = -\infty$$

Therefore, $\displaystyle\lim_{x \to 2} \frac{4x - 8}{x^2 - 4x + 4}$ **does not exist.**

The correct choice is **D.**

4.
(13)

$$\cos^{-1} -\frac{\sqrt{3}}{2} = \mathbf{150°}$$

The correct choice is **C.**

5.
(21)
The graph of g is the graph of f shifted 2 units to the right and 3 units up.

The correct choice is **C.**

6.
(44)
$$f'(3) = \lim_{x \to 3} \frac{f(x) - f(3)}{x - 3} = \lim_{x \to 3} \frac{5x^2 - 5(9)}{x - 3}$$

$$= \lim_{x \to 3} \frac{5(x^2 - 9)}{x - 3} = \lim_{x \to 3} \frac{5(x + 3)(x - 3)}{x - 3}$$

$$= \lim_{x \to 3} 5(x + 3) = \mathbf{30}$$

7.
(44)
   $u = \dfrac{v}{e^v}$ $v = 3\ln t$

$$\frac{du}{dv} = \frac{e^v - ve^v}{(e^v)^2} \qquad\qquad \frac{dv}{dt} = \frac{3}{t}$$

$$\frac{du}{dv} = \frac{1 - v}{e^v}$$

$$\frac{du}{dt} = \frac{du}{dv} \cdot \frac{dv}{dt} = \frac{1 - v}{e^v} \cdot \frac{3}{t} = \frac{1 - 3\ln t}{t^3} \cdot \frac{3}{t}$$

$$= \frac{\mathbf{3 - 9\ln t}}{t^4}$$

8.
(38)
$$\int \left(\frac{6}{x} - e^x\right) dx = 6 \int \frac{1}{x} dx - \int e^x dx$$
$$= 6 \ln |x| - e^x + C$$

9.
(31)
`nDeriv((X^4+2X3-3X)ln(X),X,`
`1.44)` yields **11.931** after rounding to three decimal places.

10.
(41)

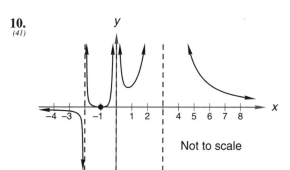

Not to scale

11.
(30)

12.
(43)

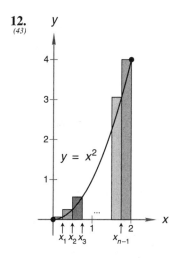

$$\Delta x = \frac{2 - 0}{n} = \frac{2}{n}$$

$$x_1 = \tfrac{2}{n}, \ x_2 = 2(\tfrac{2}{n}), \ x_3 = 3(\tfrac{2}{n}), \ \ldots, \ x_n = n(\tfrac{2}{n})$$
$$f(x_1) = (\tfrac{2}{n})^2, \ f(x_2) = 2^2(\tfrac{2}{n})^2, \ f(x_3) = 3^2(\tfrac{2}{n})^2,$$
$$\ldots, \ f(x_n) = n^2(\tfrac{2}{n})^2$$

$$S_U = \Delta x \big[f(x_1) + f(x_2) + f(x_3) + \cdots + f(x_n) \big]$$
$$= \frac{2}{n}\left[\left(\frac{2}{n}\right)^2 + 2^2\left(\frac{2}{n}\right)^2 + 3^2\left(\frac{2}{n}\right)^2 + \cdots \right.$$
$$\left. + n^2\left(\frac{2}{n}\right)^2 \right]$$
$$= \frac{2}{n}\left(\frac{2}{n}\right)^2 \big[1^2 + 2^2 + 3^2 + \cdots + n^2 \big]$$
$$= \frac{8}{n^3}\left[\frac{n(n+1)(2n+1)}{6} \right]$$
$$= \frac{4}{3}\left(\frac{2n^3 + 3n^2 + n}{n^3} \right)$$
$$A = \lim_{n \to \infty} S_U = \lim_{n \to \infty} \frac{4}{3}\left(\frac{2n^3 + 3n^2 + n}{n^3} \right)$$
$$= \lim_{n \to \infty} \frac{4}{3}\left(2 + \frac{3}{n} + \frac{1}{n^2} \right) = \frac{8}{3}$$

TEST 12, FORM A

1.
(48)
$y = x^2 \tan x$

$y' = x^2 \sec^2 x + 2x \tan x$

The correct choice is **B**.

2.
(13)
The domain of $y = \arcsin x$ is the interval $[-1, 1]$. Since $\pi \approx 3.14$, π is not in the domain of y.

The correct choice is **D**.

3.
(38)
$$\int \left(\frac{1}{u^{1/3}} + 5u^3 - 1 + 3 \sin u \right) du$$
$$= \int u^{-1/3} du + 5 \int u^3 du - \int du + 3 \int \sin u \, du$$
$$= \frac{3}{2} u^{2/3} + \frac{5u^4}{4} - u - 3 \cos u + C$$

The correct choice is **D**.

4.
(47)
$$\int_{-1}^{2} (x^3 - 2x + 2) \, dx = \frac{x^4}{4} - x^2 + 2x \bigg|_{-1}^{2}$$
$$= \frac{16}{4} - 4 + 4 - \left(\frac{(-1)^4}{4} - (-1)^2 + 2(-1) \right)$$
$$= 4 - 4 + 4 - \frac{1}{4} + 1 + 2 = \frac{27}{4}$$

The correct choice is **C**.

5. $\log_3 (x - 5) + \log_3 (x + 3) = 2$
(16)

$$\log_3 [(x - 5)(x + 3)] = 2$$

$$(x - 5)(x + 3) = 3^2$$

$$x^2 - 2x - 15 = 9$$

$$x^2 - 2x - 24 = 0$$

$$(x - 6)(x + 4) = 0$$

$$x = -4, 6$$

Since the argument of a logarithm cannot be negative, $x = 6$ is the only solution.

The correct choice is **D**.

6.
(45)

The **local minimum** occurs at **(0, 4)**.

The **local maximum** occurs at **(–1, 5)**.

7. $x^2 + y^2 = 1$
(34)

$$2x\,dx + 2y\,dy = 0$$

$$2x + 2y\frac{dy}{dx} = 0$$

$$2y\frac{dy}{dx} = -2x$$

$$\frac{dy}{dx} = -\frac{x}{y}$$

$$\frac{dy}{dx} = \frac{-\left(-\dfrac{\sqrt{2}}{2}\right)}{\dfrac{\sqrt{2}}{2}}$$

$$\frac{dy}{dx} = 1$$

8. $s(t) = 5t^3 - 3t^2 + 10$
(40)

$$v(t) = 15t^2 - 6t$$

$$v(2) = 15(4) - 6(2)$$

$$v(2) = 48\ \frac{\text{ft}}{\text{min}}$$

9.
(46)

8 ft

When $x = 5$, $y = \sqrt{64 - 25} = \sqrt{39}$.

$$x^2 + y^2 = 64$$

$$2x\frac{dx}{dt} + 2y\frac{dy}{dt} = 0$$

$$2(5)(1) + 2(\sqrt{39})\frac{dy}{dt} = 0$$

$$\frac{dy}{dt} = -\frac{5}{\sqrt{39}}\ \frac{\text{ft}}{\text{s}}$$

The top of the ladder is falling at a rate of $\dfrac{5}{\sqrt{39}}\ \dfrac{\text{ft}}{\text{s}}$.

10. $V = \frac{4}{3}\pi r^3 = \frac{4}{3}\pi\left(\frac{D}{2}\right)^3 = \frac{\pi}{6}D^3$,
(46)

where D = diameter and r = radius

$$\frac{dV}{dt} = \frac{3\pi}{6}D^2\frac{dD}{dt}$$

$$1 = \frac{\pi}{2}(12)^2\frac{dD}{dt}$$

$$1 = 72\pi\frac{dD}{dt}$$

$$\frac{dD}{dt} = \frac{1}{72\pi}\ \frac{\text{cm}}{\text{s}}$$

11.
(45)

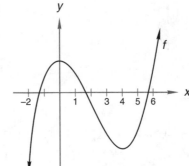

This is the basic shape of the graph of f. There are many other possible graphs of f, which are vertical translations of this one.

12. $\dfrac{d}{dx}(\cot x) = \dfrac{d}{dx}\left(\dfrac{\cos x}{\sin x}\right)$
(48)

$$= \dfrac{\sin x\,(-\sin x) - (\cos x)(\cos x)}{\sin^2 x}$$

$$= -\dfrac{\sin^2 x + \cos^2 x}{\sin^2 x}$$

$$= -\dfrac{1}{\sin^2 x}$$

$$= -\csc^2 x$$

TEST 12, FORM B

1. $y = x^3 \sec x$
(48)
$y' = x^3 \sec x \tan x + 3x^2 \sec x$

The correct choice is **C**.

2. The range of $y = \arcsin x$ is the interval $[-\frac{\pi}{2}, \frac{\pi}{2}]$,
(13)
so π is not in the range of y.

The correct choice is **A**.

3. $\displaystyle\int\left(\dfrac{1}{u^{2/3}} - 4u^3 + u - 3\cos u\right) du$
(38)

$$= \int u^{-2/3}\,du - \int 4u^3\,du + \int u\,du - 3\int \cos u\,du$$

$$= 3u^{1/3} - u^4 + \dfrac{1}{2}u^2 - 3\sin u + C$$

The correct choice is **B**.

4. $\displaystyle\int_1^2\left(e^x + \dfrac{1}{x}\right) dx = \left.(e^x + \ln|x|)\right|_1^2$
(47)

$$= e^2 + \ln 2 - (e + 0)$$

$$= e^2 + \ln 2 - e$$

$$\approx 5.3639$$

The correct choice is **D**.

5. $\log_5 120 = \dfrac{\log 120}{\log 5} \approx 2.975$
(20)

The correct choice is **B**.

6.
(40)

The graph of f has a relative minimum at about
(**0.5773, 5.4641**).

7. `nDeriv(e^(X)sin(X),X,π)` yields the
(19)
approximate result **–23.1407.**

8. $v(t) = 3t^4 - 2t^2 + 7$
(40)
$a(t) = 12t^3 - 4t$

$a(1.5) = 12(1.5)^3 - 4(1.5)$

$a(1.5) = \mathbf{34.5}\ \dfrac{\mathbf{m}}{\mathbf{s^2}}$

9.
(46)

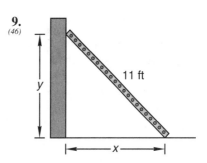

When $x = 8$, $y = \sqrt{121 - 64} = \sqrt{57}$.

$$x^2 + y^2 = 121$$

$$2x\dfrac{dx}{dt} + 2y\dfrac{dy}{dt} = 0$$

$$2(8)(2) + 2(\sqrt{57})\dfrac{dy}{dt} = 0$$

$$\dfrac{dy}{dt} = -\dfrac{16}{\sqrt{57}}\ \dfrac{\text{ft}}{\text{s}}$$

The top of the ladder is falling at a rate of $\dfrac{16}{\sqrt{57}}\ \dfrac{\text{ft}}{\text{s}}$.

10. $V = \dfrac{4}{3}\pi r^3 = \dfrac{4}{3}\pi\left(\dfrac{D}{2}\right)^3 = \dfrac{\pi}{6}D^3$
(46)
where $D = $ diameter and $r = $ radius.

$$\dfrac{dV}{dt} = \dfrac{3\pi}{6}D^2\dfrac{dD}{dt}$$

$$2 = \dfrac{\pi}{2}(10)^2\dfrac{dD}{dt}$$

$$2 = 50\pi\dfrac{dD}{dt}$$

$$\dfrac{dD}{dt} = \dfrac{1}{25\pi}\ \dfrac{\text{cm}}{\text{s}}$$

11.
(45)

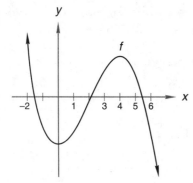

This is the basic shape of the graph of f. There are many other possible graphs of f, which are vertical translations of this one.

12.
(48)
$$\frac{d}{dx}(\tan x) = \frac{d}{dx}\left(\frac{\sin x}{\cos x}\right)$$

$$= \frac{(\cos x)(\cos x) - (\sin x)(-\sin x)}{\cos^2 x}$$

$$= \frac{\cos^2 x + \sin^2 x}{\cos^2 x}$$

$$= \frac{1}{\cos^2 x}$$

$$= \sec^2 x$$

TEST 13, FORM A

1.
(42)
$$f(x) = \frac{x - 1}{x + 1}$$

$$f'(x) = \frac{(x + 1) - (x - 1)}{(x + 1)^2} = \frac{2}{(x + 1)^2}$$

$$f'(1) = \frac{2}{(1 + 1)^2} = \frac{2}{4} = \frac{1}{2}$$

The correct choice is **D.**

2.
(51)
$$d\left(e^{x^3}\right) = e^{x^3}(3x^2\, dx)$$

Thus $\int 3x^2 e^{x^3}\, dx = e^{x^3} + C.$

The correct choice is **A.**

3.
(44)
This is, by definition, the derivative of $\sin x$ evaluated at $x = \pi$. Thus the limit is $\cos \pi = -1.$

The correct choice is **C.**

4.
(47)
$$\int_1^3 (3x^2 + 2x)\, dx = (x^3 + x^2)\Big|_1^3$$

$$= 27 + 9 - 1 - 1 = 34$$

The correct choice is **B.**

5.
(48)
$$\frac{d}{dx}(\tan x + \sec x) = \sec^2 x + \sec x \tan x$$

$$= (\sec x)(\sec x + \tan x)$$

The correct choice is **D.**

6.
(49)
$$f(x) = \frac{1}{3}x^3 - \frac{1}{2}x^2 + 3$$

$$f'(x) = x^2 - x$$

$$f''(x) = 2x - 1$$

$$2x - 1 = 0$$

$$x = \frac{1}{2}$$

If $x < \frac{1}{2}$, $f''(x) < 0$. If $x > \frac{1}{2}$, $f''(x) > 0$. Thus the point $\left(\frac{1}{2}, f\left(\frac{1}{2}\right)\right)$ is an inflection point. This is the point $\left(\frac{1}{2}, \frac{35}{12}\right)$.

7.
(6)
For x to be in the domain of f, it must satisfy $x - 5 \geq 0$ and $x \neq 0$. Both of these conditions are satisfied by the first inequality.

$$\text{Domain} = \{x \in \mathbb{R} \mid x \geq 5\}$$

8.
(50)
$$\frac{d}{dx}e^{x^2 + 1} = 2xe^{x^2 + 1}$$

$$\frac{d}{dx}\sin(x^3 - 4) = 3x^2 \cos(x^3 - 4)$$

$$y = e^{x^2 + 1}\sin(x^3 - 4)$$

$$y' = e^{x^2 + 1}\left(3x^2 \cos(x^3 - 4)\right)$$

$$\quad + 2xe^{x^2 + 1}\left(\sin(x^3 - 4)\right)$$

$$y' = xe^{x^2 + 1}\left[3x \cos(x^3 - 4) + 2\sin(x^3 - 4)\right]$$

9.
(17)
$$\lim_{n \to \infty} \frac{1 + 3n^2}{n^2 + 1000} = \lim_{n \to \infty} \frac{\frac{1}{n^2} + 3}{1 + \frac{1000}{n^2}} = 3$$

10.
(50)
$$y = (x^3 + 1)^{15}$$

$$y' = 15(x^3 + 1)^{14}(3x^2)$$

$$y' = 45x^2(x^3 + 1)^{14}$$

11.
(45)
The function g has a **relative maximum at $x = 1$.**

Note: The vertical placement of the graph is arbitrary.

12.
(52)

$x + 2y = 50$

$2y = 50 - x$

$y = 25 - \dfrac{x}{2}$

$A = xy = x\left(25 - \dfrac{x}{2}\right) = 25x - \dfrac{x^2}{2}$

$A' = 25 - x$ implies a critical number at $x = 25$. Since $A'' = -1$, the graph of A is concave down, so it has a local maximum at $x = 25$.

To maximize area, the plot must be **25 feet long and 12.5 feet wide.**

TEST 13, FORM B

1. $f(x) = \dfrac{x - 2}{x + 2}$
(42)

$f'(x) = \dfrac{(x + 2) - (x - 2)}{(x + 2)^2} = \dfrac{4}{(x + 2)^2}$

$f'(1) = \dfrac{4}{(1 + 2)^2} = \dfrac{4}{9}$

The correct choice is **C.**

2. $d\left(e^{x^4}\right) = e^{x^4}(4x^3\, dx)$
(51)

Thus $\displaystyle\int 4x^3 e^{x^4} = e^{x^4} + C.$

The correct choice is **B.**

3. This is, by definition, the derivative of $\cos x$
(44) evaluated at $x = \pi$. Thus the limit is $-\sin \pi = \mathbf{0}$.

The correct choice is **A.**

4. $\displaystyle\int_{0.75}^{2.25} (3x^2 - 2x)\, dx = x^3 - x^2 \Big|_{0.75}^{2.25}$
(47)

$= 2.25^3 - 2.25^2 - 0.75^3 + 0.75^2 = \mathbf{6.46875}$

The correct choice is **D.**

5. $\dfrac{d}{dx}(\tan x - \sec x) = \sec^2 x - \sec x \tan x$
(48)

$= (\sec x)(\sec x - \tan x)$

The correct choice is **B.**

6. $f(x) = x^3 - x^2 + \dfrac{1}{3}$
(49)

$f'(x) = 3x^2 - 2x$

$f''(x) = 6x - 2$

$0 = 2(3x - 1)$

$x = \dfrac{1}{3}$

If $x < \frac{1}{3}$, $f''(x) < 0$. If $x > \frac{1}{3}$, $f''(x) > 0$. Thus the point $\left(\frac{1}{3}, f\left(\frac{1}{3}\right)\right)$ is an inflection point. This is the point $\left(\frac{1}{3}, \frac{7}{27}\right)$.

7. For x to be in the domain of f, it must
(6) satisfy $x + 3 \geq 0$ and $x \neq 0$. Thus x must be greater than or equal to -3 and not equal to 0.

Domain $= \{x \in \mathbb{R} \mid x \geq -3 \text{ and } x \neq 0\}$

8. $\dfrac{d}{dx}(x^3 + 1)^{15} = 15(x^3 + 1)^{14}(3x^2)$
(50)

$\dfrac{d}{dx}\cos(x^2 - 3) = -\sin(x^2 - 3)\,(2x)$

$y = (x^3 + 1)^{15}\cos(x^2 - 3)$

$y' = (x^3 + 1)^{15}\left(-2x\sin(x^2 - 3)\right)$
$\qquad + 45x^2(x^3 + 1)^{14}\cos(x^2 - 3)$

$\mathbf{y' = x(x^3 + 1)^{14}\left[-2(x^3 + 1)\sin(x^2 - 3)\right.}$
$\qquad\qquad \mathbf{\left. + 45x\cos(x^2 - 3)\right]}$

9. $\displaystyle\lim_{n \to \infty} \dfrac{1 - 3n^2}{n^2 + 1000} = \lim_{n \to \infty} \dfrac{\dfrac{1}{n^2} - 3}{1 + \dfrac{1000}{n^2}} = \mathbf{-3}$
(17)

10. $y = e^{\tan x} + 1$
(50)

$y' = e^{\tan x}(\sec^2 x)$

11. The function g has a **relative minimum at $x = 2$.**
(45)

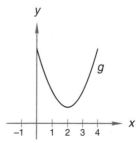

Note: The vertical placement of the graph is arbitrary.

12.
(52)

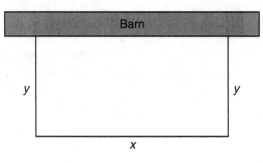

$$x + 2y = 21$$
$$2y = 21 - x$$
$$y = \frac{21}{2} - \frac{x}{2}$$

$$A = xy = x\left(\frac{21}{2} - \frac{x}{2}\right) = 10.5x - \frac{x^2}{2}$$

$A' = 10.5 - x$ implies a critical number at $x = 10.5$. Since $A'' = -1$, the graph of A is concave down, so it has a local maximum at $x = 10.5$.

To maximize area, the plot must be **10.5 meters long and 5.25 meters wide.**

TEST 14, FORM A

1. The graph of g does not have a hole at $x = 2$ and
(41) is negative on the interval $(0, 2)$. The graph of g does have a vertical asymptote at $x = -5$.

The correct choice is **B.**

2. $V = \frac{4}{3}\pi r^3$
(46)

$$\frac{dV}{dt} = 4\pi r^2 \frac{dr}{dt}$$

$$\frac{dV}{dt} = 4\pi(10)^2(2)$$

$$\frac{dV}{dt} = 800\pi \frac{\text{in.}^3}{\text{s}}$$

The correct choice is **A.**

3. $\int_1^3 (8x^3 + 5x)\, dx = \left(2x^4 + \frac{5}{2}x^2\right)\Big|_1^3$
(47)

$$= 162 + \frac{45}{2} - 2 - \frac{5}{2} = 180$$

The correct choice is **D.**

4. $\int_1^4 \ln x\, dx = \lim_{n\to\infty} \sum_{i=1}^{n} \ln (x_i)\, \Delta x$
(47)

$$= \lim_{n\to\infty} \sum_{i=1}^{n} \ln (x_i)\left(\frac{4-1}{n}\right)$$

$$= \lim_{n\to\infty} \frac{3}{n} \sum_{i=1}^{n} \ln (x_i)$$

The correct choice is **C.**

5. $x(t) = t^3 - 4t^2 - 12t + 15$
(54) $v(t) = x'(t) = 3t^2 - 8t - 12$
$a(t) = x''(t) = 6t - 8$

$$a(2) = 6(2) - 8 = 4\,\frac{\text{units}}{\text{s}^2}$$

The correct choice is **B.**

6. $h(t) = 150 + 7t - 16t^2$
(54) $v(t) = h'(t) = 7 - 32t$

The ball reaches its maximum height when the velocity is zero.

$$7 - 32t = 0$$

$$t = \frac{7}{32}\ \text{second}$$

7. $u = \sec x$
(56) $du = \sec x \tan x\, dx$

$$\int (\sec^2 x)(\sec x \tan x)\, dx$$

$$= \frac{1}{3}\int 3\,(\sec^2 x)(\sec x \tan x)\, dx$$

$$= \frac{1}{3}\int 3u^2\, du = \frac{1}{3}u^3 + C = \frac{1}{3}\sec^3 x + C$$

8. $f(x) = e^{2x} \ln (3x)$
(50)

$$f'(x) = e^{2x} \cdot \frac{3}{3x} + \ln (3x)\,(2e^{2x})$$

$$= e^{2x}\left(\frac{1}{x} + 2\ln (3x)\right)$$

9. $y = x^2 \ln x$
(49)

$$y' = x^2 \cdot \frac{1}{x} + (\ln x)(2x)$$

$$y' = x + (2x)(\ln x)$$

$$y'' = 1 + 2x\left(\frac{1}{x}\right) + 2\ln x$$

$$y'' = 1 + 2 + 2\ln x$$

$$y'' = 3 + 2\ln x$$

At $x = 1$, $y'' = 3$, so the graph is **concave upward** at $x = 1$.

10.
(40)
$$y = \frac{\sin x}{x^2 + 1}$$

$$y' = \frac{(x^2 + 1)(\cos x) - (\sin x)(2x)}{(x^2 + 1)^2}$$

At $x = 0$, $y' = 1$. Thus the slope of the normal line is -1. When $x = 0$, $y = \frac{\sin 0}{0^2 + 1} = 0$. So the equation of the line normal to the graph of $y = \frac{\sin x}{x^2 + 1}$ at $x = 0$ is

$$y - 0 = -(x - 0)$$
$$y = -x$$

11. (a)　$f(x) = \ln(1 + x)$　　　$f(0) = 0$
(55)

$$f'(x) = \frac{1}{1 + x} \qquad f'(0) = 1$$

$$f''(x) = -\frac{1}{(1 + x)^2} \qquad f''(0) = -1$$

$$f'''(x) = \frac{2}{(1 + x)^3} \qquad f'''(0) = 2$$

$$f^{(4)}(x) = -\frac{6}{(1 + x)^4} \qquad f^{(4)}(0) = -6$$

$$\vdots \qquad\qquad\qquad \vdots$$

The Maclaurin series for $f(x) = \ln(1 + x)$ is

$$0 + \frac{1x}{1} - \frac{1x^2}{2!} + \frac{2x^3}{3!} - \frac{6x^4}{4!} + \cdots$$

$$= x - \frac{x^2}{2} + \frac{x^3}{3} - \frac{x^4}{4} + \cdots$$

(b)　$\ln 2 = \ln(1 + 1)$

Replace x by 1 in $x - \frac{x^2}{2} + \frac{x^3}{3}$ to obtain

$$1 - \frac{1}{2} + \frac{1}{3} = \frac{5}{6}$$

12. (a)　$A = \int_0^4 x^2\, dx = \left.\frac{x^3}{3}\right|_0^4 = \frac{64}{3}$
(47)

(b)　$\Delta x = \dfrac{4 - 0}{n} = \dfrac{4}{n}$

$$S_L = \frac{4}{n}\left(0^2 + \left(\frac{4}{n}\right)^2 + \left(2\left(\frac{4}{n}\right)\right)^2 \right.$$

$$+ \left(3\left(\frac{4}{n}\right)\right)^2 + \cdots + \left.\left((n - 1)\left(\frac{4}{n}\right)\right)^2 \right)$$

$$= \frac{4}{n}\left(\left(\frac{4}{n}\right)^2 + 4\left(\frac{4}{n}\right)^2 + 9\left(\frac{4}{n}\right)^2 \right.$$

$$+ \cdots + \left.(n - 1)^2\left(\frac{4}{n}\right)^2 \right)$$

$$= \left(\frac{4}{n}\right)^3 (1 + 4 + 9 + \cdots + (n - 1)^2)$$

$$= \left(\frac{4}{n}\right)^3 \left(\frac{n(n - 1)(2n - 1)}{6}\right)$$

$$= \frac{64(2n^3 - 3n^2 + n)}{6n^3}$$

$$= \frac{128n^3 - 192n^2 + 64n}{6n^3}$$

$$A = \lim_{n \to \infty} S_L$$

$$= \lim_{n \to \infty} \frac{128n^3 - 192n^2 + 64n}{6n^3} = \frac{128}{6}$$

$$= \frac{64}{3}$$

Test 14, Form B

1. The graph of g has a hole at $x = -2$, is negative on
(41)　$(0, 1)$, and has a vertical asymptote at $x = 1$.

The correct choice is **D**.

2.　$V = \dfrac{4}{3}\pi r^3$
(46)

$$\frac{dV}{dt} = 4\pi r^2 \frac{dr}{dt}$$

$$\frac{dV}{dt} = 4\pi(9)^2(3)$$

$$\frac{dV}{dt} = 972\pi \ \frac{\text{cm}^3}{\text{s}}$$

The correct choice is **B**.

3. Entering `fnInt(2.7X²+3.4X,X,`
(53) `1.35,3.46)` gives approximately **52.3187**.

The correct choice is **C**.

4.　$\displaystyle\int_1^3 \ln(x)\, dx = \lim_{n \to \infty} \sum_{i=1}^{n} \ln(x_i)\, \Delta x$
(47)

$$= \lim_{n \to \infty} \sum_{i=1}^{n} \ln(x_i)\left(\frac{3 - 1}{n}\right)$$

$$= \lim_{n \to \infty} \frac{2}{n} \sum_{i=1}^{n} \ln(x_i)$$

The correct choice is **B**.

5. $x(t) = t^3 + 5t^2 - 21t + 10$
(54)

$v(t) = x'(t) = 3t^2 + 10t - 21$

$a(t) = x''(t) = 6t + 10$

$a(3.1) = 6(3.1) + 10 = \mathbf{28.6} \dfrac{\mathbf{units}}{\mathbf{s^2}}$

The correct choice is **A.**

6. $h(t) = 250 + 17t - 16t^2$
(54)

$v(t) = h'(t) = 17 - 32t$

The ball reaches its maximum height when the velocity is zero.

$17 - 32t = 0$

$$t = \frac{17}{32} \text{ second}$$

7. $u = \cos 3t$
(56)

$du = -3 \sin (3t)\, dt$

$\displaystyle\int \cos^6 (3t) \sin (3t)\, dt$

$= -\dfrac{1}{7(3)} \displaystyle\int 7\cos^6 (3t)(-3\sin(3t))\, dt$

$= -\dfrac{1}{21} \displaystyle\int 7u^6\, du$

$= -\dfrac{1}{21} u^7 + C$

$= -\dfrac{1}{21} \cos^7 (3t) + C$

8. $f(x) = e^{3x} \ln (2x)$
(50)

$f'(x) = e^{3x} \cdot \dfrac{2}{2x} + \ln(2x)(3e^{3x})$

$= e^{3x}\left(\dfrac{1}{x} + 3\ln(2x)\right)$

9. $y = x^2 e^x$
(49)

$y' = x^2 e^x + 2xe^x = (x^2 + 2x)e^x$

`nDeriv((X²+2X)e^(X),X,-1.62)` yields to approximate solution -0.3672. At $x = -1.62$, y'' is negative, so the graph is **concave downward.**

10. $y' = \dfrac{(x^2 + 1)(\cos x) - (\sin x)(2x)}{(x^2 + 1)^2}$
(40)

At $x = \pi$, $y' = \dfrac{(\pi^2 + 1)(-1)}{(\pi^2+1)^2} = \dfrac{-1}{\pi^2+1}$. So the slope of the normal line is $\pi^2 + 1$, which is approximately 10.8696. Also, when $x = \pi$, $y = 0$. So the equation of the normal line is approximately

$$y = 10.8696(x - 3.1416)$$

11. (a)
(55)

$f(x) = \ln(1 + x)$	$f(0) = 0$

$f'(x) = \dfrac{1}{1 + x}$ $f'(0) = 1$

$f''(x) = -\dfrac{1}{(1 + x)^2}$ $f''(0) = -1$

$f'''(x) = \dfrac{2}{(1 + x)^3}$ $f'''(0) = 2$

$f^{(4)}(x) = -\dfrac{6}{(1 + x)^4}$ $f^{(4)}(0) = -6$

$\vdots$ $\vdots$

The Maclaurin series for $f(x) = \ln(1 + x)$ is

$0 + \dfrac{1x}{1} - \dfrac{1x^2}{2!} + \dfrac{2x^3}{3!} - \dfrac{6x^4}{4!} + \cdots$

$= x - \dfrac{x^2}{2} + \dfrac{x^3}{3} - \dfrac{x^4}{4} + \cdots$

(b) $\ln 1.15 = \ln(1 + 0.15)$

Replace x by 0.15 in $x - \dfrac{x^2}{2} + \dfrac{x^3}{3}$ to obtain

$0.15 - \dfrac{0.15^2}{2} + \dfrac{0.15^3}{3} \approx \mathbf{0.1399}$

12. (a) $A = \displaystyle\int_0^4 x^2\, dx = \dfrac{x^3}{3}\Big|_0^4 = \dfrac{\mathbf{64}}{\mathbf{3}}$
(47,53)

(b) $\Delta x = \dfrac{4 - 0}{n} = \dfrac{4}{n}$

$S_R = \dfrac{4}{n}\left(\left(\dfrac{4}{n}\right)^2 + \left(2\left(\dfrac{4}{n}\right)\right)^2\right.$

$\left. + \left(3\left(\dfrac{4}{n}\right)\right)^2 + \cdots + \left(n\left(\dfrac{4}{n}\right)\right)^2\right)$

$= \dfrac{4}{n}\left(\left(\dfrac{4}{n}\right)^2 + 4\left(\dfrac{4}{n}\right)^2 + 9\left(\dfrac{4}{n}\right)^2\right.$

$\left. + \cdots + n^2\left(\dfrac{4}{n}\right)^2\right)$

$= \left(\dfrac{4}{n}\right)^3 (1 + 4 + 9 + \cdots + n^2)$

$= \left(\dfrac{4}{n}\right)^3 \left(\dfrac{n(n + 1)(2n + 1)}{6}\right)$

$= \dfrac{64(2n^3 + 3n^2 + n)}{6n^3}$

$= \dfrac{128n^3 + 192n^2 + 64n}{6n^3}$

$A = \lim_{n \to \infty} S_R$

$= \lim_{n \to \infty} \dfrac{128n^3 + 192n^2 + 64n}{6n^3}$

$= \dfrac{128}{6} = \dfrac{\mathbf{64}}{\mathbf{3}}$

TEST 15, FORM A

1.
(60)
$$2 - x^2 = x$$
$$x^2 + x - 2 = 0$$
$$(x + 2)(x - 1) = 0$$

The graphs intersect at $x = -2$ and $x = 1$.

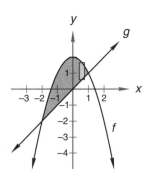

$$A = \int_{-2}^{1} \left[(2 - x^2) - x \right] dx$$

$$= \left[2x - \frac{x^3}{3} - \frac{x^2}{2} \right]_{-2}^{1}$$

$$= 2 - \frac{1}{3} - \frac{1}{2} - \left(-4 + \frac{8}{3} - 2 \right)$$

$$= \frac{9}{2}$$

The correct choice is **A.**

2.
(57)
A constant can be moved outside the integral sign, as in I, but a variable cannot, as in II. The property in III is true for all real *a, b,* and *c.*

The correct choice is **A.**

3.
(54)
$$v(t) = \frac{\ln t}{t}$$

$$v'(t) = \frac{t\left(\frac{1}{t}\right) - \ln t \,(1)}{t^2}$$

$$v'(t) = \frac{1 - \ln t}{t^2}$$

$$0 = \frac{1 - \ln t}{t^2}$$

$$\ln t = 1$$

$$t = e$$

The correct choice is **C.**

4.
(55)
$f(x) = e^x$	$f(0) = 1$
$f'(x) = e^x$	$f'(0) = 1$
$f''(x) = e^x$	$f''(0) = 1$
$\vdots$	$\vdots$

The Maclaurin series for e^x is

$$1 + x + \frac{x^2}{2!} + \frac{x^3}{3!} + \frac{x^4}{4!} + \cdots$$

The correct choice is **C.**

5.
(56)
$$u = x^3$$
$$du = 3x^2 \, dx$$

$$\int x^2 e^{x^3} \, dx = \frac{1}{3} \int 3x^2 e^{x^3} \, dx$$

$$= \frac{1}{3} \int e^u \, du$$

$$= \frac{1}{3} e^u + C$$

$$= \frac{1}{3} e^{x^3} + C$$

The correct choice is **A.**

6.
(56)
$$y = 9x - x^3$$
$$y = x(9 - x^2)$$
$$y = x(3 + x)(3 - x)$$

The graphs intersect at $x = 0$, $x = -3$, and $x = 3$.

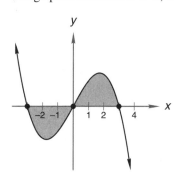

$$A = -\int_{-3}^{0} (9x - x^3) \, dx + \int_{0}^{3} (9x - x^3) \, dx$$

$$= -\left[\frac{9x^2}{2} - \frac{x^4}{4} \right]_{-3}^{0} + \left[\frac{9x^2}{2} - \frac{x^4}{4} \right]_{0}^{3}$$

$$= -\left(0 - \frac{81}{2} + \frac{81}{4} \right) + \left(\frac{81}{2} - \frac{81}{4} - 0 \right)$$

$$= -\left(-\frac{81}{4} \right) + \frac{81}{4}$$

$$= \frac{81}{2} = 40\frac{1}{2} \text{ units}^2$$

7.
(44)

$u = \cos^2 x \quad du = 2(\cos x)(-\sin x)\, dx$

$y = \cos u$

$dy = -\sin u\, du$

$dy = \left[-\sin(\cos^2 x)\right]\left[2(\cos x)(-\sin x)\, dx\right]$

$\dfrac{dy}{dx} = \left[\sin(2x)\right]\left[\sin(\cos^2 x)\right]$

8. $y = x^7 + 2$
(58)

Switch x and y and solve for y to find the inverse.

$$x = y^7 + 2$$
$$x - 2 = y^7$$
$$(x - 2)^{1/7} = y$$
$$f^{-1}(x) = (x - 2)^{1/7}$$

9.
(52)

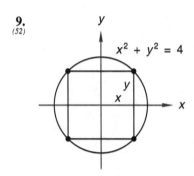

Let A be the area of the rectangle.

$A = 4xy$

$A = 4x\sqrt{4 - x^2}$

$A' = 4x\left(\dfrac{1}{2}(4 - x^2)^{-1/2}(-2x)\right) + 4\sqrt{4 - x^2}$

$A' = -4x^2(4 - x^2)^{-1/2} + 4(4 - x^2)^{1/2}$

$A' = 4(4 - x^2)^{-1/2}\left(-x^2 + (4 - x^2)\right)$

$A' = 4(4 - x^2)^{-1/2}(4 - 2x^2)$

Critical numbers occur at $x = \pm 2$ and $x = \pm\sqrt{2}$. The maximum area occurs when $x = \sqrt{2}$, and $y = \sqrt{4 - (\sqrt{2})^2} = \sqrt{4 - 2} = \sqrt{2}$. Thus the dimensions of the largest possible rectangle are **$2\sqrt{2}$ by $2\sqrt{2}$.**

10.
(58)

$\dfrac{x^2}{9} + \dfrac{y^2}{16} = 1$

$\dfrac{2x\, dx}{9} + \dfrac{2y\, dy}{16} = 0$

$\dfrac{2x}{9} + \dfrac{2y}{16} \cdot \dfrac{dy}{dx} = 0$

$\dfrac{dy}{dx} = -\dfrac{16x}{9y}$

At the point $(3, 0)$, the slope is **undefined.**

11.
(45)

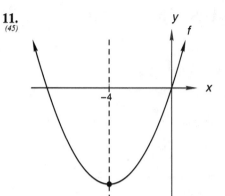

Note: The vertical position of f is arbitrary.

12. $g(x) = x^3 + 6x + 10$
(49)

$g'(x) = 3x^2 + 6$

$g''(x) = 6x$

(a) g is increasing when $g' > 0$.

$3x^2 + 6 > 0$ always

So g is increasing over the interval $(-\infty, \infty)$.

(b) g is concave down when $g'' < 0$.

$$6x < 0$$
$$x < 0$$

So g is concave down over the interval $(-\infty, 0)$.

TEST 15, FORM B

1.
(60)

$-2 + x^2 = -x$

$x^2 + x - 2 = 0$

$(x + 2)(x - 1) = 0$

The graphs intersect at $x = -2$ and $x = 1$.

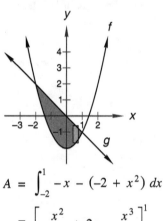

$A = \displaystyle\int_{-2}^{1} -x - (-2 + x^2)\, dx$

$= \left[-\dfrac{x^2}{2} + 2x - \dfrac{x^3}{3}\right]_{-2}^{1}$

$= -\dfrac{1}{2} + 2 - \dfrac{1}{3} - \left(-2 - 4 + \dfrac{8}{3}\right)$

$= \dfrac{9}{2}$

The correct choice is **B.**

2. A variable cannot be moved outside an integral
(57) sign, as in I, but a constant can, as in III. The
property in II is true for all real a, b, and c.

The correct choice is **C**.

3. $v(t) = \dfrac{\ln t}{t}$
(54)

$$v'(t) = \frac{t\left(\dfrac{1}{t}\right) - \ln t \,(1)}{t^2}$$

$$v'(t) = \frac{1 - \ln t}{t^2}$$

$$0 = \frac{1 - \ln t}{t^2}$$

$$\ln t = 1$$

$$t = e$$

The correct choice is **C**.

4. $\quad f(x) = e^x \qquad f(0) = 1$
(55) $\quad f'(x) = e^x \qquad f'(0) = 1$
$\quad f''(x) = e^x \qquad f''(0) = 1$
$\qquad \vdots \qquad\qquad \vdots$

The Maclaurin series for e^x is

$$1 + x + \frac{x^2}{2!} + \frac{x^3}{3!} + \frac{x^4}{4!} + \cdots$$

The correct choice is **C**.

5. $u = 2x^2 \quad du = 4x\,dx$
(56)

$$\int x \cos(2x^2)\,dx = \frac{1}{4} \int 4x \cos(2x^2)\,dx$$

$$= \frac{1}{4} \int \cos u\,du$$

$$= \frac{1}{4} \sin u + C$$

$$= \frac{1}{4} \sin(2x^2) + C$$

The correct choice is **D**.

6.
(56)

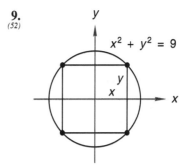

The graph of $y = xe^{-x}$ shows that the area from
-0.7 to 0 is below the x-axis while the area from 0 to

2.4 is above the x-axis. Thus the total area can be
found by entering

```
-fnInt(Xe^-X,X,-0.7,0)
+fnInt(Xe^-X,X,0,2.4),
```

which gives the approximate answer **1.0874.**

7. $\quad u = \sin^2 x \quad du = 2(\sin x)(\cos x)$
(44)

$$y = \sin u$$

$$dy = \cos u\,du$$

$$dy = \left[\cos(\sin^2 x)\right]\left[2(\sin x)(\cos x)\right]$$

$$\frac{dy}{dx} = \left[\sin(2x)\right]\left[\cos(\sin^2 x)\right]$$

8. $y = x^9 + 10$
(58)

Switch x and y and solve for y to find the inverse.

$$x = y^9 + 10$$

$$y^9 = x - 10$$

$$y = \sqrt[9]{x - 10}$$

$$f^{-1}(x) = \sqrt[9]{x - 10}$$

9.
(52)

(graph) y ; $x^2 + y^2 = 9$; y ; x ; x

Let A be the area of the rectangle.

$$A = 4xy$$

$$A = 4x\sqrt{9 - x^2}$$

$$A' = 4x\left(\frac{1}{2}(9 - x^2)^{-1/2}(-2x)\right) + 4\sqrt{9 - x^2}$$

$$A' = -4x^2(9 - x^2)^{-1/2} + 4(9 - x^2)^{1/2}$$

$$A' = 4(9 - x^2)^{-1/2}\left(-x^2 + (9 - x^2)\right)$$

$$A' = 4(9 - x^2)^{-1/2}(9 - 2x^2)$$

Critical numbers occur at $x = \pm 3$ and $x = \pm\sqrt{4.5}$.
The maximum area occurs when $x = \sqrt{4.5}$ and
$y = \sqrt{9 - (\sqrt{4.5})^2} = \sqrt{9 - 4.5} = \sqrt{4.5}$. Thus
the dimensions of the largest possible rectangle are
$3\sqrt{2}$ by $3\sqrt{2}$.

10.
(19)
$$\frac{x^2}{9} + \frac{y^2}{16} = 1$$

$$\frac{y^2}{16} = 1 - \frac{x^2}{9}$$

$$y^2 = 16\left(1 - \frac{x^2}{9}\right)$$

$$y = \pm\sqrt{16\left(1 - \frac{x^2}{9}\right)}$$

Since the point in question has a negative y-value, use

$$y = -\sqrt{16\left(1 - \frac{x^2}{9}\right)}$$

`nDeriv( -√(16(1-X²/9)),X,1)`
approximately equals **0.4714**.

11.
(45)

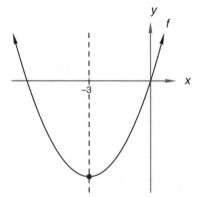

Note: The vertical placement of f is arbitrary.

12.
(49)
$$g(x) = x^3 + 6x + 10$$
$$g'(x) = 3x^2 + 6$$
$$g''(x) = 6x$$

(a) g is increasing when $g' > 0$.

    $3x^2 + 6 > 0$ always

    So g is increasing over the interval $(-\infty, \infty)$.

(b) g is concave down when $g'' < 0$.

$$6x < 0$$
$$x < 0$$

    So g is concave down over the interval $(-\infty, 0)$.

TEST 16, FORM A

1.
(64)
$$y = \arcsin x$$

$$y' = \frac{1}{\sqrt{1 - x^2}}$$

At $x = 0$, $y' = \dfrac{1}{\sqrt{1 - 0}} = 1$.

At $x = 0$, $y = \arcsin 0 = 0$.

An equation of the tangent line is

$$y - 0 = 1(x - 0)$$
$$y = x$$
$$\boldsymbol{x - y = 0}$$

The correct choice is **B**.

2.
(63)
$$f(x) = 2x^3 - 3x^2 - 12x + 1$$
$$f'(x) = 6x^2 - 6x - 12$$
$$0 = 6(x^2 - x - 2)$$
$$0 = (x - 2)(x + 1)$$
$$x = 2, -1 \text{ are critical numbers}$$

Evaluate f at each endpoint and critical number.

$$f(-3) = -44$$
$$f(-1) = 8$$
$$f(2) = -19$$
$$f(3) = -8$$

The minimum value of f on $[-3, 3]$ is **−44**.

The correct choice is **D**.

3.
(64)
$$\int_0^1 \frac{1}{x^2 + 1}\, dx = \arctan x\Big|_0^1$$

$$= \arctan 1 - \arctan 0$$

$$= \frac{\pi}{4} - 0 = \frac{\pi}{4}$$

The correct choice is **A**.

4.
(57)
$$\int_3^6 2f(x)\, dx = 2\int_3^6 f(x)\, dx$$

$$= 2\left[\int_1^6 f(x)\, dx - \int_1^3 f(x)\, dx\right]$$

$$= 2[9 - 5] = \mathbf{8}$$

The correct choice is **B**.

5.
(61)
For $x < 0$, the value of $f''(x)$ is positive, so f must be concave upward. For $x > 0$, $f''(x)$ is negative, so f must be concave downward.

The correct choice is **D**.

6. Work $= \int_2^4 2x \, dx$
(62)

$$= x^2 \Big|_2^4$$

$$= 16 - 4 = \textbf{12 joules}$$

7. $f(x) = ae^x + b$
(61)

$$f(0) = 7$$

$$ae^0 + b = 7$$

$$a + b = 7$$

$$f'(x) = ae^x$$

$$f'(0) = 2$$

$$ae^0 = 2$$

$$a = 2$$

$$\textbf{a = 2, b = 5}$$

8. $A = \int_{\ln 5}^{\ln 6} (6e^x - 5e^x) \, dx$
(60)

$$= \int_{\ln 5}^{\ln 6} e^x \, dx = e^x \Big|_{\ln 5}^{\ln 6}$$

$$= e^{\ln 6} - e^{\ln 5} = 6 - 5 = \textbf{1 unit}^2$$

9. $u = x^2 - 3x$
(51)

$$du = (2x - 3) \, dx$$

$$\int \frac{2x - 3}{x^2 - 3x} \, dx = \int \frac{1}{u} \, du$$

$$= \ln |u| + C$$

$$= \textbf{ln } |x^2 - 3x| + C$$

10. $g(x) = \dfrac{e^{2x} + x}{\sin x - e^x} + \sec x$
(42)

$$g'(x) = \frac{(\sin x - e^x)(2e^{2x} + 1)}{(\sin x - e^x)^2}$$

$$- \frac{(e^{2x} + x)(\cos x - e^x)}{(\sin x - e^x)^2}$$

$$+ \sec x \tan x$$

$$g'(0) = \frac{(-1)(3) - (1)(0)}{(-1)^2} + (1)(0) = \textbf{-3}$$

11. (a)
(47)

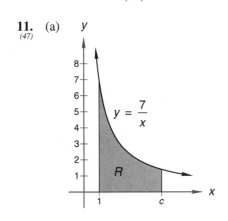

(b) $A = \int_1^c \dfrac{7}{x} \, dx = 7 \ln |x| \Big|_1^c$

$$= 7 \ln c - 7 \ln 1 = 7 \ln c$$

$$7 \ln c = 21$$

$$\ln c = 3$$

$$\textbf{c = e}^3$$

12.
(63)

Note: The value of $f(2)$ is unknown, but $f(2) < 7$.

The function f attains its **maximum value at $x = 4$** and its **minimum value at $x = 2$.**

TEST 16, FORM B

1. $y = \arctan x$
(64)

$$y' = \frac{1}{1 + x^2}$$

At $x = 0$, $y' = \dfrac{1}{1 + 0} = 1$.

At $x = 0$, $y = \arctan 0 = 0$.

An equation of the tangent line is

$$y - 0 = 1(x - 0)$$

$$\textbf{y = x}$$

The correct choice is **D.**

2. $f(x) = 2x^3 + 3x^2 - 12x - 4$
(63)

$$f'(x) = 6x^2 + 6x - 12$$

$$0 = 6(x^2 + x - 2)$$

$$0 = (x + 2)(x - 1)$$

$$x = -2, 1 \text{ are critical numbers}$$

Evaluate f at each endpoint and critical number.

$$f(-3.14) \approx 1.3405$$

$$f(-2) = 16$$

$$f(1) = -11$$

$$f(3.14) \approx 49.8171$$

The minimum value of f on $[-3.14, 3.14]$ is **-11.**

The correct choice is **C.**

3.
(64) $\displaystyle\int_0^1 \frac{1}{\sqrt{1-x^2}}\,dx = \arcsin x\big|_0^1$

$$= \arcsin 1 - \arcsin 0$$

$$= \frac{\pi}{2} - 0 = \frac{\pi}{2}$$

The correct choice is **A**.

4.
(57) $\displaystyle\int_2^7 2f(x)\,dx = 2\int_2^7 f(x)\,dx$

$$= 2\left[\int_{-1}^7 f(x)\,dx - \int_{-1}^2 f(x)\,dx\right]$$

$$= 2[11 - 4] = \mathbf{14}$$

The correct choice is **C**.

5.
(61) For $x < 0$, the value of $f''(x)$ is negative, so f must be concave downward. For $x > 0$, $f''(x)$ is positive, so f must be concave upward.

The correct choice is **A**.

6.
(62) $\displaystyle\text{Work} = \int_{1.2}^{3.7}\left(\frac{1}{3}x^3 + x^2\right)dx$

$$= \frac{x^4}{12} + \frac{x^3}{3}\bigg|_{1.2}^{3.7}$$

$$\approx \mathbf{31.7535\ joules}$$

7.
(61) $f(x) = ae^x + b$

$f(2) = 7$

$ae^2 + b = 7$

$\quad f'(x) = ae^x$

$\quad f'(1) = 2$

$\quad\quad ae = 2$

$\quad\quad a \approx \mathbf{0.7358}$

$b = 7 - ae^2 = 7 - \dfrac{2}{e}\cdot e^2 \approx \mathbf{1.5634}$

8.
(60) The graph of $y = 3^x$ is always above the graph of $y = -3^{-x}$.

$$A = \int_{-2}^2 (3^x + 3^{-x})\,dx$$

$$= \frac{3^x}{\ln 3} + \frac{1}{3^x \ln (3^{-1})}\bigg|_{-2}^2 \approx \mathbf{16.1820\ units^2}$$

9.
(51) $u = x^3 + 3x^2 - 5$

$du = 3x^2 + 6x$

$$\int \frac{3x^2 + 6x}{x^3 + 3x^2 - 5}\,dx = \int \frac{1}{u}\,du$$

$$= \ln |u| + C$$

$$= \mathbf{\ln |x^3 + 3x^2 - 5| + C}$$

10.
(42) $g(x) = \dfrac{e^{2x} - x}{\sin x + e^x} - \tan x$

$g'(x) = \dfrac{(\sin x + e^x)(2e^{2x} - 1)}{(\sin x + e^x)^2}$

$\qquad - \dfrac{(e^{2x} - x)(\cos x + e^x)}{(\sin x + e^x)^2} - \sec^2 x$

$g'(0) = \dfrac{(1)(1) - (1)(2)}{1^2} - 1^2 = \mathbf{-2}$

11. (a)
(47)

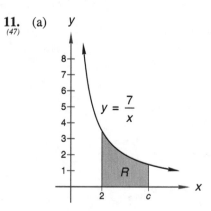

(b) $A = \displaystyle\int_2^c \frac{7}{x}\,dx = 7 \ln |x|\big|_2^c = 7 \ln c - 7 \ln 2$

$\qquad = 7(\ln c - \ln 2) = 7 \ln \dfrac{c}{2}$

$$7 \ln \frac{c}{2} = 28$$

$$\ln \frac{c}{2} = 4$$

$$\frac{c}{2} = e^4$$

$$c = \mathbf{2e^4}$$

12.
(63)

Note: The value of $f(2)$ is unknown, but $f(2) > 7$. The function f attains its **maximum value at $x = 2$** and its **minimum value at $x = 4$.**

TEST 17, FORM A

1. $f(x) = x + \sin x$
(68)

$f(-x) = -x - \sin x$

$f(-x) = -f(x)$

Since $f(-x) = -f(x)$, $f(x)$ is an odd function. Thus the graph of f is **symmetric about the origin**.

The correct choice is **C**.

2. $u = \sin(2x)$
(66)

$du = 2\cos(2x)\,dx$

At $x = 0$, $u = \sin 0 = 0$.

At $x = \dfrac{\pi}{4}$, $u = \sin\dfrac{\pi}{2} = 1$.

$\dfrac{1}{2}\displaystyle\int_0^{\pi/4} 2[\cos(2x)]e^{\sin(2x)}\,dx = \dfrac{1}{2}\int_0^1 e^u\,du$

The correct choice is **A**.

3. $f(x) = x^3 - 6x^2 + 9x$ on $[-1, 5]$
(63)

$f'(x) = 3x^2 - 12x + 9$

$0 = 3(x^2 - 4x + 3)$

$0 = (x - 1)(x - 3)$

$x = 1, 3$ are critical numbers

Evaluate f at each endpoint and critical number. $f(-1) = -16$, $f(1) = 4$, $f(3) = 0$, $f(5) = 20$

The minimum value of f on $[-1, 5]$ is **−16**.

The correct choice is **B**.

4. $y = \arctan(x^2)$
(64)

$y' = \dfrac{1}{1 + (x^2)^2}(2x)$

When $x = 1$, $y' = \dfrac{1}{1 + 1}[2(1)] = 1$.

The correct choice is **C**.

5. $y = x^8 - x^4 + 16x$ is neither even nor odd since
(68) $x^8 - x^4 + 16x^1$ has both even and odd exponents.

$y = x\cos x$ is odd since $-x\cos -x = -x\cos x$ which is $-y$.

$y = x + e^x$ is neither even nor odd since $-x + e^{-x}$ equals neither y nor $-y$.

$y = e^{x^4}$ is even since $e^{(-x)^4} = e^{x^4} = y$.

The correct choice is **D**.

6. $\qquad x = y^2 - 2$
(67)

$y^2 - y - 2 = 0$

$(y - 2)(y + 1) = 0$

$y = 2, -1$

$A = \displaystyle\int_{-1}^{2} \left[y - (y^2 - 2)\right]\,dy$

$= \dfrac{y^2}{2} - \dfrac{y^3}{3} + 2y \Big|_{-1}^{2}$

$= 2 - \dfrac{8}{3} + 4 - \left(\dfrac{1}{2} + \dfrac{1}{3} - 2\right)$

$= \dfrac{9}{2}$ **units**^{2}

7. Let $u = -x$.
(55)

$e^u = 1 + u + \dfrac{u^2}{2!} + \dfrac{u^3}{3!} + \dfrac{u^4}{4!} + \cdots$

$e^{-x} = 1 + (-x) + \dfrac{(-x)^2}{2!} + \dfrac{(-x)^3}{3!}$

$\qquad + \dfrac{(-x)^4}{4!} + \cdots$

$e^{-x} = \mathbf{1 - x +} \dfrac{x^2}{2!} - \dfrac{x^3}{3!} + \dfrac{x^4}{4!} - \cdots$

8. $\tan\theta = \dfrac{1000}{L}$
(46)

$\theta = \tan^{-1}\dfrac{1000}{L}$

$\dfrac{d\theta}{dt} = \dfrac{1}{1 + u^2}\dfrac{du}{dt}$, where $u = \dfrac{1000}{L}$

$\dfrac{d\theta}{dt} = \dfrac{1}{1 + \dfrac{1000^2}{L^2}}\left(-\dfrac{1000}{L^2} \cdot \dfrac{dL}{dt}\right)$

$\dfrac{d\theta}{dt} = -\dfrac{1000}{L^2 + 1000^2} \cdot \dfrac{dL}{dt}$

$\dfrac{d\theta}{dt} = -\dfrac{1000}{2000^2 + 1000^2}(200)$

$\dfrac{d\theta}{dt} = -\dfrac{1}{25}\dfrac{\textbf{rad}}{\textbf{s}}$

9. $u = 8 + \sin(2x)$
(66)

$du = 2\cos(2x)\,dx$

$\displaystyle\int \dfrac{8\cos(2x)}{\sqrt{8 + \sin(2x)}}\,dx = 4\int \dfrac{1}{\sqrt{u}}\,du$

$= 8\displaystyle\int \dfrac{1}{2}u^{-1/2}\,du$

$= 8u^{1/2} + C$

$= 8\sqrt{8 + \sin(2x)} + C$

10.
(48)
$$f(x) = \frac{x^2 + 1}{\sin(2x) + \tan x + 3}$$

$$f'(x) = \frac{[\sin(2x) + \tan x + 3](2x)}{[\sin(2x) + \tan x + 3]^2}$$
$$- \frac{(x^2 + 1)[2\cos(2x) + \sec^2 x]}{[\sin(2x) + \tan x + 3]^2}$$

$$f'(0) = \frac{0 - (1)(2 + 1)}{3^2} = -\frac{1}{3}$$

11. (a) $a(t) = -9.8$
(65)

$$v(t) = \int(-9.8)\,dt = -9.8t + C_1$$

$$v(0) = C_1 = -20$$

$$v(t) = -9.8t - 20$$

$$h(t) = \int v(t)\,dt = -4.9t^2 - 20t + C_2$$

$$h(0) = C_2 = 160$$

$$h(t) = -4.9t^2 - 20t + 160$$

(b) The ball hits the ground when $h(t) = 0$.

$$-4.9t^2 - 20t + 160 = 0$$

By the quadratic formula,

$$t = \frac{20 \pm \sqrt{(-20)^2 - 4(-4.9)(160)}}{2(-4.9)}$$

$$= \frac{20 \pm \sqrt{400 + 3136}}{-9.8}$$

Only the positive t-value makes sense in the context of the problem.

Thus the ball will hit the ground after $\frac{20 - \sqrt{3536}}{-9.8}$ **seconds.**

12. (a) Let $y = f(x)$. Switch x and y and solve for y to
(58) find $f^{-1}(x)$.

$$x = 7y + 6$$

$$7y = x - 6$$

$$y = \frac{x - 6}{7}$$

$$f^{-1}(x) = \frac{x - 6}{7}$$

(b) $(f \circ f^{-1})(x) = f\left(\frac{x - 6}{7}\right)$

$$= 7\left(\frac{x - 6}{7}\right) + 6$$

$$= x$$

(c)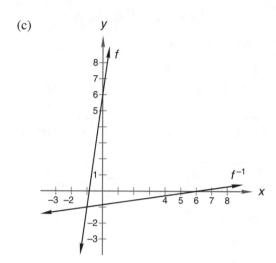

TEST 17, FORM B

1. $f(x) = x^2 \cos x$
(68)

$$f(-x) = (-x)^2 \cos(-x)$$

$$f(-x) = x^2 \cos x$$

$$f(-x) = f(x)$$

Since $f(-x) = f(x)$, f is an even function. Thus the graph of f is **symmetric about the y-axis.**

The correct choice is **A.**

2. $u = \tan(2x)$
(66)

$$du = 2\sec^2(2x)\,dx$$

At $x = 0$, $u = \tan 0 = 0$.

At $x = \frac{\pi}{8}$, $u = \tan\frac{\pi}{4} = 1$.

$$\frac{1}{2}\int_0^{\pi/8} 2\sec^2(2x)\,e^{\tan(2x)}\,dx = \frac{1}{2}\int_0^1 e^u\,du$$

The correct choice is **C.**

3.
(63)

Using the minimum feature on a graphing calculator with boundaries of 1.5 and 5 returns the minimum value of **4** at $x = 2$.

The correct choice is **B.**

4. $y = \sin^{-1}(x^2)$
(64)

$$y' = \frac{1}{\sqrt{1 - x^4}} \cdot 2x$$

At $x = 0.25$, $y' \approx \mathbf{0.5010}$

The correct choice is **D**.

5. $y = x^8 - x^4 + 16x$ is neither even nor odd since
(68) $x^8 - x^4 + 16x^1$ has both even and odd exponents.

$y = x \cos x$ is odd since $-x \cos -x = -x \cos x$
which is $-y$.

$y = x + e^x$ is neither even nor odd since
$-x + e^{-x}$ equals neither y nor $-y$.

$y = e^{x^4}$ is even since $e^{(-x)^4} = e^{x^4} = y$.

The correct choice is **B**.

6. $3 - y^2 = 2y$
(67)

$y^2 + 2y - 3 = 0$

$(y + 3)(y - 1) = 0$

$y = -3$

$$A = \int_{-3}^{1} \left[(3 - y^2) - 2y \right] dy$$

$$= 3y - \frac{y^3}{3} - y^2 \Big|_{-3}^{1}$$

$$= 3 - \frac{1}{3} - 1 - \left(-9 + \frac{27}{3} - 9 \right)$$

$$= \frac{32}{3} \text{ units}^2$$

7. Let $u = -x$.
(55)

$$e^u = 1 + u + \frac{u^2}{2!} + \frac{u^3}{3!} + \frac{u^4}{4!} + \cdots$$

$$e^{-x} = 1 + (-x) + \frac{(-x)^2}{2!} + \frac{(-x)^3}{3!}$$

$$+ \frac{(-x)^4}{4!} + \cdots$$

$$e^{-x} = 1 - x + \frac{x^2}{2!} - \frac{x^3}{3!} + \frac{x^4}{4!} - \cdots$$

8. $\tan \theta = \dfrac{1000}{L}$
(46)

$$\theta = \tan^{-1} \frac{1000}{L}$$

$$\frac{d\theta}{dt} = \frac{1}{1 + u^2} \frac{du}{dt}, \text{ where } u = \frac{1000}{L}$$

$$\frac{d\theta}{dt} = \frac{1}{1 + \dfrac{1000^2}{L^2}} \left(-\frac{1000}{L^2} \cdot \frac{dL}{dt} \right)$$

$$\frac{d\theta}{dt} = -\frac{1000}{L^2 + 1000^2} \cdot \frac{dL}{dt}$$

$$\frac{d\theta}{dt} = -\frac{1000}{1000^2 + 1000^2}(150)$$

$$\frac{d\theta}{dt} = -\frac{3}{40} \frac{\text{rad}}{\text{s}}$$

9. $u = 9 - \cos(3x)$
(66) $du = 3 \sin(3x) \, dx$

$$\int \frac{9 \sin(3x)}{\sqrt{9 - \cos(3x)}} \, dx = 3 \int \frac{1}{\sqrt{u}} \, du$$

$$= 6 \int \frac{1}{2} u^{-1/2} \, du$$

$$= 6u^{1/2} + C$$

$$= \mathbf{6\sqrt{9 - \cos(3x)} + C}$$

10. $f(x) = \dfrac{x^3 - 1}{\sin x + \tan(2x) - 4}$
(48)

$$f'(x) = \frac{[\sin x + \tan(2x) - 4](3x^2)}{[\sin x + \tan(2x) - 4]^2}$$

$$- \frac{(x^3 - 1)[\cos x + 2 \sec^2(2x)]}{[\sin x + \tan(2x) - 4]^2}$$

$$f'(0) = \frac{(0 + 0 - 4)(0) - (-1)(1 + 2(1)^2)}{(0 + 0 - 4)^2}$$

$$f'(0) = \frac{3}{16}$$

11. (a) $a(t) = -9.8$
(65)

$$v(t) = \int a(t) \, dt = -9.8t + C_1$$

$$v(0) = C_1 = -30$$
$$v(t) = \mathbf{-9.8t - 30}$$

$$h(t) = \int v(t) \, dt = -4.9t^2 - 30t + C_2$$

$$h(0) = C_2 = 220$$
$$h(t) = \mathbf{-4.9t^2 - 30t + 220}$$

(b) The ball hits the ground when $h(t) = 0$.
$$-4.9t^2 - 30t + 220 = 0$$

Only a positive t-value makes sense in the context of the problem. The TI-83 approximates the solution as **4.3055 seconds**.

12.
(58)

(a) Let $y = f(x)$. Switch x and y and solve for y to find $f^{-1}(x)$.

$$x = \frac{y - 6}{7}$$

$$7x = y - 6$$

$$y = 7x + 6$$

$$f^{-1}(x) = 7x + 6$$

(b) $(f \circ f^{-1})(x) = f(7x + 6)$

$$= \frac{7x + 6 - 6}{7}$$

$$= x$$

(c)

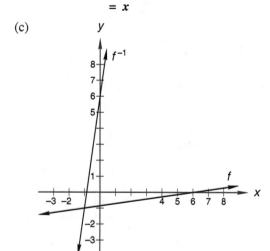

3.
(70)
$\lim\limits_{x \to 0} \dfrac{1}{x}$ is undefined since

$$\lim_{x \to 0^-} \frac{1}{x} = -\infty \quad \text{and} \quad \lim_{x \to 0^+} \frac{1}{x} = +\infty.$$

The correct choice is **D**.

4.
(70)
$\lim\limits_{x \to 2} \dfrac{f(x) + g(x)h(x)}{h(x)} = \dfrac{L + M \cdot 2}{2}$

$$= \frac{L}{2} + M$$

The correct choice is **B**.

5.
(47)
$\displaystyle\int_0^4 x^2 \, dx = \left. \frac{1}{3}x^3 \right|_0^4 = \frac{1}{3}(64 - 0) = \frac{64}{3}$ **units**^{2}

The correct choice is **C**.

6.
(69)

$$u = x \qquad\qquad dv = \cos(2x)\,dx$$

$$du = dx \qquad\qquad v = \frac{1}{2}\sin(2x)$$

$$\int x\cos(2x)\,dx = \frac{1}{2}x\sin(2x) - \int \frac{1}{2}\sin(2x)\,dx$$

$$= \frac{1}{2}x\sin(2x) + \frac{1}{4}\cos(2x) + C$$

7.
(71)

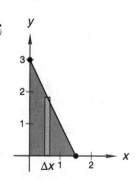

A representative disk has volume $\pi(-2x + 3)^2\,\Delta x$.

$$V = \int_0^{3/2} \pi(-2x + 3)^2\,dx$$

$$= \int_0^{3/2} \pi(4x^2 - 12x + 9)\,dx$$

$$= \pi\left[\frac{4x^3}{3} - 6x^2 + 9x \right]_0^{3/2} = \frac{9\pi}{2}\,\text{units}^3$$

8.
(72)
$f(x) = 2.7^x + 4^x + e^{x^2}$

$f'(x) = 2.7^x \ln 2.7 + 4^x \ln 4 + 2xe^{x^2}$

9.
(64)
$\displaystyle\int \frac{1}{x^2 + 4}\,dx = \frac{1}{2}\arctan\frac{x}{2} + C$

TEST 18, FORM A

1.
(71)

A representative disk has volume $\pi(x^2 + 2)^2\,\Delta x$.

$$V = \int_0^4 \pi(x^2 + 2)^2\,dx$$

The correct choice is **A**.

2.
(72)
$y = \log_6 x - \log_4 x + 5\log_7 x$

$$y' = \frac{1}{x \ln 6} - \frac{1}{x \ln 4} + \frac{5}{x \ln 7}$$

The correct choice is **A**.

10.
(66)
$u = x^2 + 1$

$du = 2x\, dx$

$$\int_0^3 x\sqrt{x^2 + 1}\; dx = \int_1^{10} \frac{1}{2}\sqrt{u}\; du$$

$$= \frac{1}{3} u^{3/2} \Big|_1^{10}$$

$$= \frac{1}{3}(10^{3/2} - 1)$$

11. (a) $A = 2xy = 2x(4 - x^2) = 8x - 2x^3$
(52)

(b) $A' = 8 - 6x^2$

$0 = 8 - 6x^2$

$6x^2 = 8$

$x = \pm \dfrac{2}{\sqrt{3}}$

Maximum area occurs when $x = \frac{2}{\sqrt{3}}$, which yields an area of

$$8\left(\frac{2}{\sqrt{3}}\right) - 2\left(\frac{2}{\sqrt{3}}\right)^3 = \frac{32}{3\sqrt{3}}\; \text{units}^2$$

$$\frac{32\sqrt{3}}{9}$$

12. (a)
(70)

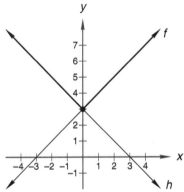

(b) Since $\lim\limits_{x \to 0} f(x) = 3$ and $\lim\limits_{x \to 0} h(x) = 3$,

$$\lim\limits_{x \to 0} g(x) = 3$$

by the squeeze theorem.

TEST 18, FORM B

1.
(71)

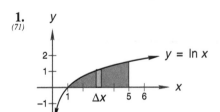

A representative disk has volume $\pi (\ln x)^2 \, \Delta x$.

$$V = \int_1^5 \pi (\ln x)^2\, dx$$

The correct choice is **B**.

2. $y = \log_6 x + 5 \log_4 x - \log_7 x$
(72)

$$y' = \frac{1}{x \ln 6} + \frac{5}{x \ln 4} - \frac{1}{x \ln 7}$$

The correct choice is **D**.

3. The expression $\lim_{x \to 0} \sin \frac{1}{x}$ is undefined since it
(70) fluctuates between -1 and $+1$ more rapidly the closer x gets to zero.

The correct choice is **C**.

4. $\lim\limits_{x \to 3} \dfrac{f(x) - g(x)h(x)}{h(x)} = \dfrac{L - M \cdot 4}{4}$
(70)

$$= \frac{L}{4} - M$$

The correct choice is **C**.

5. Xmin=-1.5, Xmax=2.25,
(53) Xscl=.25, Ymin=-3, Ymax=12,
Yscl=3, Xres=1.

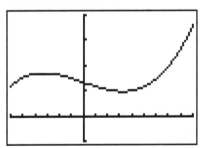

$$A = \int_{-1.5}^{2.25} (x^3 - 2x + 4)\; dx$$

$$= \frac{x^4}{4} - x^2 + 4x \Big|_{-1.5}^{2.25}$$

$$\approx 17.3291 \; \text{units}^2$$

The correct choice is **A**.

6.
(69)

$u = x$　　　　$dv = \sin(2x)\,dx$

$du = dx$　　　$v = -\dfrac{1}{2}\cos(2x)$

$\displaystyle\int x \sin(2x)\,dx$

$= -\dfrac{1}{2}x\cos(2x) + \displaystyle\int \dfrac{1}{2}\cos(2x)\,dx$

$= -\dfrac{1}{2}x\cos(2x) + \dfrac{1}{4}\sin(2x) + C$

7.
(71)

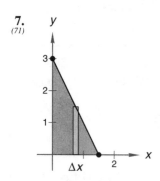

A representative disk has volume $\pi(-2x+3)^2\,\Delta x$.

$V = \displaystyle\int_0^{3/2}\pi(-2x+3)^2\,dx$

$= \displaystyle\int_0^{3/2}(4x^2 - 12x + 9)\,dx$

$= \pi\left[\dfrac{4}{3}x^3 - 6x^2 + 9x\right]_0^{3/2}$

$= \pi\left[\dfrac{9}{2} - \dfrac{27}{2} + \dfrac{27}{2}\right] = \dfrac{9\pi}{2}\ \textbf{units}^3$

8.
(72)

$f(x) = 2.7^x + 4^x + e^{x^2}$

$f'(x) = 2.7^x \ln 2.7 + 4^x \ln 4 + 2xe^{x^2}$

$f'(3) \approx \textbf{48,726.7766}$

9.
(64)

$\displaystyle\int \dfrac{1}{\sqrt{4 - x^2}}\,dx = \textbf{arcsin}\ \dfrac{x}{2} + C$

10.
(66)

$u = x^2 + 1$

$du = 2x\,dx$

$\displaystyle\int_0^3 xe^{x^2+1}\,dx = \displaystyle\int_1^{10}\dfrac{1}{2}e^u\,du$

$= \dfrac{1}{2}e^u\Big|_1^{10}$

$= \dfrac{1}{2}(e^{10} - e)$

$\approx \textbf{11,011.8738}$

11.
(52)

(a) $A = 2xy = 2x(4 - x^4) = 8x - 2x^5$

(b) $A' = 8 - 10x^4$

Using a graphing calculator to find the zeros gives $x \approx 0.9457$, which yields a maximum area of about **6.0527 units**^{2}.

12.
(70)

(a)

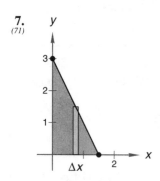

(b) Since $\displaystyle\lim_{x\to 0} f(x) = 3$ and $\displaystyle\lim_{x\to 0} h(x) = 3$,

$$\lim_{x\to 0} g(x) = \textbf{3}$$

by the squeeze theorem.

Test 19, Form A

1.
(76)

$\displaystyle\int \sin^3 x \cos^3 x\,dx = \displaystyle\int \sin^3 x (\cos^2 x) \cos x\,dx$

$= \displaystyle\int \sin^3 x (1 - \sin^2 x)\cos x\,dx$

$= \displaystyle\int (\sin^3 x - \sin^5 x)\cos x\,dx$

$u = \sin x$

$du = \cos x\,dx$

$\displaystyle\int (u^3 - u^5)\,du = \dfrac{u^4}{4} - \dfrac{u^6}{6} + C$

$= \dfrac{\sin^4 x}{4} - \dfrac{\sin^6 x}{6} + C$

The correct choice is **A.**

2.
(75)

The function f will be continuous for all real x if

$$\lim_{x\to 2^+} f(x) = f(2)$$

$$2b = 4a$$

$$b = 2a$$

The values $a = \frac{5}{6}$, $b = \frac{5}{3}$ satisfy this condition.

The correct choice is **D.**

3.
(73)

$\displaystyle\int \log_2 x\,dx = \dfrac{1}{\ln 2}(x\ln x - x) + C$

The correct choice is **C.**

4.
(34)

$$xy + y^2 = x + 1$$

$$x\,dy + y\,dx + 2y\,dy = dx$$

$$x\frac{dy}{dx} + y + 2y\frac{dy}{dx} = 1$$

$$2\frac{dy}{dx} + 1 + 2\frac{dy}{dx} = 1$$

$$\frac{dy}{dx} = 0$$

The correct choice is **B.**

5.
(73)
$$A = \int_0^5 3^x\,dx = \frac{3^x}{\ln 3}\Big|_0^5 = \frac{243}{\ln 3} - \frac{1}{\ln 3}$$

$$= \frac{242}{\ln 3}\ \text{units}^2$$

The correct choice is **C.**

6.
(71)

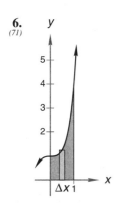

A representative disk has volume $\pi(x^3 + 1)^2\,\Delta x$.

$$V = \int_0^1 \pi(x^3 + 1)^2\,dx$$

$$= \pi\int_0^1 (x^6 + 2x^3 + 1)\,dx$$

$$= \pi\left[\frac{x^7}{7} + \frac{2x^4}{4} + x\right]_0^1$$

$$= \pi\left[\frac{1}{7} + \frac{1}{2} + 1\right] = \frac{23\pi}{14}\ \text{units}^3$$

7.
(72)
$$y = 3^{x^2 + 1} + \ln(x^3 + 1)$$

$$y' = 2x(\ln 3)3^{x^2 + 1} + \frac{3x^2}{x^3 + 1}$$

At $(0, 3)$, $y' = 2(0)(\ln 3)3^1 + \dfrac{3(0)}{0 + 1} = \mathbf{0.}$

8.
(74)

The equation of the right-hand side is
$y = 2x - 2$ or $x = \frac{y + 2}{2}$.

$$\text{Force} = \int_{y=0}^{y=2} w \cdot h \cdot (\text{area of rectangle})$$

$$= \int_0^2 1000(2 - y)\left(\frac{y + 2}{2}\right)dy$$

$$= \int_0^2 500(4 - y^2)\,dy$$

$$= 500\left(4y - \frac{y^3}{3}\right)\Big|_0^2$$

$$= 500\left(8 - \frac{8}{3}\right) = \frac{8000}{3}\ \text{newtons}$$

9.
(56)
$$\int \frac{x - 2}{\sqrt{x}}\,dx = \int\left(\frac{x}{\sqrt{x}} - \frac{2}{\sqrt{x}}\right)dx$$

$$= \int (x^{1/2} - 2x^{-1/2})\,dx$$

$$= \frac{2}{3}x^{3/2} - \frac{2x^{1/2}}{\frac{1}{2}} + C$$

$$= \frac{2}{3}x^{3/2} - 4x^{1/2} + C$$

10.
(36)
$$g(x) = x(\ln x)^3$$

$$g'(x) = x\left(\frac{3(\ln x)^2}{x}\right) + (\ln x)^3$$

$$0 = (\ln x)^2(3 + \ln x)$$

$$\ln x = 0 \qquad \text{or} \qquad 3 + \ln x = 0$$

$$x = 1 \qquad\qquad\qquad \ln x = -3$$

$$x = e^{-3}$$

11. (a) $a(t) = -9.8$
(65)

$$v(t) = \int a(t)\,dt = -9.8t + C_1$$

$$v(0) = C_1 = 49$$

$$v(t) = -9.8t + 49$$

$$h(t) = \int v(t)\,dt = -4.9t^2 + 49t + C_2$$

$$h(0) = C_2 = 10.5$$

$$h(t) = -4.9t^2 + 49t + 10.5$$

(b) The ball reaches its highest point when the velocity equals 0.

$$-9.8t + 49 = 0$$
$$9.8t = 49$$
$$t = \textbf{5 seconds}$$

(c) The maximum height of the ball is

$$h(5) = -4.9(25) + 49(5) + 10.5$$
$$= -122.5 + 245 + 10.5$$
$$= \textbf{133 meters}$$

12.
(75)
For a function f to be continuous at $x = 1$, it must be true that

$$\lim_{x \to 1^-} f(x) = \lim_{x \to 1^+} f(x) = f(1)$$

The statement does not guarantee anything about $f(1)$; therefore f is not necessarily continuous at $x = 1$.

TEST 19, FORM B

1.
(76)
$$\int \sin^3 x \cos^4 x \, dx = \int \sin x \, (\sin^2 x) \cos^4 x \, dx$$

$$= \int \sin x \, (1 - \cos^2 x) \cos^4 x \, dx$$

$$= \int (\cos^4 x - \cos^6 x) \sin x \, dx$$

$$= \int (\cos^6 x - \cos^4 x)(-\sin x) \, dx$$

$$u = \cos x$$
$$du = -\sin x \, dx$$

$$\int (u^6 - u^4) \, du = \frac{u^7}{7} - \frac{u^5}{5} + C$$

$$= \frac{\cos^7 x}{7} - \frac{\cos^5 x}{5} + C$$

The correct choice is **B**.

2.
(75)
The function f will be continuous for all real x if

$$\lim_{x \to 2^+} f(x) = f(2)$$

$$4b = 2a$$
$$2b = a$$

The values $a = \sqrt{2}$, $b = \frac{1}{\sqrt{2}}$ satisfy this condition.

The correct choice is **A**.

3.
(73)
$$\int 4^x \, dx = \frac{4^x}{\ln 4} + C$$

The correct choice is **B**.

4.
(34)
$$2xy - y^2 = 1 - x$$

$$2x \, dy + 2y \, dx - 2y \, dy = -dx$$

$$2x \frac{dy}{dx} + 2y - 2y \frac{dy}{dx} = -1$$

So at $(1, 2)$, $2 \dfrac{dy}{dx} + 4 - 4 \dfrac{dy}{dx} = -1$.

Then $2 \dfrac{dy}{dx} = 5$ or $\dfrac{dy}{dx} = \dfrac{5}{2}$.

The correct choice is **D**.

5.
(73)
$$A = \int_1^4 \log_4 x \, dx$$

$$= \frac{1}{\ln 4}(x \ln x - x)\Big|_1^4$$

$$= \frac{1}{\ln 4}(4 \ln 4 - 4 - (0 - 1))$$

$$= 4 - \frac{3}{\ln 4} \approx \textbf{1.8360 units}^2$$

The correct choice is **A**.

6.
(71)
Xmin=0, Xmax=7, Xscl=1, Ymin=0, Ymax=344, Yscl=50, Xres=1

A representative disk has volume $\pi(x^3 + 1)^2 \Delta x$.

$$V = \int_0^7 \pi(x^3 + 1)^2 \, dx$$

$$= \pi \int_0^7 (x^6 + 2x^3 + 1) \, dx$$

$$= \pi \left[\frac{x^7}{7} + \frac{2x^4}{4} + x \right]_0^7$$

$$= \pi \left(7^6 + \frac{2(7)^4}{4} + 7 \right)$$

$$= \frac{237,713\pi}{2} \textbf{ units}^3 \approx \textbf{373,398.707 units}^3$$

7. (72)
$$y = 3^{x^2+1} + \ln(x^3 + 1)$$
$$y' = 2x(\ln 3)3^{x^2+1} + \frac{3x^2}{x^3 + 1}$$

At $x = 2$, $y' = 2(2)(\ln 3)3^5 + \dfrac{3(4)}{8 + 1}$

$$\approx 1069.1845.$$

8. (74)

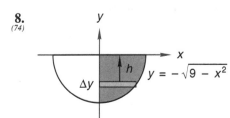

Force $= 2\displaystyle\int_{y=-3}^{y=0} w \cdot h \cdot$ (area of rectangle)

$$= 2\int_{-3}^{0} 6{,}468(-y)\sqrt{9 - y^2}\ dy$$

$$= \int_{0}^{9} 6{,}468\sqrt{u}\ du$$

$$= 6{,}468 \cdot \frac{2}{3}u^{3/2}\Big|_{0}^{9}$$

$$= 4{,}312(27 - 0) = \textbf{116,424 newtons}$$

9. (56)
$$\int \frac{x + 3}{\sqrt{x}}\ dx = \int \left(\frac{x}{\sqrt{x}} + \frac{3}{\sqrt{x}}\right) dx$$

$$= \int (x^{1/2} + 3x^{-1/2})\ dx$$

$$= \frac{2}{3}x^{3/2} + \frac{3x^{1/2}}{\frac{1}{2}} + C$$

$$= \frac{2}{3}x^{3/2} + 6x^{1/2} + C$$

10. (40)

Minimum
X=.22313095 Y=-.1680314

The minimum value of g is about $\textbf{-0.1680}$.

11. (a) $a(t) = -9.8$
(65)
$$v(t) = \int a(t)\ dt = -9.8t + C_1$$
$$v(0) = C_1 = 20$$
$$v(t) = \textbf{-9.8}t + \textbf{20}$$

$$h(t) = \int v(t)\ dt = -4.9t^2 + 20t + C_2$$
$$h(0) = C_2 = 100$$
$$h(t) = \textbf{-4.9}t^2 + \textbf{20}t + \textbf{100}$$

(b) The ball reaches its highest point when the velocity equals 0.

$$-9.8t + 20 = 0$$
$$9.8t = 20$$
$$t = \frac{100}{49}\ \text{seconds}$$

(This is approximately 2.04 seconds.)

(c) $h\left(\dfrac{100}{49}\right) \approx \textbf{120.4082 meters}$

12. For a function f to be continuous at $x = 1$, it must
(75) be true that

$$\lim_{x \to 1^-} f(x) = \lim_{x \to 1^+} f(x) = f(1)$$

The statement does not guarantee anything about $f(1)$; therefore f is not necessarily continuous at $x = 1$.

TEST 20, FORM A

1. The graph of f has a sharp corner at $x = 5$, so the
(72) derivative of f at $x = 5$ **does not exist.**

The correct choice is **D.**

2. $f(x) = \dfrac{x^2 - x - 2}{x - 1} = x - \dfrac{2}{x - 1}$
(80)

The denominator of $x - 1$ means f has a vertical asymptote at $x = 1.$ The divided form shows that $f(x) \approx x$ for large values of x. Thus f has an asymptote of $y = x.$

The correct choice is **D.**

3. Since g is continuous with $g(-1) = 4$ and
(75) $g(3) = -2$, the Intermediate Value Theorem says that $g(x) = 0$ for at least one value between $x = -1$ and $x = 3$. This means **the graph of g must cross the x-axis between $x = -1$ and $x = 3$.**

The correct choice is **C.**

4. Use L'Hôpital's Rule.
(79)
$$\lim_{x \to \infty} \frac{x^2 + \cos x}{x^2 + 5} = \lim_{x \to \infty} \frac{2x - \sin x}{2x}$$

$$= \lim_{x \to \infty}\left(1 - \frac{\sin x}{2x}\right)$$

$$= 1$$

The correct choice is **C.**

5.
(64)
$$\int_0^1 \frac{3}{1+x^2} \, dx = 3 \arctan x \Big|_0^1$$

$$= 3(\arctan(1) - \arctan(0))$$

$$= 3\left(\frac{\pi}{4} - 0\right) = \frac{3\pi}{4}$$

The correct choice is **A.**

6.
(76)
$$\int \cos^3 x \, dx = \int (\cos^2 x)(\cos x) \, dx$$

$$= \int (1 - \sin^2 x)(\cos x) \, dx$$

$$= \int (\cos x) \, dx - \int \sin^2 x \cos x \, dx$$

$$= \sin x - \frac{\sin^3 x}{3} + C$$

7. Use L'Hôpital's Rule.
(79)

$$\lim_{x \to 0} \frac{e^{2x} - 1}{\tan x} = \lim_{x \to 0} \frac{2e^{2x}}{\sec^2 x}$$

$$= \frac{2e^0}{\sec^2 0} = \frac{2}{1} = 2$$

8. The zeros are $x = 2$ and $x = -1$. There is a
(80) vertical asymptote at $x = 3$. Since $y = \frac{x^2 - x - 2}{x - 3}$
$= x + 2 + \frac{4}{x - 3}$, the line $y = x + 2$ is also an asymptote.

9. $u = \sin x + 3$
(66)
$du = \cos x \, dx$

$$\int_0^{\pi/2} \frac{\cos x}{\sqrt{\sin x + 3}} \, dx = \int_3^4 \frac{1}{\sqrt{u}} \, du$$

$$= \int_3^4 u^{-1/2} \, du = 2u^{1/2} \Big|_3^4$$

$$= 2\sqrt{4} - 2\sqrt{3}$$

$$= 4 - 2\sqrt{3}$$

10. $y = \log_2 x$
(72)

$$y' = \frac{1}{x \ln 2}$$

At $x = 3$, $y' = \frac{1}{3 \ln 2}$.

So the slope of the line normal to the graph is **$-3 \ln 2$.**

11. (a) $a(t) = 6t - 4$
(78)

$$v(t) = \int a(t) \, dt = 3t^2 - 4t + C$$

$v(1) = 1$ implies $C = 2$

$$v(t) = 3t^2 - 4t + 2$$

$$x(t) = \int v(t) \, dt = t^3 - 2t^2 + 2t + C$$

$x(0) = 3$ implies $C = 3$

$$x(t) = t^3 - 2t^2 + 2t + 3$$

(b) The velocity is increasing when $v'(t) > 0$. Since $v'(t) = a(t) = 6t - 4$, the velocity is increasing when $6t - 4 > 0$, or $t > \frac{2}{3}$.

12.
(77)

(a) Force $= \displaystyle\int_0^2 9800(2 - y)(4) \, dy$

$$= \int_0^2 39{,}200(2 - y) \, dy$$

$$= 39{,}200\left(2y - \frac{y^2}{2}\right)\Big|_0^2$$

$$= 39{,}200(4 - 2)$$

$$= \textbf{78{,}400 newtons}$$

(b) Work $= \displaystyle\int_0^2 (2 - y)(9800)[4(7)] \, dy$

$$= \int_0^2 274{,}400(2 - y) \, dy$$

$$= 274{,}400\left(2y - \frac{y^2}{2}\right)\Big|_0^2$$

$$= 274{,}400(4 - 2)$$

$$= \textbf{548{,}800 joules}$$

TEST 20, FORM B

1. (72) The graph of f has a slope of +1 when $x > 2$, so $f'(5) = $ **1.**

The correct choice is **B.**

2. (80) $f(x) = \dfrac{x^2 - x - 2}{x^2 - 1} = \dfrac{(x-2)(x+1)}{(x-1)(x+1)} = \dfrac{x-2}{x-1}$

The denominator of $x - 1$ means f has a vertical asymptote at $x = $ **1.** For large values of x, $f(x) \approx 1$, so f has a horizontal asymptote at $y = $ **1.**

The correct choice is **C.**

3. (75) Since g is continuous and $g(-4) = -2$ and $g(3) = 3$, the Intermediate Value Theorem says that $g(x) = 0$ for at least one value between $x = -4$ and $x = 3$. This means **the graph of g must cross the x-axis between $x = -4$ and $x = 3$.**

The correct choice is **D.**

4. (79) Use L'Hôpital's Rule.

$$\lim_{x \to \infty} \frac{x - \cos x}{x^2 + 5x + 6} = \lim_{x \to \infty} \frac{1 + \sin x}{2x + 5}$$

Since $\sin x$ varies from -1 to 1, the numerator varies between 0 and 3 while the denominator grows infinitely large. Thus the limit is **0.**

The correct choice is **A.**

5. (53) In the absence of an effective integration technique, resort to numeric integration on the graphing calculator. `fnInt(3ln(X)/(1+X²),X, 1.2,3.9)` equals approximately **0.9346 units².**

The correct choice is **C.**

6. (76)
$$\int \sin^3 x \, dx = \int (\sin^2 x)(\sin x) \, dx$$
$$= \int (1 - \cos^2 x)(\sin x) \, dx$$
$$= \int (\sin x) \, dx - \int \cos^2 x \sin x \, dx$$
$$= -\cos x + \frac{\cos^3 x}{3} + C$$

7. (79) Use L'Hôpital's Rule.
$$\lim_{x \to 0} \frac{\sin x}{e^{2x} - 1} = \lim_{x \to 0} \frac{\cos x}{2e^{2x}}$$
$$= \frac{\cos 0}{2e^0} = \frac{1}{2}$$

8. (80) The zeros are $x = -3$ and $x = -1$. There is a vertical asymptote at $x = 1$. Since $y = \dfrac{x^2 + 4x + 3}{x - 1} = x + 5 + \dfrac{8}{x-1}$, the line $y = x + 5$ is also an asymptote.

9. (66) $u = \cos x + 3x$

$du = (-\sin x + 3) \, dx$

$$\int_0^{\pi/2} \frac{3 - \sin x}{\sqrt{\cos x + 3x}} \, dx = \int_1^{3\pi/2} \frac{1}{\sqrt{u}} \, du$$
$$= \int_1^{3\pi/2} u^{-1/2} \, du$$
$$= 2u^{1/2} \Big|_1^{3\pi/2}$$
$$= 2\sqrt{\frac{3\pi}{2}} - 2$$
$$= \sqrt{6\pi} - 2$$

10. (72) $y = -\log_4 x$

$$y' = -\frac{1}{x \ln 4}$$

At $x = 5$, $y' = -\dfrac{1}{5 \ln 4}$.

So the slope of the line normal to the graph is **5 ln 4.**

11. (78) (a) $a(t) = 8t - 7$

$$v(t) = \int a(t) \, dt = 4t^2 - 7t + C$$

$v(1) = 1$ implies $C = 4$

$$v(t) = 4t^2 - 7t + 4$$

$$x(t) = \int v(t) \, dt = \frac{4}{3}t^3 - \frac{7}{2}t^2 + 4t + C$$

$x(0) = -5$ implies $C = -5$

$$x(t) = \frac{4}{3}t^3 - \frac{7}{2}t^2 + 4t - 5$$

(b) The velocity is increasing when $v'(t) > 0$. Since $v'(t) = a(t) = 8t - 7$, the velocity is increasing when $8t - 7 > 0$, or $t > \frac{7}{8}$.

12.
(77)

(a) Force $= \displaystyle\int_{y=0}^{y=3} 9800(3 - y)(5)\, dy$

$= \displaystyle\int_0^3 49{,}000(3 - y)\, dy$

$= 49{,}000\left(3y - \dfrac{y^2}{2}\right)\Big|_0^3$

$= 49{,}000\left(9 - \dfrac{9}{2}\right)$

$= \mathbf{220{,}500\ newtons}$

(b) Work $= \displaystyle\int_0^3 (3 - y)(9800)[5(8)]\, dy$

$= \displaystyle\int_0^3 392{,}000(3 - y)\, dy$

$= 392{,}000\left(3y - \dfrac{y^2}{2}\right)\Big|_0^3$

$= 392{,}000\left(\dfrac{9}{2}\right)$

$= \mathbf{1{,}764{,}000\ joules}$

TEST 21, FORM A

1.
(82)
To make the function f continuous at $x = 1$, a and b must make the left- and right-hand limits equal. That is, a and b must satisfy $a(1)^2 = b(1) + 3$ or $a = b + 3$. This eliminates choices C and D. For f to be differentiable at $x = 1$, the left- and right-hand limits of f' must be equal. That is, $2a(1) = 1$ or $2a = b$. This eliminates choice B.

The correct choice is **A**.

2.
(79)
$\displaystyle\lim_{x \to 0} \dfrac{6x^2}{3 \sin (4x)}$

$= \displaystyle\lim_{x \to 0} \dfrac{12x}{12 \cos (4x)}$

$= \dfrac{12(0)}{12 \cos (0)} = \mathbf{0}$

The correct choice is **A**.

3.
(68)
Choice A is even since $f(-x) = \sin \cos (-x)$ $= \sin \cos x = f(x)$.

The correct choice is **A**.

4.
(82)
The graphs of $y = \dfrac{|x|}{x}$ and $y = \dfrac{x - 2}{x^2}$ are not continuous at $x = 0$, so choices A and B can be immediately discarded. The graph of $y = 5x^2$ is a parabola, so it is both differentiable and continuous everywhere. The graph of $y = x^{2/3} + 5$ is continuous at $x = 0$, but the left- and right-hand limits of the derivative are not equal at $x = 0$.

$y' = \dfrac{2}{3}x^{-1/3} = \dfrac{\frac{2}{3}}{x^{1/3}}$

$\displaystyle\lim_{x \to 0^+} \dfrac{\frac{2}{3}}{x^{1/3}} = \infty$ $\displaystyle\lim_{x \to 0^-} \dfrac{\frac{2}{3}}{x^{1/3}} = -\infty$

So the function $y = x^{2/3} + 5$ is not differentiable at $x = 0$.

The correct choice is **C**.

5.
(69)
Finding the intersection of f and g,

$$xe^x = e^x$$
$$x = 1$$

So the integral goes from $x = 0$ to $x = 1$. On this interval, $e^x \geq xe^x$.

Area $= \displaystyle\int_0^1 (e^x - xe^x)\, dx$

$= \displaystyle\int_0^1 e^x\, dx - \int_0^1 xe^x\, dx$

$= e^x\Big|_0^1 - \displaystyle\int_0^1 xe^x\, dx$

$= e^1 - e^0 - \left[xe^x - e^x\right]_0^1$

$= e - 1 - \left[e^1 - e^1 - (0 - e^0)\right]$

$= e - 1 - 1$

$= \mathbf{(e - 2)\ unit^2}$

6.
(62)
By Hooke's law, the force on the spring is $F = kx = 2.5x$. The work done on the spring is

$W = \displaystyle\int_1^4 2.5x\, dx = \dfrac{2.5x^2}{2}\Big|_1^4 = \dfrac{2.5}{2}(16 - 1)$

$= \dfrac{2.5(15)}{2} = \dfrac{75}{4}\ \mathbf{joules}$

7.
(84)
$y = x^{2 \sin x}$

$\ln y = 2 \sin x \ln x$

$\dfrac{y'}{y} = 2\left[(\sin x)\left(\dfrac{1}{x}\right) + (\ln x)(\cos x)\right]$

$y' = 2y\left[\dfrac{\sin x}{x} + (\ln x)(\cos x)\right]$ or

$y' = 2x^{2 \sin x}\left[\dfrac{\sin x}{x} + (\ln x)(\cos x)\right]$

8.
(83)
$$\int 4\cos^2 x\,dx$$

$$= \int 4\left[\frac{1}{2} + \frac{1}{2}\cos{(2x)}\right]dx$$

$$= \int [2 + 2\cos{(2x)}]\,dx$$

$$= 2x + \sin{(2x)} + C$$

9.
(31)
$$y = x^2 e^{x+3}$$
$$y' = x^2 e^{x+3} + e^{x+3}(2x)$$
$$y' = (x^2 + 2x)e^{x+3}$$

10.
(79)
$$\lim_{x\to 2} \frac{x^3 - x^2 - x - 2}{x - 2}$$

$$= \lim_{x\to 2} \frac{3x^2 - 2x - 1}{1}$$

$$= 3(2)^2 - 2(2) - 1 = 7$$

11.
(71,81)
(a) Use the disk method.

$$V = \int_0^1 \pi(x^2)^2\,dx$$

$$= \pi \int_0^1 x^4\,dx$$

$$= \pi\frac{x^5}{5}\bigg|_0^1$$

$$= \frac{\pi}{5}\ \text{unit}^3$$

(b) Use the washer method.

$$V = \int_0^1 \pi\left[1^2 - (\sqrt{y})^2\right]dy$$

$$= \pi \int_0^1 (1 - y)\,dy$$

$$= \pi\left(y - \frac{y^2}{2}\right)\bigg|_0^1$$

$$= \frac{\pi}{2}\ \text{units}^3$$

12.
(80)
(a) $f(x) = \dfrac{2x + 4}{x^2 - 5x + 4} = \dfrac{2x + 4}{(x - 1)(x - 4)}$ The x-axis is the horizontal asymptote because the degree of the numerator is less than the degree of the denominator. The vertical asymptotes are apparent from the factored denominator.
$$y = 0,\ x = 4,\ x = 1$$

(b)

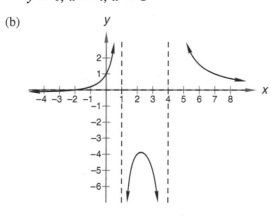

1.
(82)
To make the function f continuous at $x = 1$, a and b must make the left- and right-hand limits equal. That is, a and b must satisfy $a(1) + 3 = b(1)^2$ or $a + 3 = b$. This eliminates choices C and D. For f to be differentiable at $x = 1$, the left- and right-hand limits of f' must be equal. That is, $a = 2b(1)$ or $a = 2b$. This eliminates choice A.

The correct choice is **B.**

2.
(79)
$$\lim_{x\to 0} \frac{6x}{3\sin{(4x)}}$$

$$= \lim_{x\to 0} \frac{6}{12\cos{(4x)}}$$

$$= \frac{6}{12(1)} = \frac{1}{2}$$

The correct choice is **C.**

3.
(68)
The function $\sin{(x^3)}$ is odd since $f(-x)$ $= \sin{[(-x)^3]} = \sin{(-x^3)} = -\sin x = -f(x)$.

The correct choice is **B.**

4.
(82)
The graphs of $y = \frac{|x|}{x}$ and $y = \frac{x-2}{x^2}$ are not continuous at $x = 0$, so choices A and B can be discarded immediately. The graph of $y = x^{2/3} + 5$ is continuous at $x = 0$, but the left- and right-hand derivatives are not equal at $x = 0$.

$$y' = \frac{2}{3}x^{-1/3} = \frac{\frac{2}{3}}{x^{1/3}}$$

$$\lim_{x\to 0^+} \frac{\frac{2}{3}}{x^{1/3}} = \infty \qquad \lim_{x\to 0^-} \frac{\frac{2}{3}}{x^{1/3}} = -\infty$$

So $y = x^{2/3} + 5$ is not differentiable at $x = 0$. The graph of $y = 5x^2$ is a parabola, so it is both continuous and differentiable everywhere.

The correct choice is **D.**

5.
(60)

The graphs intersect at $x = 1$, so the definite integral goes from $x = 0$ to $x = 1$.

$$A = \int_0^1 (e^x - x^2 e^x)\,dx$$

Using fnInt gives $A = $ **1 unit².**

6.
(62)
By Hooke's law, the force on the spring is $F = kx = 2.5x$. The work done on the spring is

$$W = \int_{2}^{4} 2.5x \, dx = \left. \frac{2.5x^2}{2} \right|_{2}^{4} = \frac{2.5}{2}(16 - 4)$$

$$= 2.5(6) = \textbf{15 joules}$$

7.
(84)
$y = x^{2\cos x}$

$\ln y = 2 \cos x \ln x$

$$\frac{y'}{y} = 2 \left[(\cos x)\left(\frac{1}{x}\right) + (\ln x)(-\sin x) \right]$$

$$y' = 2y \left[\frac{\cos x}{x} - (\ln x)(\sin x) \right] \text{ or }$$

$$y' = 2x^{2\cos x} \left[\frac{\cos x}{x} - (\ln x)(\sin x) \right]$$

8.
(83)
$\displaystyle \int 4 \sin^2 x \, dx = \int 4 \left[\frac{1}{2} - \frac{1}{2} \cos(2x) \right] dx$

$$= \int [2 - 2\cos(2x)] \, dx$$

$$= 2x - \sin(2x) + C$$

9.
(31)
$y = x^3 e^{2x}$

$y' = x^3(2e^{2x}) + e^{2x}(3x^2)$

$y' = (2x^3 + 3x^2)e^{2x}$

10.
(79)
$\displaystyle \lim_{x \to 2} \frac{x^4 - x^3 - x - 6}{x - 2}$

$$= \lim_{x \to 2} \frac{4x^3 - 3x^2 - 1}{1}$$

$$= 4(2)^3 - 3(2)^2 - 1$$

$$= 32 - 12 - 1 = \textbf{19}$$

11.
(71,81)
(a) Use the disk method.

$$V = \int_{x=0}^{x=1} \pi (x^3)^2 \, dx = \int_{0}^{1} \pi x^6 \, dx$$

Using fnInt gives $V = \textbf{0.4488 unit}^3$.

(b) Use the washer method.

$$V = \int_{y=0}^{y=1} \pi \left[1^2 - (\sqrt[3]{y})^2 \right] dy$$

$$= \int_{0}^{1} \pi \left[1 - y^{2/3} \right] dy$$

Using fnInt gives $V = \textbf{1.2566 units}^3$.

12.
(80)
(a) $f(x) = \frac{2x+4}{x^2 - 7x + 6} = \frac{2x+4}{(x-1)(x-6)}$ The x-axis is the horizontal asymptote because the degree of the numerator is less than the degree of the denominator. The vertical asymptotes are apparent from the factored denominator.

$y = 0, \ x = 6, \ x = 1$

(b)

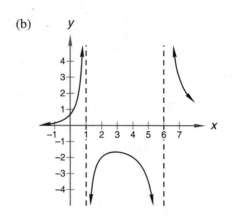

TEST 22, FORM A

1.
(86)
The function $f(x) = \cos x$ is even while $g(x) = x^5 + x^3 + 3x$ is odd. Their product, $(fg)(x)$, is also odd. An odd function integrated over a symmetric interval, $\int_{-k}^{k} (fg)(x) \, dx$, is **zero**.

The correct choice is **B**.

2.
(79)
$\displaystyle \lim_{x \to 1} \frac{x^5 - 1}{x - 1} = \lim_{x \to 1} \frac{5x^4}{1} = \frac{5(1)^4}{1} = \textbf{5}$

The correct choice is **B**.

3.
(84)
$y = x^{\ln x}$

$\ln y = \ln x \ln x = (\ln x)^2$

$\displaystyle \frac{dy}{y} = 2(\ln x)\left(\frac{1}{x}\right) dx$

$\displaystyle \frac{dy}{dx} = \frac{2y \ln x}{x}$

$\displaystyle \frac{dy}{dx} = \frac{2x^{\ln x} \ln x}{x}$

The correct choice is **B**.

4.
(85)
The function $f(x) = x^{2/3}$ is continuous on $[-8, 8]$, but is not differentiable on $[-8, 8]$. This occurs because there is a cusp at $x = 0$.

This can be proven by examining the left- and right-hand derivatives at $x = 0$.

$$f' = \frac{\frac{2}{3}}{x^{1/3}}$$

$$\lim_{x \to 0^+} f'(x) = \infty \qquad \lim_{x \to 0^-} f'(x) = -\infty$$

Since the two are not equal, the derivative does not exist at $x = 0$, and the conditions of the mean value theorem are not met.

The correct choice is **C**.

5. *(88)*

$$\frac{dy}{dx} = 9y^4$$

$$\frac{dy}{y^4} = 9\, dx$$

$$\int y^{-4}\, dy = \int 9\, dx$$

$$-\frac{1}{3}y^{-3} = 9x + C$$

$$y^{-3} = -27x + C$$

$$1^{-3} = -27(0) + C$$

$$1 = C$$

$$y^{-3} = -27x + C$$

$$y^{-3} = -27\left(\frac{1}{3}\right) + 1$$

$$y^{-3} = -8$$

$$y = -\frac{1}{2}$$

6. *(64,66)*

$$\int \frac{9 + x}{1 + x^2}\, dx$$

$$= \int \frac{9}{1 + x^2}\, dx + \int \frac{x}{1 + x^2}\, dx$$

$$= 9 \arctan(x) + \int \frac{x}{1 + x^2}\, dx$$

$$= 9 \arctan(x) + \frac{1}{2} \ln(1 + x^2) + C$$

7. *(88)* $x^2\, dx + 3y\, dy = 0$

$$\int x^2\, dx = \int -3y\, dy$$

$$\frac{x^3}{3} = -\frac{3y^2}{2} + C$$

$$\frac{x^3}{3} + \frac{3y^2}{2} = C$$

8. *(63)* $f(x) = \dfrac{x^2 - 3x - 4}{x + 2}$

$$f'(x) = \frac{(x + 2)(2x - 3) - (x^2 - 3x - 4)(1)}{(x + 2)^2}$$

$$f'(x) = \frac{2x^2 + x - 6 - x^2 + 3x + 4}{(x + 2)^2}$$

$$f'(x) = \frac{x^2 + 4x - 2}{(x + 2)^2}$$

The critical numbers are those values of x in the domain of f for which $f'(x) = 0$ or $f'(x)$ is undefined. Although $f'(-2)$ is undefined, -2 is not in the domain of f, so it is not a critical number. This leaves those x-values for which $f'(x) = 0$.

$$x = \frac{-4 \pm \sqrt{16 + 8}}{2}$$

$$= -2 \pm \frac{\sqrt{24}}{2}$$

$$= -2 \pm \sqrt{6}$$

The critical numbers are $-2 + \sqrt{6}$ and $-2 - \sqrt{6}$.

9. *(19)* $\lim\limits_{h \to 0} \dfrac{\sin(x + h) - \sin(x)}{h} = \cos x$

10. *(85)*

$$f(x) = 3 \cos x$$

$$f'(x) = -3 \sin x$$

Since f is continuous on $\left[\frac{\pi}{2}, \frac{3\pi}{2}\right]$ and differentiable on $\left(\frac{\pi}{2}, \frac{3\pi}{2}\right)$, and since $f\left(\frac{\pi}{2}\right) = f\left(\frac{3\pi}{2}\right) = 0$, Rolle's theorem guarantees that a value c exists in $\left[\frac{\pi}{2}, \frac{3\pi}{2}\right]$ such that $f'(c) = 0$.

$$-3 \sin c = 0$$

$$\sin c = 0$$

$$c = \pi$$

11. *(81,87)*

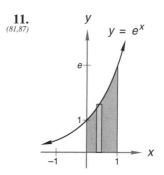

Use the shell method.

$$V = \int_0^1 2\pi x e^x\, dx$$

$$= 2\pi \left[x e^x - e^x \right]_0^1$$

$$= 2\pi \left[e^1 - e^1 - (0 - 1) \right]$$

$$= 2\pi \text{ units}^3$$

12.
(26)

$$A(t) = A_0 e^{rt}$$
$$10,000 = A_0 e^{0.08(10)}$$
$$A_0 = 10,000 e^{-0.8} \approx \textbf{\$4493.29}$$

TEST 22, FORM B

1.
(86)
The functions $f(x) = \cos x$ and $g(x) = x^4 + x^2$ are even, so their product, $(fg)(x)$, is even as well. An even function integrated over a symmetric interval, $\int_{-k}^{k} (fg)(x)\, dx$, is twice the value of $\int_{0}^{k} (fg)(x)\, dx$, or $2(12) = \textbf{24.}$

The correct choice is **D.**

2.
(79)
$$\lim_{x \to 1} \frac{x^3 - 1}{x - 1} = \lim_{x \to 1} \frac{3x^2}{1} = 3(1)^2 = \textbf{3}$$

The correct choice is **B.**

3.
(84)
$$y = x^{e^x}$$
$$\ln y = e^x \ln x$$
$$\frac{dy}{y} = e^x\, dx \ln x + \frac{e^x}{x}\, dx$$
$$\frac{dy}{dx} = ye^x\left(\ln x + \frac{1}{x}\right)$$
$$\frac{dy}{dx} = x^{e^x} e^x\left(\ln x + \frac{1}{x}\right)$$

The correct choice is **A.**

4.
(85)
To satisfy the conditions of the mean value theorem, $f(x) = x^{3/2}$ must be continuous on $[-8, 8]$ and differentiable on $(-8, 8)$. Since $x^{3/2} = (\sqrt{x})^3$, $f(x)$ is not defined for negative numbers, so it is not continuous on $[-8, 8]$.

The correct choice is **D.**

5.
(88)
$$\frac{dy}{dx} = 8y^5$$
$$\frac{dy}{y^5} = 8\, dx$$
$$\int y^{-5}\, dy = \int 8\, dx$$
$$-\frac{1}{4}y^{-4} = 8x + C$$
$$y^{-4} = -32x + C$$
$$1^{-4} = -32\left(\frac{1}{2}\right) + C$$
$$17 = C$$
$$y^{-4} = -32x + 17$$
$$y^{-4} = -32\left(-\frac{1}{4}\right) + 17$$
$$y^{-4} = 25$$
$$y = 25^{-1/4} = \textbf{5}^{-1/2} \approx \textbf{0.4472}$$

6.
(64,66)
$$\int \frac{7 + 2x}{1 + x^2}\, dx$$
$$= \int \frac{7}{1 + x^2}\, dx + \int \frac{2x}{1 + x^2}\, dx$$
$$= 7 \arctan(x) + \int \frac{2x}{1 + x^2}\, dx$$
$$= \textbf{7 arctan}(x) + \ln(1 + x^2) + C$$

7.
(88)
$$x^2\, dx - 3y^2\, dy = 0$$
$$\int x^2\, dx = \int 3y^2\, dy$$
$$\frac{x^3}{3} = y^3 + C$$
$$\frac{x^3}{3} - y^3 = C$$

8.
(63)
$$f(x) = \frac{x^2 - 3x + 5}{x - 4}$$
$$f'(x) = \frac{(x - 4)(2x - 3) - (x^2 - 3x + 5)(1)}{(x - 4)^2}$$
$$= \frac{2x^2 - 11x + 12 - x^2 + 3x - 5}{(x - 4)^2}$$
$$= \frac{x^2 - 8x + 7}{(x - 4)^2}$$

The critical numbers are those values of x in the domain of f for which $f'(x) = 0$ or $f'(x)$ is undefined. Although $f'(4)$ is undefined, 4 is not in the domain of f, so it is not a critical number. This leaves those x-values for which $f'(x) = 0$.

$$x^2 - 8x + 7 = 0$$
$$(x - 7)(x - 1) = 0$$

So $x = \textbf{1, 7}$ are the critical numbers of $f(x)$.

9.
(19)
$$\lim_{h \to 0} \frac{\cos(x + h) - \cos(x)}{h} = \textbf{sin } x$$

10.
(85)
$$f(x) = 3 \cos(2x)$$
$$f'(x) = -6 \sin(2x)$$

Since f is continuous on $\left[\frac{\pi}{4}, \frac{3\pi}{4}\right]$ and differentiable on $\left(\frac{\pi}{4}, \frac{3\pi}{4}\right)$, and since $f\left(\frac{\pi}{4}\right) = f\left(\frac{3\pi}{4}\right) = 0$, Rolle's theorem guarantees that a value c exists in $\left[\frac{\pi}{4}, \frac{3\pi}{4}\right]$ such that $f'(c) = 0$.

$$-6 \sin(2c) = 0$$
$$\sin(2c) = 0$$
$$2c = \pi$$
$$c = \frac{\pi}{2}$$

11.
(81,87)

Use the shell method.

$$V = \int_1^2 2\pi x e^x \, dx$$

$$= 2\pi [x e^x - e^x]_1^2$$

$$= 2\pi(2e^2 - e^2 - e + e)$$

$$= 2\pi e^2 \text{ units}^3$$

12.
(26)
$$A_t = A_0 e^{rt}$$

$$20{,}000 = A_0 e^{0.08(10)}$$

$$A_0 = 20{,}000 e^{-0.8} \approx \$8986.58$$

TEST 23, FORM A

1. $x(t) = 8t - 3t^2$
(90)

$v(t) = 8 - 6t$

The zero of $v(t)$ is at $t = \frac{4}{3}$. To determine the total distance, the position function can be evaluated at 1, $\frac{4}{3}$, and 2.

$$x(1) = 8(1) - 3(1)^2 = 5 = \frac{15}{3}$$

$$x\left(\frac{4}{3}\right) = 8\left(\frac{4}{3}\right) - 3\left(\frac{4}{3}\right)^2 = \frac{16}{3}$$

$$x(2) = 8(2) - 3(2)^2 = 4 = \frac{12}{3}$$

Sum of the distances traveled:

$$\left(\frac{16}{3} - \frac{15}{3}\right) + \left(\frac{16}{3} - \frac{12}{3}\right) = \frac{5}{3}$$

The correct choice is **C.**

2. $\dfrac{1}{2-0} \displaystyle\int_0^2 \sqrt{x} \, dx = \dfrac{1}{2} \displaystyle\int_0^2 x^{1/2} \, dx$
(89)

$$= \frac{1}{2} \cdot \frac{2}{3} x^{3/2} \Big|_0^2$$

$$= \frac{1}{3}(2)^{3/2} = \frac{2}{3}\sqrt{2}$$

The correct choice is **C.**

3. $\displaystyle\lim_{x \to (\pi/2)^-} (\tan x - \sec x)$
(91)

$$= \lim_{x \to (\pi/2)^-} \frac{\sin x - 1}{\cos x}$$

$$= \lim_{x \to (\pi/2)^-} \frac{\cos x}{-\sin x}$$

$$= \frac{0}{-1} = \mathbf{0}$$

The correct choice is **B.**

4. The integral $\int_{-\pi}^{\pi} \cos^2 (2x) \, dx$ is an even function to
(83) be evaluated over a symmetric interval, so it simplifies to

$$2 \int_0^\pi \cos^2 (2x) \, dx = 2 \int_0^\pi \left[\frac{1}{2} + \frac{1}{2} \cos (4x)\right] dx$$

$$= \left[x + \frac{1}{4} \sin (4x)\right]_0^\pi$$

$$= \pi + 0 - (0 + 0) = \pi$$

The correct choice is **C.**

5.
(34)
$$\tan (xy) = x$$

$$\sec^2 (xy)\left[x \frac{dy}{dx} + y\right] = 1$$

$$x \frac{dy}{dx} + y = \cos^2 (xy)$$

$$x \frac{dy}{dx} = \cos^2 (xy) - y$$

$$\frac{dy}{dx} = \frac{\cos^2 (xy) - y}{x}$$

6. Average value $= \dfrac{1}{5} \displaystyle\int_0^5 (3x^2 - 12x + 10) \, dx$
(89)

$$= \frac{1}{5}[x^3 - 6x^2 + 10x]\Big|_0^5$$

$$= \frac{1}{5}(25) = 5$$

The mean value theorem for integrals guarantees a value c such that $f(c) = 5$.

$$3c^2 - 12c + 10 = 5$$

$$3c^2 - 12c + 5 = 0$$

By the quadratic formula,

$$c = \frac{12 \pm \sqrt{144 - 60}}{6} = 2 \pm \frac{\sqrt{84}}{6}$$

$$= 2 \pm \frac{\sqrt{21}}{3}$$

Both $2 - \frac{\sqrt{21}}{3}$ and $2 + \frac{\sqrt{21}}{3}$ are in the interval $[0, 5]$, so either can be chosen for c.

7.
(87)

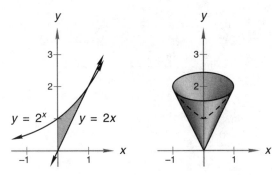

Use the shell method.

$$V = \int_0^1 2\pi x(2^x - 2x)\, dx$$

$$= 2\pi \int_0^1 x 2^x \, dx - 4\pi \int_0^1 x^2 \, dx$$

Integrate by parts.

$$V = 2\pi\left[\frac{x 2^x}{\ln 2} - \frac{2^x}{(\ln 2)^2}\right]_0^1 - \frac{4\pi x^3}{3}\Big|_0^1$$

$$= 2\pi\left(\frac{2}{\ln 2} - \frac{2}{(\ln 2)^2} - 0 + \frac{1}{(\ln 2)^2}\right) - \frac{4\pi}{3}$$

$$= \left[2\pi\left(\frac{2}{\ln 2} - \frac{1}{(\ln 2)^2}\right) - \frac{4\pi}{3}\right] \text{unit}^3$$

8. $\dfrac{dy}{dx} = 7y^2$
(88)

$$\frac{dy}{y^2} = 7\, dx$$

$$-\frac{1}{y} = 7x + C$$

$$y = -\frac{1}{7x + C}$$

9. $f(x) = x^3 + x - 1;\ f'(x) = 3x^2 + 1$
(92)

$$(f^{-1})'(-1) = \frac{1}{f'(f^{-1}(-1))} = \frac{1}{f'(0)}$$

$$= \frac{1}{3(0)^2 + 1} = 1$$

10. $\lim\limits_{x\to\infty} e^{-x} \ln(x^5) = \lim\limits_{x\to\infty} \dfrac{\ln(x^5)}{e^x}$
(91)

$$= \lim_{x\to\infty} \frac{\frac{5x^4}{x^5}}{e^x} = \lim_{x\to\infty} \frac{5}{xe^x} = 0$$

11.
(81,87)

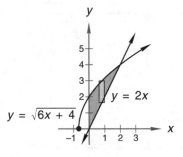

(a) $A = \displaystyle\int_0^2 \left(\sqrt{6x + 4} - 2x\right) dx$

$$= \left[\frac{1}{9}(6x + 4)^{3/2} - x^2\right]_0^2$$

$$= \frac{1}{9}(64) - 4 - \left(\frac{8}{9} - 0\right)$$

$$= \frac{56}{9} - 4 = \frac{20}{9}\text{units}^2$$

(b) Use the washer method.

$$V = \int_0^2 \pi\left[(\sqrt{6x + 4})^2 - (2x)^2\right] dx$$

(c) Use the shell method.

$$V = \int_0^2 2\pi x(\sqrt{6x + 4} - 2x)\, dx$$

12. (a) $a(t) = 6t - 17$
(90)

$$v(t) = 3t^2 - 17t + C$$

$$v(2) = 3(2)^2 - 17(2) + C$$

$$10 = 12 - 34 + C$$

$$32 = C$$

$$v(t) = 3t^2 - 17t + 32$$

(b) Average velocity

$$= \frac{1}{3 - 0}\int_0^3 (3t^2 - 17t + 32)\, dt$$

$$= \frac{1}{3}\left[t^3 - \frac{17t^2}{2} + 32t\right]_0^3$$

$$= \frac{1}{3}\left[\frac{93}{2}\right]$$

$$= \frac{31}{2}\text{ units per second}$$

$$= 15.5 = 15\tfrac{1}{2}$$

TEST 23, FORM B

1.
(83) The integral $\int_{-\pi}^{\pi} \sin^2 (2x)\, dx$ is an even function to be evaluated over a symmetric interval, so it simplifies to

$$2 \int_0^{\pi} \sin^2 (2x)\, dx = 2 \int_0^{\pi} \left[\frac{1}{2} - \frac{\cos (4x)}{2} \right] dx$$

$$= \left[x - \frac{1}{4} \sin (4x) \right]_0^{\pi}$$

$$= \pi - 0 - 0 + 0 = \pi$$

The correct choice is **C**.

2.
(89)
$$\frac{1}{2 - 0} \int_0^2 \sqrt[3]{x}\, dx = \frac{1}{2} \int_0^2 x^{1/3}\, dx$$

$$= \frac{1}{2} \cdot \frac{3}{4} x^{4/3} \Big|_0^2$$

$$= \frac{3}{8} (2)^{4/3} = \frac{3\sqrt[3]{2}}{4}$$

The correct choice is **B**.

3.
(91)
$$\lim_{x \to 0^+} (\cot x - \csc x) = \lim_{x \to 0^+} \frac{\cos x - 1}{\sin x}$$

$$= \lim_{x \to 0^+} \frac{-\sin x}{\cos x} = \frac{0}{1} = 0$$

The correct choice is **B**.

4.
(90)
$$x(t) = 7t - 2t^2$$
$$v(t) = 7 - 4t$$

The zero of $v(t)$ is at $t = \frac{7}{4}$. To determine the total distance, the position function can be evaluated at 1, $\frac{7}{4}$, and 2.

$$x(1) = 7(1) - 2(1)^2 = 5$$

$$x\left(\frac{7}{4}\right) = 7\left(\frac{7}{4}\right) - 2\left(\frac{7}{4}\right)^2 = \frac{49}{8}$$

$$x(2) = 7(2) - 2(2)^2 = 6$$

Sum of the distances traveled:

$$\left(\frac{49}{8} - \frac{40}{8}\right) + \left(\frac{49}{8} - \frac{48}{8}\right) = \frac{10}{8} = \frac{5}{4} \text{ units}$$

5.
(34)
$$\tan (xy) = y$$

$$\sec^2 (xy) \left[x \frac{dy}{dx} + y \right] = \frac{dy}{dx}$$

$$x \frac{dy}{dx} + y = \cos^2 (xy) \frac{dy}{dx}$$

$$\cos^2 (xy) \frac{dy}{dx} - x \frac{dy}{dx} = y$$

$$\frac{dy}{dx} = \frac{y}{\cos^2 (xy) - x}$$

6.
(89)
$$\frac{1}{5 - 1} \int_1^5 (3x^2 - 12x + 10)\, dx$$

$$= \frac{1}{4} [x^3 - 6x^2 + 10x] \Big|_1^5$$

$$= 5$$

The mean value theorem for integrals guarantees a value c such that $f(c) = 5$.

$$3c^2 - 12c + 10 = 5$$

$$3c^2 - 12c + 5 = 0$$

By the quadratic formula,

$$c = \frac{12 \pm \sqrt{144 - 120}}{6}$$

$$= 2 \pm \frac{\sqrt{6}}{3}$$

Only $2 \pm \dfrac{\sqrt{6}}{3}$ is in the interval $[1, 5]$.

7.
(87)

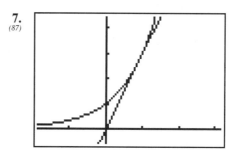

Use the shell method.

$$V = \int_0^1 2\pi x (3^x - 3x)\, dx$$

$$\approx 0.4627 \text{ using } \mathsf{fnInt}.$$

8.
(88)
$$\frac{dy}{dx} = 9y^{-2}$$

$$y^2\, dy = 9\, dx$$

$$\frac{y^3}{3} = 9x + C$$

$$y^3 = 27x + C$$

9.
(92) $f(x) = x^3 + 4x - 7;\ f'(x) = 3x^2 + 4$

$$(f^{-1})(-7) = \frac{1}{f'(f^{-1}(-7))} = \frac{1}{f'(0)}$$

$$= \frac{1}{3(0)^2 + 4} = \frac{1}{4}$$

10.
(91)
$$\lim_{x \to \infty} e^{-x} \ln (x^7) = \lim_{x \to \infty} \frac{\ln (x^7)}{e^x}$$

$$= \lim_{x \to \infty} \frac{\frac{7x^6}{x^7}}{e^x} = \lim_{x \to \infty} \frac{7}{xe^x} = 0$$

11.
(81,87)

Intersection
X=1   Y=3

(a) $A = \int_0^1 (\sqrt{6x + 3} - 3x)\, dx$

$= \left[\frac{1}{9}(6x + 3)^{3/2} - \frac{3}{2}x^2 \right]_0^1$

$= 3 - \frac{3}{2} - \frac{1}{9}\sqrt[3]{27}$

$\approx 0.9226 \text{ unit}^2$

(b) Use the washer method.

$V = \int_0^1 \pi\left[(\sqrt{6x + 3})^2 - (3x)^2\right] dx$

Using fnInt, $V \approx 9.4248 \text{ units}^3$.

(c) Use the shell method.

$V = \int_0^1 2\pi x(\sqrt{6x + 3} - 3x)\, dx$

Using fnInt, $V \approx 1.9822 \text{ units}^3$.

12. (a) $a(t) = 6t - 17$
(90)

$v(t) = 3t^2 - 17t + C$

$v(2) = 3(2)^2 - 17(2) + C$

$3 = 12 - 34 + C$

$25 = C$

$v(t) = 3t^2 - 17t + 25$

(b) Average velocity

$= \frac{1}{3 - 0} \int_0^3 (3t^2 - 17t + 25)\, dt$

$= \frac{1}{3}\left[t^3 - 17\frac{t^2}{2} + 25t \right]_0^3$

$= \frac{1}{3}\left[27 - \frac{153}{2} + 75 \right]$

$= \frac{1}{3}\left[\frac{51}{2} \right]$

$= \frac{17}{2} \text{ units per second}$

TEST 24, FORM A

1. $f(x) = x^3 + x;\ f'(x) = 3x^2 + 1$
(92)

$g'(2) = \dfrac{1}{f'(g(2))}$

Since g is the inverse of f, $g(2)$ is the solution of $x^3 + x = 2$, which by inspection is $x = 1$.

$g'(2) = \dfrac{1}{f'(1)} = \dfrac{1}{3(1)^2 + 1} = \dfrac{1}{4}$

The correct choice is **B**.

2. $\int_{-3}^3 |x + 2|\, dx$
(96)

$= \int_{-3}^{-2} -(x + 2)\, dx + \int_{-2}^3 (x + 2)\, dx$

$= \left[-\frac{x^2}{2} - 2x \right]_{-3}^{-2} + \left[\frac{x^2}{2} + 2x \right]_{-2}^3$

$= \left(-2 + 4 + \frac{9}{2} - 6 \right) + \left(\frac{9}{2} + 6 - 2 + 4 \right)$

$= 13$

The correct choice is **C**.

3. $\displaystyle\lim_{x \to 0} x \csc x = \lim_{x \to 0} \frac{x}{\sin x} = \lim_{x \to 0} \frac{1}{\cos x} = 1$
(91)

The correct choice is **C**.

4. The graph of $f(|x|)$ takes the graph of $f(x)$
(96) for $x \geq 0$ and reflects it about the y-axis. Since the x-value for which $f(x)$ is 0 or -12 are not known, the validity of choices B and D cannot be determined. Choice A is false because $|f(x)| = 12$ at the point where $f(x) = -12$. Since $-12 \leq f(x) \leq 8$, the maximum of $|f(x)|$ must be 12.

The correct choice is **C**.

5.
(88)
$\dfrac{dy}{dx} = \dfrac{1 - 2x}{2y}$

$2y\, dy = (1 - 2x)\, dx$

$y^2 = x - x^2 + C$

$x^2 - x + y^2 = C$

The coefficients of the squared terms are equal, so the equation describes a family of circles.

The correct choice is **A**.

6. $v(t) = \dfrac{t - 2}{t} = 1 - \dfrac{2}{t}$
(54)

$a(t) = \dfrac{2}{t^2}$

As t gets large, $a(t)$ approaches **0**.

---

7. (66) $u = 1 - x$

$du = -dx$

$$\int \frac{2}{\sqrt{1-x}}\, dx = \int 2(1-x)^{-1/2}\, dx$$

$$= -\int 2u^{-1/2}\, du$$

$$= -2\frac{u^{1/2}}{\frac{1}{2}} + C$$

$$= -4\sqrt{1-x} + C$$

8. (85) $f(x) = 3x^2 + 4x - 1;\ f'(x) = 6x + 4$

$$\frac{f(3) - f(1)}{3 - 1} = \frac{38 - 6}{2} = 16$$

$$f'(c) = 16$$

$$6c + 4 = 16$$

$$6c = 12$$

$$c = 2$$

9. (94) Use the disk method.

$y = x^3$

A representative disk has volume $\pi(1 - x)^2 \Delta y$.

$$V = \pi \int_0^1 (1 - x)^2\, dy$$

$$= \pi \int_0^1 (1 - y^{1/3})^2\, dy$$

$$= \pi \int_0^1 (1 - 2y^{1/3} + y^{2/3})\, dy$$

$$= \pi \left[y - 2\left(\frac{3}{4}\right)y^{4/3} + \frac{3}{5}y^{5/3} \right]_0^1$$

$$= \pi \left[1 - \frac{3}{2} + \frac{3}{5} \right] = \frac{\pi}{10}\ \textbf{units}^3$$

10. (49) $y = \frac{1}{3}x^3 - 5x^2 + 21x - 3$

$y' = x^2 - 10x + 21$

$y'' = 2x - 10$

The graph is concave down when $y'' < 0$.

$2x - 10 < 0$

$2x < 10$

$x < 5$

The interval over which the graph is concave down is $(-\infty, \mathbf{5})$.

11. (93) (a) $f(x) = x^3 + 4x^2 - 21x$

$$= x(x^2 + 4x - 21)$$

$$= x(x + 7)(x - 3)$$

The roots are $x = \mathbf{-7, 0, 3}$.

(b) $f'(x) = 3x^2 + 8x - 21$

$x_1 = 2$

$$x_2 = x_1 - \frac{f(x_1)}{f'(x_1)}$$

$$x_2 = 2 - \frac{f(2)}{f'(2)} = 2 - \frac{(-18)}{7} = \frac{32}{7}$$

This is a **rough approximation** $\left(\frac{32}{7} \approx 4.5714\right)$ of the root $x = 3$.

12. (95) (a) Dividing the interval $[1, 4]$ into 3 subdivisions requires 4 values.

x	1	2	3	4
y	1	8	27	64

$$A \approx \frac{4 - 1}{2(3)}[1 + 2(8) + 2(27) + 64]$$

$$\approx \frac{3}{6}[1 + 16 + 54 + 64] = \frac{135}{2} = 67.5$$

(b) $A = \int_1^4 x^3\, dx = \left.\frac{x^4}{4}\right|_1^4 = 64 - \frac{1}{4}$

$$= 63\frac{3}{4} = \frac{255}{4}$$

The trapezoidal rule gave a larger value since $\frac{135}{2} = \frac{270}{4}$.

TEST 24, FORM B

1. (92) $f(x) = x^3 + 2x;\ f'(x) = 3x^2 + 2$

$$g'(3) = \frac{1}{f'(g(3))}$$

Since g is the inverse of f, $g(3)$ is the solution of $x^3 + 2x = 3$, which by inspection is $x = 1$.

$$g'(3) = \frac{1}{f'(1)} = \frac{1}{3(1)^2 + 2} = \frac{1}{5}$$

The correct choice is **A**.

2.
(88)
$$\frac{dy}{dx} = \frac{1 + 2x}{2y}$$
$$2y\,dy = (1 + 2x)\,dx$$
$$y^2 = x + x^2 + C$$
$$y^2 - x^2 - x = C$$

The coefficients of the squared terms have opposite signs, so the equation describes a family of hyperbolas.

The correct choice is **C**.

3.
(91)
$$\lim_{x \to 0} x^{-3} \sin x = \lim_{x \to 0} \frac{\sin x}{x^3}$$
$$= \lim_{x \to 0} \frac{\cos x}{3x^2} = +\infty$$

The correct choice is **D**.

4. Choice A is false since $|f(x)| = 12$ where
(96) $f(x) = -12$. The value of 0 is not on the graph of $f(x)$, so it is not on $f(|x|)$, eliminating choice B. The validity of D cannot be determined since it is not known where $f(x) = -12$ occurs along the x-axis. Since $-12 \le f(x) \le -8$, the maximum of $|f(x)| = |-12| = 12$.

The correct choice is **C**.

5.
(96)
$$\int_{-3}^{3} |x - 2|\,dx$$
$$= \int_{-3}^{2} -(x - 2)\,dx + \int_{2}^{3} (x - 2)\,dx$$
$$= \left[-\frac{x^2}{2} + 2x\right]_{-3}^{2} + \left[\frac{x^2}{2} - 2x\right]_{2}^{3}$$
$$= \left[-2 + 4 + \frac{9}{2} + 6\right] + \left[\frac{9}{2} - 6 - 2 + 4\right]$$
$$= 13$$

6.
(54)
$$v(t) = \frac{t}{t - 2}$$
$$a(t) = \frac{(t - 2) - t}{(t - 2)^2} = \frac{-2}{(t - 2)^2}$$

As t gets large, $a(t)$ approaches **0**.

7.
(66)
$$u = 1 + x$$
$$du = dx$$
$$\int \frac{2}{\sqrt{1 + x}}\,dx = \int 2(1 + x)^{-1/2}\,dx$$
$$= \int 2u^{-1/2}\,du$$
$$= \frac{2u^{1/2}}{\frac{1}{2}} + C$$
$$= 4u^{1/2} + C$$
$$= 4\sqrt{1 + x} + C$$

8. $f(x) = x^2 + 8x - 1;\ f'(x) = 2x + 8$
(85)
$$\frac{f(3) - f(1)}{3 - 1} = \frac{32 - 8}{2} = 12$$
$$f'(c) = 12$$
$$2c + 8 = 12$$
$$2c = 4$$
$$c = 2$$

9.
(94)

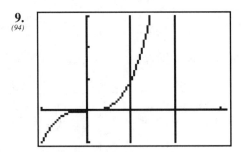

Use the washer method.
$$V = \int_{y=0}^{y=1} \pi\left[(2 - x)^2 - (2 - 1)^2\right]\,dy$$
$$= \int_{0}^{1} \pi\left[(2 - y^{1/3})^2 - 1\right]\,dy$$

Using `fnInt` gives $V \approx$ **1.8850 units³**.

10.
(49)
$$y = \frac{1}{3}x^3 - 5x^2 + 21x - 3$$
$$y' = x^2 - 10x + 21$$
$$y'' = 2x - 10$$

The graph is concave up when $y'' > 0$.
$$2x - 10 > 0$$
$$2x > 10$$
$$x > 5$$

The interval over which the graph is concave up is **(5, ∞)**.

11. (a)
(93)

Using the `2:zero` feature on the `CALCULATE` screen, the roots are approximately **-7.2041**, **0.9061**, and **2.2980**.

(b) $f'(x) = 3x^2 + 8x - 21$

$x_1 = 4$

$x_2 = 4 - \dfrac{f(4)}{f'(4)} = 4 - \dfrac{59}{59} = \mathbf{3}$

$x_3 = 3 - \dfrac{f(3)}{f'(3)} = 3 - \dfrac{15}{30} = \mathbf{2.5}$

This is **a rough approximation** of the largest root, 2.2980.

12. (a) Dividing the interval [1, 4] into 3 subdivisions
(95) requires 4 values.

x	1	2	3	4
y	1	8	27	64

$A \approx \dfrac{4 - 1}{2(3)}[1 + 2(8) + 2(27) + 64]$

$= \dfrac{3}{6}[1 + 16 + 54 + 64] = \mathbf{67.5 \ units^2}$

(b) $A = \displaystyle\int_1^4 x^3 \, dx = \dfrac{x^4}{4}\Big|_1^4 = 64 - \dfrac{1}{4}$

$= \mathbf{63.75 \ units^2}$

This is a smaller value than the trapezoidal approximation.

(c) $E \le \dfrac{(b - a)^3}{12n^2}\left(\max |f''(x)|\right) < 0.001$

With $f''(x) = 6x$, $\max |f''(x)|$ is $6 \cdot 4 = 24$ on the interval [1, 4].

$\dfrac{(4 - 1)^3}{12n^2}(24) < 0.001$

$n^2 > \dfrac{3^3(24)}{(12)(0.001)}$

$n > 232.3790$

Using **233 subdivisions** ensures the error will be less than 0.001.

TEST 25, FORM A

1. $x^2 = 4y$
(97)

$V = \displaystyle\int_{y=0}^{y=2} x^2 \, dy$

$= \displaystyle\int_0^2 4y \, dy$

$= 2y^2\Big|_0^2 = \mathbf{8 \ units^3}$

The correct choice is **A**.

2. The cosine function ranges from -1 to $+1$, so
(96) $\cos x - \dfrac{1}{2}$ ranges from $-\dfrac{3}{2}$ to $\dfrac{1}{2}$. The maximum absolute value in this range is $\dfrac{3}{2}$.

The correct choice is **C**.

3. By the Fundamental Theorem of Calculus,
(98) $F'(x) = e^{-x^2}$.

The correct choice is **C**.

4. Let $f(x) = x^{1/4}$, $x = 81$, $\Delta x = -3$.
(99) Then $\Delta y = 81^{1/4} - 78^{1/4}$

$\approx dy$

$= f'(81)(-3)$

$= \dfrac{1}{4}(81)^{-3/4}(-3)$

$= \dfrac{-3}{4(27)} = -\dfrac{1}{36}$

So $78^{1/4} \approx 81^{1/4} - \dfrac{1}{36} = 3 - \dfrac{1}{36}$

The correct choice is **C**.

5.
(85)
By the mean value theorem, **B** must be true. If $x_1 > x_2$ and $f(x_2) > f(x_1)$, then $\frac{f(x_1) - f(x_2)}{x_1 - x_2}$ would be negative and there would have to be a number c between x_2 and x_1 such that $f'(c) = \frac{f(x_1) - f(x_2)}{x_1 - x_2}$. But that cannot happen because $f'(x) > 0$ for all x. The other options can be ruled out by counterexample. For A, let $f(x) = x$. Then $f(x) < 0$ when $x < 0$. For C, let $f(x) = x^3 + x$. Then f is concave downward when $x < 0$. For D, let $f(x) = e^x$. Then f is concave upward everywhere.

The correct choice is **B**.

6.
(100)
$\int \tan^3 x \, dx$

$= \int \tan x \, (\tan^2 x) \, dx$

$= \int \tan x \, (\sec^2 x - 1) \, dx$

$= \int (\tan x)(\sec^2 x) \, dx - \int \tan x \, dx$

$= \frac{\tan^2 x}{2} - \int \tan x \, dx$

$= \frac{\tan^2 x}{2} - \int \frac{\sin x}{\cos x} \, dx$

$= \frac{\tan^2 x}{2} + \ln |\cos x| + C$

7.
(95)

x	0	$\frac{1}{2}$	1	$\frac{3}{2}$	2
y	1	$\frac{5}{4}$	2	$\frac{13}{4}$	5

$A \approx \frac{2 - 0}{2(4)}\left[1 + 2\left(\frac{5}{4}\right) + 2(2) + 2\left(\frac{13}{4}\right) + 5\right]$

$\approx \frac{1}{4}\left[1 + \frac{10}{4} + 4 + \frac{26}{4} + 5\right] = \frac{19}{4}$

8.
(93)
If $x_1 = 0$, then $f(x_1) = x_1^3 + 7x_1 - 1 = -1$ and $f'(x_1) = 3x_1^2 + 7 = 7$.

$x_2 = x_1 - \frac{f(x_1)}{f'(x_1)}$

$= 0 - \frac{-1}{7} = \frac{1}{7}$

9.
(91)
$\lim_{x \to 0} 5x \csc (2x) = \lim_{x \to 0} \frac{5x}{\sin (2x)} = \frac{5}{2}$

10.
(71)

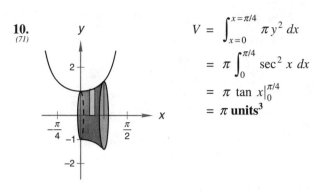

$V = \int_{x=0}^{x=\pi/4} \pi y^2 \, dx$

$= \pi \int_0^{\pi/4} \sec^2 x \, dx$

$= \pi \tan x \Big|_0^{\pi/4}$

$= \pi \text{ units}^3$

11.
(92)
(a) $f^{-1}(4)$ equals x when $f(x) = x^3 + 3x = 4$. The apparent solution is $x = 1$, so $f^{-1}(4) = \mathbf{1}$.

(b) $(f^{-1})'(4) = \frac{1}{f'(f^{-1}(4))} = \frac{1}{f'(1)}$

$= \frac{1}{3(1)^2 + 3} = \frac{1}{6}$

12.
(46)
$V = \frac{1}{3}\pi r^2 h$

$\frac{dV}{dt} = \frac{\pi}{3}\left(r^2 \frac{dh}{dt} + 2rh \frac{dr}{dt}\right)$

$\frac{dV}{dt} = \frac{\pi}{3}[3^2(8) + 2(3)(12)(-2)]$

$\frac{dV}{dt} = \frac{\pi}{3}(-72)$

$\frac{dV}{dt} = -24\pi \text{ cm}^3\text{/s}$

TEST 25, FORM B

1.
(97)

$-x^2 = 4y$

$-x^2 = 4y$

$V = \int_{y=-2}^{y=0} x^2 \, dy$

$= \int_{-2}^{0} -4y \, dy$

$= -2y^2 \Big|_{-2}^{0} = 8 \text{ units}^3$

The correct choice is **A**.

2.
(96) The sine function ranges from -1 to 1 even when its argument is $3x$, so $\sin(3x) - \frac{1}{2}$ ranges from $-\frac{3}{2}$ to $\frac{1}{2}$. The maximum absolute value in this range is $\frac{3}{2}$.

The correct choice is **C**.

3.
(98) By the Fundamental Theorem of Calculus, $F'(u) = e^{-u^2}$.

The correct choice is **C**.

4.
(99) Let $f(x) = x^{1/4}$, $x = 81$, $\Delta x = -3$.

$$\Delta y = 81^{1/4} - 78^{1/4}$$
$$\approx dy$$
$$= f'(81)(-3)$$
$$= \frac{1}{4}(81)^{-3/4}(-3)$$
$$= \frac{-3}{4(27)} = -\frac{1}{36}$$

$$78^{1/4} \approx 81^{1/4} - \frac{1}{36} = 3 - \frac{1}{36}$$

The correct choice is **C**.

5.
(49) By definition of concavity, **D** is true and C is false. The other choices can be ruled out by counterexample. Let $f(x) = -x^2$. Then $f(x) \leq 0$ for all x. Also $f(1) < f(0)$ even though $1 > 0$.

The correct choice is **D**.

6.
(100) $\int \cot^3 x \, dx$

$$= \int \cot x \, (\cot^2 x) \, dx$$
$$= \int \cot x \, (\csc^2 x - 1) \, dx$$
$$= \int (\cot x)(\csc^2 x) \, dx - \int \cot x \, dx$$
$$= -\frac{\cot^2 x}{2} - \int \cot x \, dx$$
$$= -\frac{\cot^2 x}{2} - \int \frac{\cos x}{\sin x} \, dx$$
$$= -\frac{\cot^2 x}{2} - \ln|\sin x| + C$$

7.
(95) Let `Y₁=1/√(X²+1)` and set `Tblstart=0` and `ΔTbl=(1/3)`. This produces the following:

X	Y₁
0	1
.33333	.94868
.66667	.83205
1	.70711
1.3333	.6
1.6667	.5145
2	.44721

X=0

$$A \approx \frac{2 - 0}{2(6)}[1 + 2(0.94868 + 0.83205$$
$$+ 0.70711 + 0.6 + 0.5145) + 0.44721]$$
$$= \mathbf{1.4420}$$

8.
(93) Let `Y₁=X³+7X−1`.

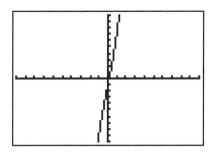

The graph shows the root is near $x = 0$.

Let `Y₂=nDeriv(Y₁,X,X)`.

```
0→X
              0
X-Y₁/Y₂→X
     .1428571224
     .142444261
     .1424442506
     .1424442506
```

The root is approximately **0.14244425**.

9.
(91) $\displaystyle\lim_{x \to 0} \pi x \csc(2x) = \lim_{x \to 0} \frac{\pi x}{\sin(2x)} = \frac{\pi}{2}$

10.
(71)

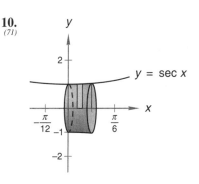

$$V = \int_{x=0}^{x=\pi/12} \pi y^2 \, dx$$
$$= \pi \int_0^{\pi/12} \sec^2 x \, dx$$
$$= \pi \tan x \Big|_0^{\pi/12}$$
$$\approx \pi \tan \frac{\pi}{12} \text{ unit}^3$$

11.
(92)
(a) $f^{-1}(3)$ equals x when $f(x) = x^5 + 2x = 3$. The apparent solution is $x = 1$, so $f^{-1}(3) = \mathbf{1}$.

(b) $(f^{-1})'(3) = \dfrac{1}{f'(f^{-1}(3))} = \dfrac{1}{f'(1)}$

$= \dfrac{1}{5(1)^4 + 2} = \dfrac{1}{7}$

12.
(46)
$V = \dfrac{1}{3}\pi r^2 h$

$\dfrac{dV}{dt} = \dfrac{\pi}{3}\left(r^2 \dfrac{dh}{dt} + 2rh \dfrac{dr}{dt} \right)$

$\dfrac{dV}{dt} = \dfrac{\pi}{3}[3^2(6) + 2(3)(12)(-1)]$

$\dfrac{dV}{dt} \approx -18.8496 \ \dfrac{\mathbf{cm}^3}{\mathbf{s}}$

TEST 26, FORM A

1.
(90)
$v(t) = \dfrac{1}{3}t^3 - \dfrac{7}{2}t^2 + 12t$

$a(t) = t^2 - 7t + 12$

$t^2 - 7t + 12 = 0$

$(t - 4)(t - 3) = 0$

$t = \mathbf{3, 4}$

The correct choice is **D**.

2.
(79)
Use L'Hôpital's Rule.

$\displaystyle\lim_{x \to 0} \dfrac{5x}{\sin(6x)} = \lim_{x \to 0} \dfrac{5}{6\cos(6x)} = \dfrac{5}{6}$

The correct choice is **B**.

3.
(79)
Use L'Hôpital's Rule four times.

$\displaystyle\lim_{x \to \infty} x^4 e^{-x} = \lim_{x \to \infty} \dfrac{x^4}{e^x} = \lim_{x \to \infty} \dfrac{4x^3}{e^x}$

$= \displaystyle\lim_{x \to \infty} \dfrac{12x^2}{e^x} = \lim_{x \to \infty} \dfrac{24x}{e^x} = \lim_{x \to \infty} \dfrac{24}{e^x} = \mathbf{0}$

The correct choice is **B**.

4.
(87)

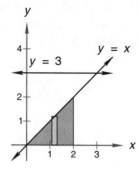

Use the washer method.

$V = \pi \displaystyle\int_0^2 [9 - (3 - x)^2] \, dx$

$= \pi \displaystyle\int_0^2 [9 - (9 - 6x + x^2)] \, dx$

$= \pi \displaystyle\int_0^2 (6x - x^2) \, dx$

$= \pi\left[3x^2 - \dfrac{x^3}{3} \right]_0^2 = \dfrac{28}{3}\pi \ \mathbf{units}^3$

5.
(96)
$\displaystyle\int_0^5 |x - 3| \, dx = \int_0^3 -(x - 3) \, dx + \int_3^5 (x - 3) \, dx$

$= \left[-\dfrac{x^2}{2} + 3x \right]_0^3 + \left[\dfrac{x^2}{2} - 3x \right]_3^5$

$= \left(-\dfrac{9}{2} + 9 \right) + \left(\dfrac{25}{2} - 15 - \dfrac{9}{2} + 9 \right) = \dfrac{\mathbf{13}}{\mathbf{2}}$

6.
(100)
$u = \tan x$

$du = \sec^2 x \, dx$

$\displaystyle\int \pi \sec^2 x \, e^{\tan x} \, dx = \int \pi e^u \, du$

$= \pi e^u + C$

$= \pi e^{\tan x} + \mathbf{C}$

7.
(63)
On the interval $(1, 4)$, the slope is positive and increasing, so the graph is concave up. On the interval $(4, 8)$, the slope is negative and also increasing, so the graph is still concave up. This produces a cusp at $x = 4$.

8.
(76)

$u = \cos x$

$du = -\sin x \, dx$

$\int \sin^3 x \, dx = \int (\sin x)(\sin^2 x) \, dx$

$= \int (\sin x)(1 - \cos^2 x) \, dx$

$= -\int (1 - u^2) \, du$

$= -u + \dfrac{u^3}{3} + C$

$= -\cos x + \dfrac{\cos^3 x}{3} + C$

9. By the Fundamental Theorem of Calculus,
(98)

$f(x) = (\cos x)e^{x+2}$

$f(0) = (\cos 0)e^{0+2} = e^2$

10. For $\frac{dy}{dx} = x$ the slope at any point equals its
(104) x-coordinate, so all points along a given vertical line have the same slope. In the slope field below, consecutive dots are one unit apart.

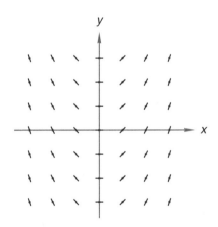

11. Let $y = e^x$ and show that $\dfrac{dy}{dx} = e^x$.
(102)

$y = e^x$

$x = \ln y$

$1 = \dfrac{1}{y} \cdot \dfrac{dy}{dx}$

$y = \dfrac{dy}{dx}$

$e^x = \dfrac{dy}{dx}$

12. $\displaystyle \lim_{h \to 0} \frac{\sin(x+h) - \sin(x)}{h}$
(101)

$= \displaystyle \lim_{h \to 0} \frac{\sin x \cos h + \cos x \sin h - \sin x}{h}$

$= \displaystyle \lim_{h \to 0} \frac{\sin x \cos h - \sin x + \cos x \sin h}{h}$

$= \displaystyle \lim_{h \to 0} \sin x \left(\frac{\cos h - 1}{h} \right) + \lim_{h \to 0} \cos x \left(\frac{\sin h}{h} \right)$

$= \sin x \displaystyle \lim_{h \to 0} \left(\frac{\cos h - 1}{h} \right) + \cos x \lim_{h \to 0} \frac{\sin h}{h}$

$= (\sin x)(0) + (\cos x)(1) = \cos x$

TEST 26, FORM B

1. Use L'Hôpital's Rule.
(79)

$\displaystyle \lim_{x \to 0} \frac{7x}{\sin(8x)} = \lim_{x \to 0} \frac{7}{8 \cos(8x)} = \frac{7}{8} = 0.875$

The correct choice is **B.**

2. $\displaystyle \lim_{x \to \infty} x^{-4} e^x$
(87)

$= \displaystyle \lim_{x \to \infty} \frac{e^x}{x^4}$

$= \displaystyle \lim_{x \to \infty} \frac{e^x}{24}$

$= +\infty$

The correct choice is **D.**

3. $v(t) = t^3 - 7t^2 + 12t$
(90) $a(t) = 3t^2 - 14t + 12$

Using the calculator to determine the zeros of this function gives $t = $ **1.1315** and **3.5352.**

4.
(87)

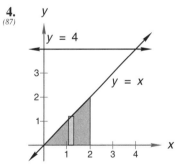

Use the washer method.

$V = \pi \displaystyle \int_0^2 \left[16 - (4 - x)^2 \right] dx$

$= \pi \displaystyle \int_0^2 \left[16 - (16 - 8x + x^2) \right] dx$

$= \pi \displaystyle \int_0^2 (8x - x^2) \, dx = \pi \left[4x^2 - \frac{x^3}{3} \right]_0^2$

$= \dfrac{40\pi}{3} \text{ units}^3$

5. $\int_0^8 |2x - 3|\, dx$
(59)

$$= \int_0^{1.5} (-2x + 3)\, dx + \int_{1.5}^8 (2x - 3)\, dx$$

$$= [-x^2 + 3x]_0^{1.5} + [x^2 - 3x]_{1.5}^8$$

$$= \mathbf{44.5}$$

6. $u = \sec x$
(100)

$du = \sec x \tan x\, dx$

$$\int 3 \sec x \tan x\, e^{\sec x}\, dx = \int 3e^u\, du$$

$$= 3e^u + C$$

$$= 3e^{\sec x} + C$$

7. On the interval $(1, 4)$, the slope is positive and
(63) increasing, so the graph is concave up. On the interval $(4, 8)$, the slope is positive and decreasing, so the graph is concave down. This indicates an inflection point at $x = 4$.

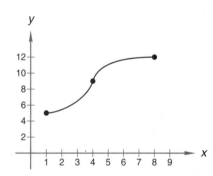

8. $u = \sin x$
(76)

$du = \cos x\, dx$

$$\int \cos^3 x\, dx = \int (\cos x)(\cos^2 x)\, dx$$

$$= \int (\cos x)(1 - \sin^2 x)\, dx$$

$$= \int (1 - u^2)\, du = u - \frac{u^3}{3} + C$$

$$= \sin x - \frac{\sin^3 x}{3} + C$$

9. By the Fundamental Theorem of Calculus,
(98)

$$f(x) = \sin\left(x + \frac{\pi}{4}\right) e^{x+2}$$

$$f(0) = \left(\sin \frac{\pi}{4}\right) e^2 \approx \mathbf{5.2249}$$

10. For $\frac{dy}{dx} = y$ the slope at any point equals its
(104) y-coordinate, so all points on a given horizontal line have the same slope. In the slope field below, consecutive dots are one unit apart.

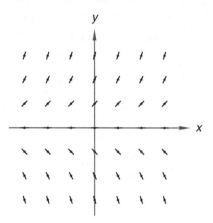

11. Let $y = e^x$ and show that $\dfrac{dy}{dx} = e^x$.
(102)

$$y = e^x$$

$$x = \ln y$$

$$1 = \frac{1}{y} \cdot \frac{dy}{dx}$$

$$y = \frac{dy}{dx}$$

$$e^x = \frac{dy}{dx}$$

12. $\displaystyle\lim_{h \to 0} \frac{\sin(x + h) - \sin(x)}{h}$
(101)

$$= \lim_{h \to 0} \frac{\sin x \cos h + \cos x \sin h - \sin x}{h}$$

$$= \lim_{h \to 0} \frac{\sin x \cos h - \sin x + \cos x \sin h}{h}$$

$$= \lim_{h \to 0} \sin x \left(\frac{\cos h - 1}{h}\right) + \lim_{h \to 0} \cos x \left(\frac{\sin h}{h}\right)$$

$$= \sin x \lim_{h \to 0} \left(\frac{\cos h - 1}{h}\right) + \cos x \lim_{h \to 0} \frac{\sin h}{h}$$

$$= (\sin x)(0) + (\cos x)(1)$$

$$= \cos x$$

TEST 27, FORM A

1. $3\langle 4, -1 \rangle - 2\langle -2, -3 \rangle = \langle 12, -3 \rangle + \langle 4, 6 \rangle$
(93)

$$= \langle 16, 3 \rangle = \mathbf{16}\hat{\imath} + \mathbf{3}\hat{\jmath}$$

The correct choice is **B.**

2. $\displaystyle \lim_{n \to \infty} a_n = \lim_{n \to \infty} \frac{5 - 3n - n^2}{n^3}$
(105)

$\displaystyle = \lim_{n \to \infty} \left(\frac{5}{n^3} - \frac{3}{n^2} - \frac{1}{n} \right) = 0$

$\displaystyle \lim_{n \to \infty} a_n = \lim_{n \to \infty} \frac{n^3}{3^n} = \lim_{n \to \infty} \frac{3n^2}{3^n(\ln 3)}$

$\displaystyle = \lim_{n \to \infty} \frac{6n}{3^n(\ln 3)^2} = \lim_{n \to \infty} \frac{6}{3^n(\ln 3)^3}$

$= 0$

$\displaystyle \lim_{n \to \infty} a_n = \lim_{n \to \infty} \frac{3^n}{2^n} = \lim_{n \to \infty} \left(\frac{3}{2} \right)^n = \infty$

The correct choice is **D.**

3. $\displaystyle \lim_{x \to \infty} \left(1 + \frac{1}{x} \right)^{5x} = \lim_{x \to \infty} \left[\left(1 + \frac{1}{x} \right)^x \right]^5$
(102)

$\displaystyle = \left[\lim_{x \to \infty} \left(1 + \frac{1}{x} \right)^x \right]^5$

$= e^5$

The correct choice is **B.**

4. $r = \cos \theta$
(107)

$\displaystyle \sqrt{x^2 + y^2} = \frac{x}{\sqrt{x^2 + y^2}}$

$x^2 + y^2 = x$

The correct choice is **A.**

5. $\displaystyle x_2 = x_1 - \frac{f(x_1)}{f'(x_1)}$
(93)

$\displaystyle = \frac{3}{2} - \frac{\left(\frac{3}{2} \right)^2 - 2}{2\left(\frac{3}{2} \right)}$

$\displaystyle = \frac{17}{12}$

6. $\displaystyle \frac{1}{e - 1} \int_1^e \frac{1}{x}\, dx = \frac{1}{e - 1} \ln x \Big|_1^e$
(89)

$\displaystyle = \frac{1}{e - 1}(\ln e - \ln 1)$

$\displaystyle = \frac{1}{e - 1}$

7. Let $I = \int e^x \sin x\, dx$ and integrate by parts.
(69)

$u = e^x \qquad\qquad v = -\cos x$

$du = e^x\, dx \qquad dv = \sin x\, dx$

$\displaystyle I = -e^x \cos x - \int (-\cos x)e^x\, dx$

$\displaystyle = -e^x \cos x + \int \cos x \, e^x\, dx$

Integrate by parts again.

$u = e^x \qquad\qquad v = \sin x$

$du = e^x\, dx \qquad dv = \cos x\, dx$

$\displaystyle I = -e^x \cos x + \left[e^x \sin x - \int (\sin x)e^x\, dx \right]$

$I = -e^x \cos x + e^x \sin x - I$

$2I = -e^x \cos x + e^x \sin x$

$\displaystyle I = \frac{-e^x \cos x + e^x \sin x}{2}$

8. $y = 7x^2 - 2x + 1$
(108)

$y' = 14x - 2$

$y' = 14(1) - 2$

$y' = 12$

The vector $\vec{v} = \langle 1, 12 \rangle$ is parallel to the line tangent to the curve at $(1, 6)$ because its slope is 12. Divide $\vec{v}$ by $|\vec{v}|$, which is $\sqrt{145}$, to get the unit vector $\left\langle \frac{1}{\sqrt{145}}, \frac{12}{\sqrt{145}} \right\rangle$. The other possible answer is $\left\langle -\frac{1}{\sqrt{145}}, -\frac{12}{\sqrt{145}} \right\rangle$.

9.
(55)

n	$g^{(n)}(x)$	$g^{(n)}(0)$
0	$\ln(x + 1)$	0
1	$\dfrac{1}{1 + x}$	1
2	$-\dfrac{1}{(1 + x)^2}$	-1
3	$\dfrac{2}{(1 + x)^3}$	2
4	$-\dfrac{6}{(1 + x)^4}$	-6
$\vdots$	$\vdots$	$\vdots$

$\displaystyle 0 + 1x - \frac{1x^2}{2!} + \frac{2x^3}{3!} - \frac{6x^4}{4!} + \cdots$

$\displaystyle = x - \frac{x^2}{2} + \frac{x^3}{3} - \frac{x^4}{4} + \cdots$

10. Let $\varepsilon > 0$ and $f(x) = 2x + 3$, and work back-
(103) ward to find $\delta(\varepsilon)$.

$$7 - \varepsilon < 2x + 3 < 7 + \varepsilon$$

$$4 - \varepsilon < 2x < 4 + \varepsilon$$

$$2 - \frac{\varepsilon}{2} < x < 2 + \frac{\varepsilon}{2}$$

Thus, let $\delta(\varepsilon) = \dfrac{\varepsilon}{2}$ and work forward.

$$|x - 2| < \delta(\varepsilon)$$

$$|x - 2| < \frac{\varepsilon}{2}$$

$$2|x - 2| < \varepsilon$$

$$|2x - 4| < \varepsilon$$

$$|(2x + 3) - 7| < \varepsilon$$

$$|f(x) - 7| < \varepsilon$$

Therefore $\lim\limits_{x \to 2} f(x) = 7$.

11. (a) $f(x) = \dfrac{3}{2}x^{2/3} + 3x^{1/3}$
(63)

$$f'(x) = x^{-1/3} + x^{-2/3}$$

$$f'(x) = x^{-2/3}[x^{1/3} + 1]$$

The first derivative is zero when x is 0 or -1.
The boundary numbers are -8 and 8.

$$f(-8) = 0$$

$$f(-1) = -\frac{3}{2}$$

$$f(0) = 0$$

$$f(8) = 12$$

Absolute maximum: **12**

Absolute minimum: $-\dfrac{3}{2}$.

(b) $f''(x) = -\dfrac{1}{3}x^{-4/3} - \dfrac{2}{3}x^{-5/3}$

$$f''(x) = -\frac{1}{3}x^{-5/3}\left(x^{1/3} + 2\right)$$

$$0 = -\frac{1}{3}x^{-5/3}\left(x^{1/3} + 2\right)$$

$$-8 = x$$

$f''(x)$ is undefined when $x = 0$.

Function f is concave up on the interval **$(-8, 0)$**.

12. (a) $x = 3t$
(106)

$$t = \frac{x}{3}$$

$$y = t^2 + 1$$

$$y = \left(\frac{x}{3}\right)^2 + 1$$

$$y = \frac{x^2}{9} + 1$$

(b)

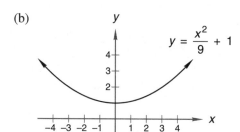

TEST 27, FORM B

1. $-2\langle 4, -1\rangle + 3\langle -1, -3\rangle = \langle -8, 2\rangle + \langle -3, -9\rangle$
(108)
$$= \langle -11, -7\rangle = -11\hat{i} - 7\hat{j}$$

The correct choice is **D.**

2. $\lim\limits_{n \to \infty} a_n = \lim\limits_{n \to \infty} \dfrac{5 - 3n - n^2}{n^3}$
(105)

$$= \lim\limits_{n \to \infty} \left(\frac{5}{n^3} - \frac{3}{n^2} - \frac{1}{n}\right) = 0$$

$$\lim\limits_{n \to \infty} a_n = \lim\limits_{n \to \infty} \frac{3^n}{n^4} = \lim\limits_{n \to \infty} \frac{3^n(\ln 3)}{4n^3}$$

$$= \lim\limits_{n \to \infty} \frac{3^n(\ln 3)^2}{12n^2} = \lim\limits_{n \to \infty} \frac{3^n(\ln 3)^3}{24n}$$

$$= \lim\limits_{n \to \infty} \frac{3^n(\ln 3)^4}{24} = \infty$$

$$\lim\limits_{n \to \infty} a_n = \lim\limits_{n \to \infty} \frac{3^n}{2^n} = \lim\limits_{n \to \infty} \left(\frac{3}{2}\right)^n = \infty$$

The correct choice is **A.**

3. $\lim\limits_{x \to \infty} \left(1 + \dfrac{1}{x}\right)^{8x} = \lim\limits_{x \to \infty} \left[\left(1 + \dfrac{1}{x}\right)^x\right]^8$
(102)

$$= \left[\lim\limits_{x \to \infty} \left(1 + \frac{1}{x}\right)^x\right]^8 = e^8$$

The correct choice is **B.**

4.
(107)
$$r = \sin\theta$$

$$\sqrt{x^2 + y^2} = \frac{y}{\sqrt{x^2 + y^2}}$$

$$x^2 + y^2 = y$$

The correct choice is **B.**

5.
(93)
$$y = f(x) = x^2 - 2 \qquad y' = f'(x) = 2x$$

$$x_1 = 1.5$$

$$x_2 = 1.5 - \frac{f(1.5)}{f'(1.5)} = 1.4166667$$

$$x_3 = 1.4166667 - \frac{f(1.4166667)}{f'(1.4166667)} = \mathbf{1.4142}$$

6.
(89)
$$\frac{1}{e-1} \int_1^e \frac{1}{x}\, dx = \frac{1}{e-1} \ln x \Big|_1^e$$

$$= \frac{1}{e-1}(\ln e - \ln 1)$$

$$= \frac{1}{e-1}$$

7. Let $I = \displaystyle\int e^x \cos x\, dx$ and integrate by parts.
(69)

$$u = e^x \qquad\qquad v = \sin x$$
$$du = e^x\, dx \qquad dv = \cos x\, dx$$

$$I = e^x \sin x - \int (\sin x)e^x\, dx$$

Integrate by parts again.

$$u = e^x \qquad\qquad v = -\cos x$$
$$du = e^x\, dx \qquad dv = \sin x\, dx$$

$$I = e^x \sin x - \left[-e^x \cos x + \int (\cos x)e^x\, dx \right]$$

$$I = e^x \sin x + e^x \cos x - I$$

$$2I = e^x \sin x + e^x \cos x$$

$$I = \frac{e^x \sin x + e^x \cos x}{2}$$

8.
(108)
$$y = 7x^2 - 12x + 1$$

$$y' = 14x - 12$$

$$y' = 14(2) - 12$$

$$y' = 16$$

The vector $\vec{v} = \langle 1, 16 \rangle$ is parallel to the line tangent to the curve at $(2, 5)$ because its slope is 16. Divide $\vec{v}$ by $|\vec{v}|$, which is $\sqrt{257}$, to get the unit vector $\left\langle \frac{1}{\sqrt{257}}, \frac{16}{\sqrt{257}} \right\rangle$. The other possible answer is $\left\langle -\frac{1}{\sqrt{257}}, -\frac{16}{\sqrt{257}} \right\rangle.$

9.
(55)

n	$g^{(n)}(x)$	$g^{(n)}(0)$
0	$\ln(x+1)$	0
1	$\dfrac{1}{1+x}$	1
2	$-\dfrac{1}{(1+x)^2}$	-1
3	$\dfrac{2}{(1+x)^3}$	2
4	$-\dfrac{6}{(1+x)^4}$	-6
$\vdots$	$\vdots$	$\vdots$

$$0 + 1x - \frac{1x^2}{2!} + \frac{2x^3}{3!} - \frac{6x^4}{4!} + \cdots$$

$$= x - \frac{x^2}{2} + \frac{x^3}{3} - \frac{x^4}{4} + \cdots$$

$$\ln 1.3 \approx 0.3 - \frac{0.3^2}{2} + \frac{0.3^3}{3} = \mathbf{0.264}$$

10. Let $f(x) = 3x + 1$ and $\varepsilon > 0$, and work backward
(103) to find $\delta(\varepsilon)$.

$$16 - \varepsilon < 3x + 1 < 16 + \varepsilon$$

$$15 - \varepsilon < 3x < 15 + \varepsilon$$

$$5 - \frac{\varepsilon}{3} < x < 5 + \frac{\varepsilon}{3}$$

Thus let $\delta(\varepsilon) = \dfrac{\varepsilon}{3}$ and work forward.

$$|x - 5| < \delta(\varepsilon)$$

$$|x - 5| < \frac{\varepsilon}{3}$$

$$3|x - 5| < \varepsilon$$

$$|3x - 15| < \varepsilon$$

$$|(3x + 1) - 16| < \varepsilon$$

$$|f(x) - 16| < \varepsilon$$

Therefore $\lim\limits_{x \to 5} f(x) = 16.$

11. (a) $f(x) = \dfrac{3}{2}x^{2/3} + 3x^{1/3}$
(63)

$f'(x) = x^{-1/3} + x^{-2/3}$

$f'(x) = x^{-2/3}[x^{1/3} + 1]$

The first derivative is zero when z is 0. The boundary numbers are –8 and 0.

$f(-8) = 0$

$f(-1) = -\dfrac{3}{2}$

$f(0) = 0$

Absolute maximum: **0**

Absolute minimum: $-\dfrac{3}{2}$

(b) $f''(x) = -\dfrac{1}{3}x^{-4/3} - \dfrac{2}{3}x^{-5/3}$

$f''(x) = -\dfrac{1}{3}x^{-5/3}(x^{1/3} + 2)$

$0 = -\dfrac{1}{3}x^{-5/3}(x^{1/3} + 2)$

$-8 = x$

$f''(x)$ is undefined when $x = 0$

Function f is concave up on the interval **(–8, 0)**.

12. (a) $x = 3t$
(106)

$t = \dfrac{x}{3}$

$y = t^3 + 1$

$y = \left(\dfrac{x}{3}\right)^3 + 1$

$y = \dfrac{x^3}{27} + 1$

(b)

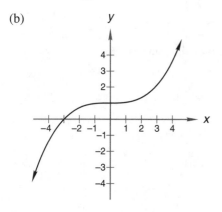

TEST 28, FORM A

1. $L_0^1 = \displaystyle\int_0^1 \sqrt{1 + [y'(x)]^2}\, dx$
(109)

$= \displaystyle\int_0^1 \sqrt{1 + \left(\dfrac{\sec x \tan x}{\sec x}\right)^2}\, dx$

$= \displaystyle\int_0^1 \sqrt{1 + \tan^2 x}\, dx$

$= \displaystyle\int_0^1 \sec x\, dx$

The correct choice is **A**.

2. $y = 3x^2 - 8x + 4;\ y' = 6x - 8$
(108)
At $(2, 0)$, $y' = 4$. Thus the normal vector must have a slope that is the negative reciprocal of 4, which is $-\frac{1}{4}$. Two such vectors are $\langle -4, 1\rangle$ and $\langle 4, -1\rangle$. Divide these vectors by their length, $\sqrt{17}$, to get unit normal vectors. Thus both $\left\langle -\frac{4}{\sqrt{17}}, \frac{1}{\sqrt{17}}\right\rangle$ and $\left\langle \frac{4}{\sqrt{17}}, -\frac{1}{\sqrt{17}}\right\rangle$ fulfill the requirements of the problem.

The correct choice is **D**.

3. $\displaystyle\lim_{x \to 0^+} \ln x^x = \lim_{x \to 0^+} x \ln x$
(111)

$= \displaystyle\lim_{x \to 0^+} \dfrac{\ln x}{\dfrac{1}{x}} = \lim_{x \to 0^+} \dfrac{\dfrac{1}{x}}{-\dfrac{1}{x^2}} = \lim_{x \to 0^+} -x = 0$

$\displaystyle\lim_{x \to 0^+} x^x = e^0 = 1$

The correct choice is **C**.

4.
(106)
$$x = 3 \sin t$$
$$x^2 = 9 \sin^2 t$$
$$x^2 = 9(1 - \cos^2 t)$$
$$x^2 = 9\left(1 - \dfrac{y^2}{16}\right)$$
$$\dfrac{x^2}{9} + \dfrac{y^2}{16} = 1$$

This is an **ellipse** centered at the origin.

The correct choice is **C**.

5. $u = \sin \dfrac{\pi}{2}x$
(66)

$du = \dfrac{\pi}{2} \cos \dfrac{\pi}{2}x\, dx$

$u(0) = 0 \quad u(1) = 0$

$\displaystyle\int_0^1 \sin^3 \dfrac{\pi}{2}x \cos \dfrac{\pi}{2}x\, dx = \dfrac{2}{\pi} \int_0^1 u^3\, du$

The correct choice is **C**.

6.
(106)
$$y = 7 \cos t \qquad x = 5 \sin t$$

$$\frac{dy}{dt} = -7 \sin t \qquad \frac{dx}{dt} = 5 \cos t$$

$$\frac{dy}{dx} = \frac{-7 \sin t}{5 \cos t} = -\frac{7}{5} \tan t$$

7.
(107)
$$x^2 + y^2 - 2x + 4y = 0$$
$$r^2 - 2r \cos \theta + 4r \sin \theta = 0$$

8. Use L'Hôpital's Rule.
(79)

$$\lim_{x \to 0^+} \left(\frac{1}{x^2} - \frac{1}{\sin x} \right) = \lim_{x \to 0^+} \frac{\sin x - x^2}{x^2 \sin x}$$

$$= \lim_{x \to 0^+} \frac{\cos x - 2x}{x^2 \cos x + 2x \sin x} = +\infty$$

9.
(58)
$$2xy - 4x^2 + y^2 = 20$$

$$2 \left(x \frac{dy}{dx} + y \right) - 8x + 2y \frac{dy}{dx} = 0$$

$$2x \frac{dy}{dx} + 2y \frac{dy}{dx} = 8x - 2y$$

$$\frac{dy}{dx} = \frac{8x - 2y}{2x + 2y}$$

$$\frac{dy}{dx}\bigg|_{(1,4)} = \frac{8(1) - 2(4)}{2(1) + 2(4)}$$

$$\frac{dy}{dx}\bigg|_{(1,4)} = 0$$

$$y(1.1) \approx y(1) + \frac{dy}{dx}\bigg|_{(1,4)} (1.1 - 1)$$

$$y(1.1) \approx 4 + 0(0.1)$$

$$y(1.1) \approx 4$$

10.
(94)

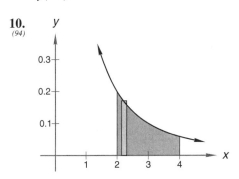

Use the shell method.

$$V = \int_2^4 2\pi r y \, dx = 2\pi \int_2^4 \frac{x}{x^2 - 1} \, dx$$

$$u = x^2 - 1 \qquad du = 2x \, dx$$

$$V = \pi \int_3^{15} \frac{1}{u} \, du = \pi \ln u \big|_3^{15}$$

$$= \pi(\ln 15 - \ln 3) = \pi \ln 5 \text{ units}^3$$

11. (a) The numerators are multiples of 3. The first
(105) denominator is 2, and each following
denominator is 5 times the previous one.

$$a_n = \frac{3^n}{2(5^{n-1})}, \qquad n = 1, 2, 3, \ldots$$

$$a_n = \frac{5}{2} \left(\frac{3}{5} \right)^n, \qquad n = 1, 2, 3, \ldots$$

(b) $\displaystyle \lim_{n \to \infty} a_n = \lim_{n \to \infty} \frac{5}{2} \left(\frac{3}{5} \right)^n = 0$

The sequence **converges to zero.**

12. $\displaystyle L_0^1 = \int_0^1 \sqrt{1 + [f'(x)]^2} \, dx$
(109)

$$= \int_0^1 \sqrt{1 + x^2} \, dx$$

Use the trigonometric substitution $x = \tan \theta$. Thus
$dx = \sec^2 \theta \, d\theta$.

$$L_0^1 = \int_0^{\pi/4} \sqrt{1 + \tan^2 \theta} \, \sec^2 \theta \, d\theta$$

$$= \int_0^{\pi/4} \sec^3 \theta \, d\theta$$

$$= \left[\frac{\sec \theta \tan \theta}{2} + \frac{\ln |\sec \theta + \tan \theta|}{2} \right]_0^{\pi/4}$$

$$= \frac{\sqrt{2} + \ln (1 + \sqrt{2})}{2} \text{ units}$$

TEST 28, FORM B

1. $\displaystyle L_0^1 = \int_0^1 \sqrt{1 + [y'(x)]^2} \, dx$
(109)

$$= \int_0^1 \sqrt{1 + \left(\frac{-\csc x \cot x}{\csc x} \right)^2} \, dx$$

$$= \int_0^1 \sqrt{1 + \cot^2 x} \, dx$$

$$= \int_0^1 \csc x \, dx$$

The correct choice is **A.**

2. $y = x^2 - 4x + 4; \quad y' = 2x - 4$
(108)
At $(4, 4)$, $y' = 4$. Thus the normal vector must
have a slope that is the negative reciprocal of 4,
which is $-\frac{1}{4}$. Two such vectors are $\langle -4, 1 \rangle$ and $\langle 4, -1 \rangle$.
Divide these vectors by their length, $\sqrt{17}$, to get unit
normal vectors. Thus both $\left\langle -\frac{4}{\sqrt{17}}, \frac{1}{\sqrt{17}} \right\rangle$ and
$\left\langle \frac{4}{\sqrt{17}}, -\frac{1}{\sqrt{17}} \right\rangle$ fulfill the requirements of the problem.

The correct choice is **D.**

3.
(111)
$$\lim_{x \to 0^+} \ln(x^{2x}) = \lim_{x \to 0^+} 2x \ln x$$

$$= \lim_{x \to 0^+} \frac{\ln x}{\frac{1}{2x}} = \lim_{x \to 0^+} \frac{\frac{1}{x}}{\frac{-1}{2x^2}} = \lim_{x \to 0^+} -2x = 0$$

$$\lim_{x \to 0^+} x^{2x} = e^0 = \mathbf{1}$$

The correct choice is **C**.

4.
(106)
$$x = 3 \sin t$$

$$x^2 = 9 \sin^2 t$$

$$x^2 = 9(1 - \cos^2 t)$$

$$x^2 = 9\left(1 - \frac{y^2}{9}\right)$$

$$x^2 + y^2 = 9$$

This is a **circle** of radius 3 centered at the origin.

The correct choice is **B**.

5.
(66)
$$u = \cos \frac{\pi}{2} x$$

$$du = -\frac{\pi}{2} \sin \frac{\pi}{2} x \, dx$$

$$u(0) = 1 \quad u(1) = 0$$

$$\int_0^1 \cos^3 \frac{\pi}{2} x \sin \frac{\pi}{2} x \, dx = -\frac{2}{\pi} \int_1^0 u^3 \, du$$

The correct choice is **C**.

6.
(106)
$$y = 7 \cos t \qquad x = 5 \sin t$$

$$\frac{dy}{dt} = -7 \sin t \qquad \frac{dx}{dt} = 5 \cos t$$

$$\frac{dy}{dx} = \frac{-7 \sin t}{5 \cos t} = \frac{-7}{5} \tan t$$

$$\frac{dy}{dx}\bigg|_{t = \pi/6} = -\frac{7}{5} \tan \frac{\pi}{6} \approx \mathbf{-0.8083}$$

7.
(107)
$$x^2 + y^2 + 3x - 5y = 0$$
$$r^2 + 3r \cos \theta - 5r \sin \theta = 0$$

8.
(79)
Use L'Hôpital's Rule.

$$\lim_{x \to 0^+} \left(\frac{1}{x} - \frac{1}{2 \sin x}\right) = \lim_{x \to 0^+} \frac{2 \sin x - x}{2x \sin x}$$

$$= \lim_{x \to 0^+} \frac{2 \cos x - 1}{2x \cos x + 2 \sin x} = +\infty$$

9.
(58)
$$2xy - 4x^2 + y^2 = 20$$

$$2\left(x \frac{dy}{dx} + y\right) - 8x + 2y \frac{dy}{dx} = 0$$

$$2x \frac{dy}{dx} + 2y \frac{dy}{dx} = 8x - 2y$$

$$\frac{dy}{dx} = \frac{8x - 2y}{2x + 2y}$$

$$\frac{dy}{dx}\bigg|_{(1,4)} = \frac{8(1) - 2(4)}{2(1) + 2(4)}$$

$$\frac{dy}{dx}\bigg|_{(1,4)} = 0$$

$$y(0.9) \approx y(1) + \frac{dy}{dx}\bigg|_{(1,4)} (0.9 - 1)$$

$$y(0.9) \approx 4 + 0(-0.1)$$

$$y(0.9) \approx \mathbf{4}$$

10.
(94)

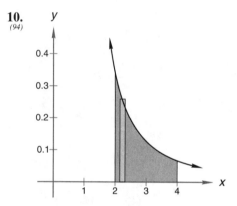

Use the shell method.

$$V = \int_2^4 2\pi r y \, dx = 2\pi \int_2^4 \frac{x}{x^2 + 1} \, dx$$

$$u = x^2 + 1 \quad du = 2x \, dx$$

$$V = \pi \int_5^{17} \frac{1}{u} \, du = \pi \ln u \big|_5^{17}$$

$$= \pi(\mathbf{ln\ 17 - ln\ 5})\ \mathbf{units}^3$$

11.
(105)
(a) The first numerator is 3, and each following numerator is 3 times the previous one. The first denominator is 2, and each following denominator is 5 times the previous one.

$$a_n = \frac{3^{n+1}}{2(5^n)}, \qquad n = 1, 2, 3, \ldots$$

$$a_n = \frac{3}{2}\left(\frac{3}{5}\right)^n, \ n = \mathbf{1, 2, 3, \ldots}$$

(b) $$\lim_{n \to \infty} a_n = \lim_{n \to \infty} \frac{3}{2}\left(\frac{3}{5}\right)^n = 0$$

The sequence **converges to zero**.

12. $L_0^1 = \int_0^1 \sqrt{1 + [f'(x)]^2}\ dx$
(109)

$\qquad = \int_0^1 \sqrt{1 + \dfrac{9x^4}{4}}\ dx$

From **fnInt** the arc length is approximately **1.1825 units.**

TEST 29, FORM A

1. The third partial sum is the sum of the first three terms.
(116)

$$\frac{3}{2} + \frac{3}{4} + \frac{3}{8} = \frac{21}{8}$$

The correct choice is **D.**

2. $r = 4 \cos \theta$
(107)

$$\sqrt{x^2 + y^2} = \frac{4x}{\sqrt{x^2 + y^2}}$$

$$x^2 + y^2 = 4x$$

$$(x^2 - 4x) + y^2 = 0$$

$$(x - 2)^2 - 4 + y^2 = 0$$

$$(x - 2)^2 + y^2 = 2^2$$

This describes a circle of radius 2 centered at (2, 0).

The correct choice is **B.**

3. $\displaystyle\int_{-1}^{1} \frac{dx}{x^2 + 5x + 6} = \int_{-1}^{1} \frac{dx}{(x + 2)(x + 3)}$
(115)

$$= \int_{-1}^{1} \left(\frac{1}{x + 2} - \frac{1}{x + 3} \right) dx$$

$$= \Big[\ln |x + 2| - \ln |x + 3| \Big]_{-1}^{1}$$

$$= \ln 3 - \ln 1 - \ln 4 + \ln 2$$

$$= \ln \frac{3}{2}$$

The correct choice is **A.**

4. In this slope field $\frac{dy}{dx}$ is zero whenever x or y is zero.
(104) Among these choices only the differential equation $\frac{dy}{dx} = x^2 y^2$ satisfies this condition.

The correct choice is **B.**

5. For a function multiplied by a minus sign to equal
(96) its absolute value, the function must be either negative or zero.

The correct choice is **C.**

6. Use trigonometric substitution.
(113)

$$x = 2 \sin \theta$$

$$dx = 2 \cos \theta\ d\theta$$

$$\int_0^1 \frac{1}{(4 - x^2)^{3/2}}\ dx = \int_0^{\pi/6} \frac{2 \cos \theta\ d\theta}{(4 - 4 \sin^2 \theta)^{3/2}}$$

$$= \frac{1}{4} \int_0^{\pi/6} \frac{\cos \theta\ d\theta}{\cos^3 \theta}$$

$$= \frac{1}{4} \int_0^{\pi/6} \sec^2 \theta\ d\theta$$

$$= \frac{1}{4} \tan \theta \Big|_0^{\pi/6}$$

$$= \mathbf{\frac{1}{4\sqrt{3}}}$$

7. The described ellipse, $\frac{x^2}{16} + \frac{y^2}{64} = 1$, is centered at
(97) the origin. The vertical cross sections run parallel to the x-axis with each side having a length of $2x$.

$$V = \int_{y=-8}^{y=8} (2x)^2\ dy$$

$$= \int_{-8}^{8} (64 - y^2)\ dy$$

$$= \left[64y - \frac{y^3}{3} \right]_{-8}^{8}$$

$$= 1024 - \frac{1024}{3} = \mathbf{\frac{2048}{3}}\ \textbf{units}^3$$

8. $\displaystyle\lim_{x \to 0^+} \ln (e^x - 1)^x = \lim_{x \to 0^+} x \ln (e^x - 1)$
(111)

$$= \lim_{x \to 0^+} \frac{\ln (e^x - 1)}{\frac{1}{x}} = \lim_{x \to 0^+} \frac{\frac{e^x}{e^x - 1}}{-\frac{1}{x^2}}$$

$$= \lim_{x \to 0^+} \frac{-x^2 e^x}{e^x - 1} = \lim_{x \to 0^+} \frac{-x^2 e^x - 2xe^x}{e^x}$$

$$= \lim_{x \to 0^+} (-x^2 - 2x) = 0$$

$$\lim_{x \to 0^+} (e^x - 1)^x = e^0 = 1$$

9. $y = (2t + 5)^{1/2} \qquad x = t - t^2$
(106)

$$\frac{dy}{dt} = (2t + 5)^{-1/2} \qquad \frac{dx}{dt} = 1 - 2t$$

$$\frac{dy}{dx}\Big|_{t=2} = \frac{(2t + 5)^{-1/2}}{1 - 2t}\Big|_2 = -\frac{1}{9}$$

10.
(102)
$$\lim_{n \to \infty} \left(\frac{n + 3}{n}\right)^n = \lim_{n \to \infty} \left(1 + \frac{3}{n}\right)^n = e^3$$

The sequence **converges to e^3.**

11.
(90)
(a) The particle can only be at rest when $v(t) = 0$, which never occurs for the given velocity function; so the particle is **never at rest.**

(b) $v(t) = (16 - t^2)^{-1/2}$

$$a(t) = -\frac{1}{2}(16 - t^2)^{-3/2}(-2t)$$

$$a(t) = t(16 - t^2)^{-3/2}$$

$$a(1) = 1(15)^{-3/2}$$

$$a(1) = \frac{1}{15^{3/2}}$$

12.
(114)
$$L_0^2 = \int_0^2 \sqrt{\left(\frac{dx}{dt}\right)^2 + \left(\frac{dy}{dt}\right)^2} \, dt$$

$$= \int_0^2 \sqrt{(3 - 3t^2)^2 + (6t)^2} \, dt$$

$$= \int_0^2 \sqrt{9t^4 + 18t^2 + 9} \, dt$$

$$= 3\int_0^2 (t^2 + 1) \, dt$$

$$= 3\left(\frac{t^3}{3} + t\right)\Big|_0^2 = 3\left(\frac{8}{3} + 2\right)$$

$$= \textbf{14 units}$$

TEST 29, FORM B

1.
(116)
The fourth partial sum is just the sum of the first 4 terms of $\sum_{n=1}^{\infty} \frac{3}{2^n}$

$$\frac{3}{2} + \frac{3}{4} + \frac{3}{8} + \frac{3}{16} = \frac{45}{16}$$

The correct choice is **C.**

2.
(107)

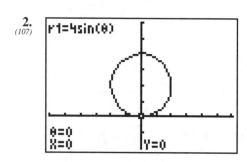

The graph describes a circle of radius 2 centered at $(0, 2)$ that touches the x-axis only at $(0, 0)$.

The correct choice is **C.**

3.
(115)
$$\int \frac{dx}{x^2 + 5x + 6}$$

$$= \int \frac{dx}{(x + 2)(x + 3)}$$

$$= \int \left(\frac{1}{x + 2} - \frac{1}{x + 3}\right) dx$$

$$= \ln|x + 2| - \ln|x + 3| + C$$

$$= \ln\left|\frac{x + 2}{x + 3}\right| + C$$

The correct choice is **A.**

4.
(96)
For a function to equal its absolute value, the function must be either positive or zero.

The correct choice is **B.**

5.
(104)
In this slope field $\frac{dy}{dx}$ is zero whenever x or y is zero. Among these choices only the differential equation $\frac{dy}{dx} = x^2 y^2$ satisfies this condition.

The correct choice is **D.**

6.
(113)
Use trigonometric substitution.

$$x = 2\sin\theta$$

$$dx = 2\cos\theta \, d\theta$$

$$\int \frac{1}{(4 - x^2)^{3/2}} \, dx = \int \frac{2\cos\theta \, d\theta}{(4 - 4\sin^2\theta)^{3/2}}$$

$$= \frac{1}{4}\int \sec^2\theta \, d\theta$$

$$= \frac{1}{4}\tan\theta + C$$

7.
(97)
The described ellipse, $\frac{x^2}{64} + \frac{y^2}{16} = 1$, is centered at the origin. The vertical cross sections run parallel to the y-axis with each side having a length of $2y$.

$$V = \int_{x=-8}^{x=8} (2y)^2 \, dx$$

$$= \int_{-8}^{8} (64 - x^2) \, dx$$

$$= \left[64x - \frac{x^3}{3}\right]_{-8}^{8}$$

$$= 1024 - \frac{1024}{3} = \frac{2048}{3} \text{ units}^3$$

8.
(111)
$$\lim_{x\to 0^+} \ln(e^x - 1)^{2x} = \lim_{x\to 0^+} 2x \ln(e^x - 1)$$

$$= \lim_{x\to 0^+} \frac{\ln(e^x - 1)}{\dfrac{1}{2x}} = \lim_{x\to 0^+} \frac{\dfrac{e^x}{e^x - 1}}{-\dfrac{1}{2x^2}}$$

$$= \lim_{x\to 0^+} \frac{-2x^2 e^x}{e^x - 1} = \lim_{x\to 0^+} \frac{-2x^2 e^x - 4xe^x}{e^x}$$

$$= \lim_{x\to 0^+} (-2x^2 - 4x) = 0$$

$$\lim_{x\to 0^+} (e^x - 1)^{2x} = e^0 = \mathbf{1}$$

9.
(106)
$$y = (2t + 5)^{1/2} \qquad\qquad x = t - t^2$$

$$\frac{dy}{dt} = (2t + 5)^{-1/2} \qquad\qquad \frac{dx}{dt} = 1 - 2t$$

$$\left.\frac{dy}{dx}\right|_{t=8} = \left.\frac{(2t + 5)^{-1/2}}{1 - 2t}\right|_8 = \frac{[2(8) + 5]^{-1/2}}{1 - 2(8)}$$

$$\approx \mathbf{-0.0145}$$

10.
(102)
$$\lim_{n\to\infty} \left(\frac{n + 2}{n}\right)^n = \lim_{n\to\infty} \left(1 + \frac{2}{n}\right)^n = e^2$$

The sequence **converges to e^2.**

11.
(90)
(a) The particle can only be at rest when $v(t) = 0$, which never occurs for the given velocity function; so the particle is **never at rest.**

(b) $v(t) = (16 + t^2)^{-1/2}$

$$a(t) = -\frac{1}{2}(16 + t^2)^{-3/2}(2t)$$

$$a(t) = -t(16 + t^2)^{-3/2}$$

$$a(1) = \mathbf{-0.0143}$$

12.
(114)
$$L_0^5 = \int_0^5 \sqrt{\left(\frac{dx}{dt}\right)^2 + \left(\frac{dy}{dt}\right)^2}\; dt$$

$$= \int_0^5 \sqrt{(3 - 3t^2)^2 + (6t)^2}\; dt$$

$$= \int_0^5 (3 + t^3)\; dt$$

$$= \left[3t + t^3\right]_0^5$$

$$= \mathbf{140\ units}$$

TEST 30, FORM A

1.
(118)
The equation $r = 2 - 2\sin\theta$ has the form $r = a \pm b\sin\theta$ with $\frac{a}{b} = \frac{2}{2} = 1$. Thus its graph is a **cardioid.**

The correct choice is **C.**

2.
(107)
$$\int \log_5 (2x)\, dx = \frac{1}{2}\int \log_5 u\, du$$

$$= \frac{1}{2\ln 5}(u\ln u - u) + C$$

$$= \frac{1}{2\ln 5}\left[2x\ln(2x) - 2x\right] + C$$

$$= \frac{x}{\ln 5}\left[\ln(2x) - 1\right] + C$$

The correct choice is **D.**

3.
(117)
I. $\sum_{n=1}^{\infty} \frac{3}{3^n} = \sum_{n=1}^{\infty} 3\left(\frac{1}{3}\right)^n$ is a convergent geometric series, since $r = \frac{1}{3} < 1$.

II. $\sum_{n=1}^{\infty} \frac{4^n}{3^n} = \sum_{n=0}^{\infty} \left(\frac{4}{3}\right)\left(\frac{4}{3}\right)^n$ is a divergent geometric series, since $r = \frac{4}{3} > 1$.

III. $\sum_{n=1}^{\infty} \frac{1}{2^{n+1}} = \frac{1}{2}\sum_{n=1}^{\infty} \left(\frac{1}{2}\right)^n$ is a convergent geometric series, since $r = \frac{1}{2} < 1$.

The correct choice is **C.**

4.
(119)
$$y = t^3 \qquad\qquad x = 2t^2$$

$$\frac{dy}{dt} = 3t^2 \qquad\qquad \frac{dx}{dt} = 4t$$

$$\frac{dy}{dx} = \frac{3t^2}{4t} = \frac{3t}{4}$$

$$\frac{d^2y}{dx^2} = \frac{\dfrac{d}{dt}\left(\dfrac{3t}{4}\right)}{\dfrac{dx}{dt}} = \frac{\dfrac{3}{4}}{4t} = \frac{3}{16t}$$

$$\left.\frac{d^2y}{dx^2}\right|_{t=3} = \frac{3}{16(3)} = \frac{1}{16}$$

The correct choice is **A.**

5.
(117)
$$\sum_{n=1}^{\infty} \frac{3^{n+1}}{4^n} = \sum_{n=0}^{\infty} \left(\frac{9}{4}\right)\left(\frac{3}{4}\right)^n = \frac{\dfrac{9}{4}}{1 - \dfrac{3}{4}} = \mathbf{9}$$

6.
(120)

$$\frac{1}{x^2(x+1)} = \frac{A}{x} + \frac{B}{x^2} + \frac{C}{x+1}$$

$$1 = Ax(x+1) + B(x+1) + Cx^2$$

$x = 0:$ $B = 1$

$x = -1:$ $C = 1$

$x = 1:$ $A = -1$

$$\int \frac{1}{x^2(x+1)} \, dx$$

$$= \int \left(\frac{-1}{x} + \frac{1}{x^2} + \frac{1}{x+1}\right) dx$$

$$= -\ln |x| - \frac{1}{x} + \ln |x+1| + C$$

$$= \ln \left|\frac{x+1}{x}\right| - \frac{1}{x} + C$$

7.
(99)

$$y = x^{1/3}$$

$$dy = \frac{1}{3} x^{-2/3} \, dx$$

$$\sqrt[3]{65} \times \sqrt[3]{64} + dy = 4 + \frac{1}{3}(64)^{-2/3}(1)$$

$$= 4 + \frac{1}{48}$$

8.
(119)

$$y = 2t + 3 \qquad x = t^2 + t$$

$$\frac{dy}{dt} = 2 \qquad \frac{dx}{dt} = 2t + 1$$

$$\frac{dy}{dt} = \frac{2}{2t+1}$$

$$\frac{dy}{dx}\bigg|_{t=1} = \frac{2}{3}$$

$$y - 5 = \frac{2}{3}(x - 2)$$

9.
(108)

$y = 3x^2 - 4x + 12; \; y' = 6x - 4$

At $x = 1$, $y' = 2$. The unit normal vector has a slope equal to the negative reciprocal of 2, which is $-\frac{1}{2}$. One normal vector is $\langle -2, 1 \rangle$. Dividing this vector by its length produces the unit normal vector $\left\langle -\frac{2}{\sqrt{5}}, \frac{1}{\sqrt{5}} \right\rangle$. The other possible solution is $\left\langle \frac{2}{\sqrt{5}}, -\frac{1}{\sqrt{5}} \right\rangle$.

10.
(98)

$$\frac{d}{dx}\int_1^x \cos(t^3) \, dt = \cos(x^3)$$

11.
(117)

$$d = 12 + 2\left[12\left(\frac{4}{7}\right)\right] + 2\left[12\left(\frac{4}{7}\right)^2\right]$$

$$+ 2\left[12\left(\frac{4}{7}\right)^3\right] + \cdots$$

$$= 12 + 2(12)\left[\left(\frac{4}{7}\right) + \left(\frac{4}{7}\right)^2 + \left(\frac{4}{7}\right)^3 + \cdots\right]$$

$$= 12 + 24\sum_{n=1}^{\infty}\left(\frac{4}{7}\right)^n = 12 + 24\left(\frac{\frac{4}{7}}{1 - \frac{4}{7}}\right)$$

$$= 12 + 24\left(\frac{4}{3}\right) = \textbf{44 feet}$$

12.
(109)

$$y = \frac{1}{3}(x^2 + 2)^{3/2}$$

$$y' = \frac{1}{2}(x^2 + 2)^{1/2}(2x) = x(x^2 + 2)^{1/2}$$

$$L_0^1 = \int_0^1 \sqrt{1 + [x(x^2 + 2)^{1/2}]^2} \, dx$$

$$= \int_0^1 \sqrt{1 + x^2(x^2 + 2)} \, dx$$

$$= \int_0^1 \sqrt{1 + x^4 + 2x^2} \, dx$$

$$= \int_0^1 (x^2 + 1) \, dx$$

$$= \frac{x^3}{3} + x \bigg|_0^1 = \frac{4}{3} \textbf{ units}$$

Test 30, Form B

1.
(118)

This graph is a **cardioid.**

The correct choice is **C.**

2.
(73) $\displaystyle \int \log_7 (2x)\, dx = \frac{1}{2} \int \log_7 u\, du$

$$= \frac{1}{2}\, \frac{1}{\ln 7}\, (u \ln u - u) + C$$

$$= \frac{1}{2 \ln 7}\, [2x \ln (2x) - 2x] + C$$

$$= \frac{x}{\ln 7}\, [\ln (2x) - 1] + C$$

The correct choice is **D**.

3. I.
(117) $\displaystyle \sum_{n=1}^{\infty} \frac{3}{3^n} = \sum_{n=1}^{\infty} 3\left(\frac{1}{3}\right)^n$ is a convergent geometric series, since $r = \frac{1}{3} < 1$.

II. $\displaystyle \sum_{n=1}^{\infty} \frac{\pi^n}{3^n} = \sum_{n=0}^{\infty} \left(\frac{\pi}{3}\right)\left(\frac{\pi}{3}\right)^n$ is a divergent geometric series, since $r = \frac{\pi}{3} < 1$.

III. $\displaystyle \sum_{n=1}^{\infty} \frac{1}{2^{n+1}} = \frac{1}{2}\sum_{n=1}^{\infty} \left(\frac{1}{2}\right)^n$ is a convergent geometric series, since $r = \frac{1}{2} < 1$.

The correct choice is **C**.

4.
(119) $\qquad y = t^3 \qquad\qquad x = 2t^2$

$$\frac{dy}{dt} = 3t^2 \qquad\qquad \frac{dx}{dt} = 4t$$

$$\frac{dy}{dx} = \frac{3t^2}{4t} = \frac{3t}{4}$$

$$\frac{d^2 y}{dx^2} = \frac{\dfrac{d}{dt}\left(\dfrac{3t}{4}\right)}{\dfrac{dx}{dt}} = \frac{\dfrac{3}{4}}{4t} = \frac{3}{16t}$$

$$\left.\frac{d^2 y}{dx^2}\right|_{t=1} = \frac{3}{16(1)} = \frac{3}{16}$$

The correct choice is **A**.

5.
(117) $\displaystyle \sum_{n=2}^{\infty} \frac{3^{n+1}}{4^n} = \sum_{n=0}^{\infty} \left(\frac{27}{16}\right)\left(\frac{3}{4}\right)^n$

$$= \frac{\dfrac{27}{16}}{1 - \dfrac{3}{4}} = \frac{\dfrac{27}{16}}{\dfrac{1}{4}} = \frac{27}{4} = \textbf{6.75}$$

6.
(120) $\displaystyle \frac{2}{x^2(x+1)} = \frac{A}{x} + \frac{B}{x^2} + \frac{C}{x+1}$

$$2 = Ax(x+1) + B(x+1) + Cx^2$$

$$x = 0: \qquad B = 2$$

$$x = -1: \qquad C = 2$$

$$x = 1: \qquad A = -2$$

$$\int \frac{2}{x^2(x+1)}\, dx$$

$$= \int \left(\frac{-2}{x} + \frac{2}{x^2} + \frac{2}{x+1}\right) dx$$

$$= -2 \ln |x| - \frac{2}{x} + 2 \ln |x+1| + C$$

$$= 2 \ln \left|\frac{x+1}{x}\right| - \frac{2}{x} + C$$

7.
(99) $y = x^{1/3}$

$$dy = \frac{1}{3} x^{-2/3}\, dx$$

$$\sqrt[3]{66} = \sqrt[3]{64} + dy = 4 + \frac{1}{3}(64)^{-2/3}(2)$$

$$= 4 + \frac{1}{24}$$

8.
(119) $\qquad y = 2t + 3 \qquad x = t^2 + t$

$$\frac{dy}{dt} = 2 \qquad\qquad \frac{dx}{dt} = 2t + 1$$

$$\frac{dy}{dx} = \frac{2}{2t + 1}$$

$$\left.\frac{dy}{dx}\right|_{t=4} = \frac{2}{9}$$

$$y - 11 = \frac{2}{9}(x - 20)$$

9. $y = 8x^2 - 14x + 13;\ y' = 16x - 14$
(108)

At $x = 1$, $y' = 2$. The unit normal vector has a slope equal to the negative reciprocal of 2, which is $-\frac{1}{2}$. One normal vector is $\langle -2, 1 \rangle$. Dividing this vector by its length produces the unit normal vector $\left\langle -\frac{2}{\sqrt{5}}, \frac{1}{\sqrt{5}} \right\rangle$. The other possible solution is $\left\langle \frac{2}{\sqrt{5}}, -\frac{1}{\sqrt{5}} \right\rangle$.

10. $\displaystyle \frac{d}{dx}\int_1^x \ln (t^3)\, dt = \ln (x^3)$
(98)

11.
(117)
$$d = 10 + 2\left[10\left(\frac{4}{7}\right)\right] + 2\left[10\left(\frac{4}{7}\right)^2\right]$$

$$+ 2\left[10\left(\frac{4}{7}\right)^3\right] + \cdots$$

$$= 10 + 2(10)\left[\left(\frac{4}{7}\right) + \left(\frac{4}{7}\right)^2 + \left(\frac{4}{7}\right)^3 + \cdots\right]$$

$$= 10 + 20\sum_{n=1}^{\infty}\left(\frac{4}{7}\right)^n = 10 + 20\left(\frac{\frac{4}{7}}{1 - \frac{4}{7}}\right)$$

$$= 10 + 20\left(\frac{4}{3}\right) = \mathbf{36\frac{2}{3}\ feet}$$

12.
(109)
$$y = \frac{1}{3}(x^2 + 2)^{3/2}$$

$$y' = \frac{1}{2}(x^2 + 2)^{1/2}(2x) = x(x^2 + 2)^{1/2}$$

$$L_0^4 = \int_0^4 \sqrt{1 + \left[x(x^2 + 2)^{1/2}\right]^2}\ dx$$

$$= \int_0^4 \sqrt{1 + x^2(x^2 + 2)}\ dx$$

$$= \int_0^4 \sqrt{1 + x^4 + 2x^2}\ dx$$

$$= \int_0^4 (x^2 + 1)\ dx$$

$$= \frac{x^3}{4} + x\Big|_0^4 = \frac{\mathbf{101}}{\mathbf{4}}\ \mathbf{units}$$

TEST 31, FORM A

1.
(121)
Choice A, $\sum_{n=1}^{\infty}\left(\frac{2}{3}\right)^n$, is a geometric series with $r = \frac{2}{3} < 1$, so it converges.

The series in B, $\sum_{n=1}^{\infty}\frac{2n}{3}$, will diverge by the divergence theorem since

$$\lim_{n\to\infty} a_n = \lim_{n\to\infty}\frac{2n}{3} = +\infty$$

For the series in C, $\sum_{n=1}^{\infty}\frac{1+n}{n}$,

$$\lim_{n\to\infty} a_n = \lim_{n\to\infty}\frac{\frac{1}{n} + 1}{1} = 1$$

so the series diverges by the divergence theorem.

The correct choice is **A**.

2.
(86)
$$f(-x) = \frac{\sin(-x)}{-x} = \frac{-\sin x}{-x} = \frac{\sin x}{x} = f(x)$$

So $\dfrac{\sin x}{x}$ is an even function, and therefore

$$\int_1^k \frac{\sin x}{x}\ dx = \int_k^{-1} \frac{\sin x}{x}\ dx = \mathbf{1}$$

The correct choice is **A**.

3.
(106)
$$y = te^t \qquad x = t^3$$

$$\frac{dy}{dt} = te^t + e^t \qquad \frac{dx}{dt} = 3t^2$$

$$\frac{dy}{dx} = \frac{te^t + e^t}{3t^2}$$

$$\frac{dy}{dx}\Big|_{t=2} = \frac{2e^2 + e^2}{12} > 0$$

The slope does not correspond to a vertical or horizontal line.

The correct choice is **B**.

4.
(124)
$$x^2 + y^2 = 25$$

$$2x + 2y\frac{dy}{dx} = 0$$

$$\frac{dy}{dx} = -\frac{x}{y}$$

$$\frac{d^2y}{dx^2} = \frac{-y + x\dfrac{dy}{dx}}{y^2}$$

$$\frac{d^2y}{dx^2} = \frac{-y - \dfrac{x^2}{y}}{y^2}$$

$$\frac{d^2y}{dx^2}\Big|_{(0,5)} = \frac{-5 - 0}{25} = -\frac{\mathbf{1}}{\mathbf{5}}$$

5.
(115)
$$\frac{1}{x(x+3)} = \frac{A}{x} + \frac{B}{x+3}$$

$$1 = A(x+3) + Bx$$

Letting $x = 0$ gives $A = \dfrac{1}{3}$.

Letting $x = -3$ gives $B = -\dfrac{1}{3}$.

$$\int \frac{1}{x(x+3)}\ dx = \int \frac{\frac{1}{3}}{x}\ dx + \int \frac{-\frac{1}{3}}{x+3}\ dx$$

$$= \frac{1}{3}\ln|x| - \frac{1}{3}\ln|x+3| + C$$

6.
(121)
$$\sum_{n=3}^{\infty} \frac{1}{n(n+2)} = \sum_{n=3}^{\infty} \frac{\frac{1}{2}}{n} - \sum_{n=3}^{\infty} \frac{\frac{1}{2}}{n+2}$$

$$= \sum_{n=3}^{\infty} \frac{\frac{1}{2}}{n} - \sum_{n=5}^{\infty} \frac{\frac{1}{2}}{n}$$

$$= \frac{\frac{1}{2}}{3} + \frac{\frac{1}{2}}{4} + \sum_{n=5}^{\infty} \frac{\frac{1}{2}}{n} - \sum_{n=5}^{\infty} \frac{\frac{1}{2}}{n}$$

$$= \frac{1}{6} + \frac{1}{8} = \frac{7}{24}$$

7.
(123)
$$\vec{f}(t) = \ln(t)\,\hat{i} - \sqrt{t+2}\,\hat{j}$$

$$\vec{f}'(t) = \frac{1}{t}\hat{i} - \frac{1}{2\sqrt{t+2}}\hat{j}$$

8.
(107)
$$x^2 + 4y^2 = 9$$
$$x^2 + y^2 + 3y^2 = 9$$
$$r^2 + 3(r\sin\theta)^2 = 9$$
$$r^2 + 3r^2\sin^2\theta = 9$$

9. Rewriting $y = \sqrt{4 - x^2}$ as $x^2 + y^2 = 4$
(22) reveals the equation of a circle. The graph is a quarter circle of radius 2, so the area must be $\frac{1}{4}(\pi \cdot 2^2) = \pi$ **units^2.**

10.
(55)

n	$f^{(n)}(x)$	$f^{(n)}(0)$
0	$\sin x$	0
1	$\cos x$	1
2	$-\sin x$	0
3	$-\cos x$	-1
4	$\sin x$	0
5	$\cos x$	1
$\vdots$	$\vdots$	$\vdots$

$$\sin x \approx x - \frac{x^3}{3!} + \frac{x^5}{5!}$$

$$\sin 0.5 \approx 0.5 - \frac{0.5^3}{6} + \frac{0.5^5}{120}$$

$$\sin 0.5 \approx \frac{1}{2} - \frac{1}{48} + \frac{1}{3840}$$

$$\sin 0.5 \approx \frac{1841}{3840}$$

11.
(121)
$$\lim_{n\to\infty} a_n = \lim_{n\to\infty} \frac{n}{n+1} = \lim_{n\to\infty} \frac{1}{1 + \frac{1}{n}} = 1$$

Since the limit is not zero, the series **diverges** by the divergence theorem.

12.
(122)
$$u = x^2 \qquad dv = \cos x\,dx$$
$$du = 2x\,dx \qquad v = \sin x$$

$$\int x^2 \cos x\,dx = x^2 \sin x - \int 2x \sin x\,dx$$

$$u = 2x \qquad dv = \sin x\,dx$$
$$du = 2\,dx \qquad v = -\cos x$$

$$= x^2 \sin x - \left[-2x \cos x - \int -2\cos x\,dx \right]$$

$$= x^2 \sin x + 2x \cos x - 2\sin x + C$$

TEST 31, FORM B

1. Choice A, $\sum_{n=1}^{\infty} \left(\frac{4}{3}\right)^n$, is a geometric series with
(121) $r = \frac{4}{3} > 1$, so it diverges.

The series in B, $\sum_{n=1}^{\infty} \frac{2n}{3}$, will diverge by the divergence theorem since

$$\lim_{n\to\infty} a_n = \lim_{n\to\infty} \frac{2n}{3} = +\infty$$

For the series in C, $\sum_{n=1}^{\infty} \frac{1+n}{n}$,

$$\lim_{n\to\infty} a_n = \lim_{n\to\infty} \frac{\frac{1}{n} + 1}{1} = 1$$

so the series diverges by the divergence theorem.

The correct choice is **D.**

2.
(86)
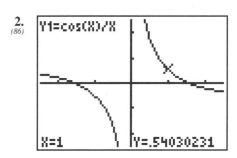

The graph of $\frac{\cos x}{x}$ reveals the symmetry of an odd function, so

$$\int_{-k}^{-1} \frac{\cos x}{x}\,dx = -\int_{1}^{k} \frac{\cos x}{x}\,dx = -0.1$$

The correct choice is **C.**

3.
(106)
After graphing the function, the `CALCULATE` menu option `2: dy/dx` can be used to investigate the slope of the curve around $t = 1$.

The slope at $t = 1$ is positive.

The correct choice is **B.**

4.
(124)
$$x^2 - y^2 = -25$$

$$2x - 2y\frac{dy}{dx} = 0$$

$$\frac{dy}{dx} = \frac{x}{y}$$

$$\frac{d^2y}{dx^2} = \frac{y(1) - x\frac{dy}{dx}}{y^2}$$

$$\frac{d^2y}{dx^2} = \frac{y - x\left(\frac{x}{y}\right)}{y^2} = \frac{y - \frac{x^2}{y}}{y^2}$$

$$\left.\frac{d^2y}{dx^2}\right|_{(0,5)} = \frac{5 - 0}{25} = \frac{1}{5}$$

5.
(115)
$$\frac{4}{x(x-3)} = \frac{A}{x} + \frac{B}{x-3}$$

$$4 = A(x-3) + Bx$$

Letting $x = 0$ gives $A = -\frac{4}{3}$

Letting $x = 3$ gives $B = \frac{4}{3}$

$$\int \frac{4}{x(x-3)}\, dx$$

$$= \int \frac{-\frac{4}{3}}{x}\, dx + \int \frac{\frac{4}{3}}{x+3}\, dx$$

$$= -\frac{4}{3}\ln|x| + \frac{4}{3}\ln|x+3| + C$$

6.
(121)
$$\sum_{n=2}^{\infty} \frac{1}{n(n+2)} = \sum_{n=2}^{\infty} \frac{\frac{1}{2}}{n} - \sum_{n=2}^{\infty} \frac{\frac{1}{2}}{n+2}$$

$$= \sum_{n=2}^{\infty} \frac{\frac{1}{2}}{n} - \sum_{n=4}^{\infty} \frac{\frac{1}{2}}{n}$$

$$= \frac{\frac{1}{2}}{2} + \frac{\frac{1}{2}}{3} + \sum_{n=4}^{\infty} \frac{\frac{1}{2}}{n} - \sum_{n=4}^{\infty} \frac{\frac{1}{2}}{n}$$

$$= \frac{1}{4} + \frac{1}{6} = \frac{5}{12}$$

7.
(123)
$$\vec{f}(t) = (\cos t)\hat{i} - \sqrt{t+2}\,\hat{j}$$

$$\vec{f}'(t) = -(\sin t)\hat{i} - \frac{1}{2\sqrt{t+2}}\,\hat{j}$$

8.
(107)
$$4x^2 + y^2 = 9$$

$$3x^2 + x^2 + y^2 = 9$$

$$3(r\cos\theta)^2 + r^2 = 9$$

$$\mathbf{3\,r^2\cos^2\theta + r^2 = 9}$$

9.
(22)

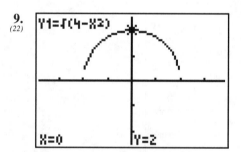

The graph is a semicircle of radius 2, so the area is $\frac{1}{2}\pi(2)^2 = \mathbf{2\pi\ units^2.}$

10.
(55)

n	$f^{(n)}(x)$	$f^{(n)}(0)$
0	$\sin x$	0
1	$\cos x$	1
2	$-\sin x$	0
3	$-\cos x$	-1
4	$\sin x$	0
5	$\cos x$	1
6	$-\sin x$	0
7	$-\cos x$	-1
$\vdots$	$\vdots$	$\vdots$

$$\sin x \approx x - \frac{x^3}{3!} + \frac{x^5}{5!} - \frac{x^7}{7!}$$

$$\sin x \approx x - \frac{x^3}{3!} + \frac{x^5}{5!} - \frac{x^7}{7!}$$

$$\sin 0.5 \approx 0.5 - \frac{0.5^3}{3!} + \frac{0.5^5}{5!} - \frac{0.5^7}{7!}$$

$$\sin 0.5 \approx \frac{1}{2} - \frac{1}{48} + \frac{1}{3840} - \frac{1}{645,120}$$

$$\sin 0.5 \approx \frac{309,287}{645,120}$$

11.
(121)
$$\lim_{n \to \infty} a_n = \lim_{n \to \infty} \frac{3n}{4n + 1} = \lim_{n \to \infty} \frac{3}{4} = \frac{3}{4}$$

Since the limit is not zero, the series **diverges** by the divergence theorem.

12.
(122)
$$u = x^2 \qquad dv = \sin x \, dx$$
$$du = 2x \, dx \qquad v = -\cos x$$

$$\int x^2 \sin x \, dx = -x^2 \cos x + \int 2x \cos x \, dx$$

$$u = 2x \qquad dv = \cos x \, dx$$
$$du = 2 \, dx \qquad v = \sin x$$

$$= -x^2 \cos x + \left[2x \sin x - \int 2 \sin x \, dx \right]$$

$$= -x^2 \cos x + 2x \sin x + 2 \cos x + C$$

TEST 32, FORM A

1.
(127,128)
Choice A, $\sum_{n=1}^{\infty} \frac{2n}{n^2} = 2 \sum_{n=1}^{\infty} \frac{1}{n}$, is the harmonic series multiplied by 2, so it diverges.

For B, note that $n^2 + 1 > n^2$, so $\frac{1}{n^2 + 1} < \frac{1}{n^2}$ for all $n \geq 1$. Since $\sum_{n=1}^{\infty} \frac{1}{n^2}$ is a convergent p-series, $\sum_{n=1}^{\infty} \frac{1}{n^2 + 1}$ converges by the basic comparison test.

Choice C, $\sum_{n=1}^{\infty} \frac{3n}{n^3} = 3 \sum_{n=1}^{\infty} \frac{1}{n^2}$, is a convergent p-series.

The correct choice is **A**.

2.
(79)
$$\lim_{x \to \infty} \frac{x^2 + x \ln x}{1 + x^2} = \lim_{x \to \infty} \frac{2x + \frac{x}{x} + \ln x}{2x}$$

$$= \lim_{x \to \infty} \frac{2x + 1 + \ln x}{2x}$$

$$= \lim_{x \to \infty} \frac{2 + 0 + \frac{1}{x}}{2}$$

$$= \frac{2}{2} = 1$$

The correct choice is **B**.

3.
(118)
The graph of $a \pm b \cos \theta$ with $\frac{a}{b} < 1$ describes a limaçon with an inner loop. So $r = 3 + 4 \cos \theta$ is a **limaçon**.

The correct choice is **C**.

4.
(112)
When terms of the form $a^2 - x^2$ appear in the integrand, the substitution $x = a \sin \theta$ is useful. Thus, $x = 3 \sin \theta$ is appropriate for $\int \frac{4}{\sqrt{9 - x^2}} \, dx$ because it simplifies the integral to $\int 4 \, d\theta$.

The correct choice is **A**.

5.
(84)
$$f(x) = x^x$$

$$\ln f(x) = x \ln x$$

$$\frac{d[\ln f(x)]}{dx} = x\left(\frac{1}{x}\right) + (\ln x)(1)$$

$$\frac{f'(x)}{f(x)} = 1 + \ln x$$

$$f'(x) = x^x(1 + \ln x)$$

$$f'(2) = 2^2(1 + \ln 2) = \mathbf{4 + 4 \ln 2}$$

6.
(128)
$u = \ln x \quad du = \frac{1}{x} \, dx$

$$\int_2^{\infty} \frac{1}{x \ln x} \, dx = \int_{\ln 2}^{\infty} \frac{1}{u} \, du$$

$$= \ln |u| \Big\|_{\ln 2}^{\infty}$$

$$= \lim_{b \to \infty} \ln b - \ln (\ln 2) = \infty$$

Since the integral diverges, the series also **diverges**.

7.
(126)
$$\frac{x + 1}{(x^2 + 1)(x - 1)} = \frac{Ax + B}{x^2 + 1} + \frac{C}{x - 1}$$

$$x + 1 = (Ax + B)(x - 1) + C(x^2 + 1)$$

$$x = 1: \qquad 2 = 2C$$
$$\qquad\qquad C = 1$$

$$x = 0: \qquad 1 = -B + C = -B + 1$$
$$\qquad\qquad B = 0$$

$$x = 2: \qquad 3 = 2A(1) + 1(5)$$
$$\qquad\qquad 2A = -2$$
$$\qquad\qquad A = -1$$

$$\int \frac{x + 1}{(x^2 + 1)(x - 1)} \, dx$$

$$= \int \left(\frac{-x}{x^2 + 1} + \frac{1}{x - 1} \right) dx$$

$$= -\frac{1}{2} \ln |x^2 + 1| + \ln |x - 1| + C$$

8.
(127)
$$\sum_{n=1}^{\infty} \frac{18}{\sqrt[6]{n^{13}}} = 18 \sum_{n=1}^{\infty} \frac{1}{n^{13/6}}$$

This is a p-series with $p = \frac{13}{6}$, which is larger than 1. So the series **converges.**

9.
(119)
$$y = 5t - 4 \qquad x = 2t^2 + 5$$

$$\frac{dy}{dt} = 5 \qquad \frac{dx}{dt} = 4t$$

$$\frac{dy}{dx} = \frac{5}{4t}$$

$$\frac{d^2y}{dx^2} = \frac{\frac{d}{dt}\left(\frac{dy}{dx}\right)}{\frac{dx}{dt}} = \frac{\frac{-5}{4t^2}}{4t} = \frac{-5}{16t^3}$$

$$\left.\frac{d^2y}{dx^2}\right|_{t=1} = -\frac{5}{16}$$

Thus the curve is **concave down.**

10.
(88)
$$\frac{dy}{dx} = \frac{y}{x}$$

$$\frac{dy}{y} = \frac{dx}{x}$$

$$\ln|y| = \ln|x| + C$$

$$|y| = e^{\ln|x| + C}$$

$$|y| = e^{\ln|x|}e^{C}$$

$$|y| = |x|e^{C} = k|x|$$

Since the graph passes through $(1, 4)$, $k = 4$ and the equation of the curve is $|y| = 4|x|$.

11.
(125)

$$y = \frac{1}{x^2}$$

(a)
$$A = \int_5^{\infty} \frac{1}{x^2}\, dx$$

$$= \lim_{b \to \infty} \int_5^b x^{-2}\, dx$$

$$= \lim_{b \to \infty} \left[-x^{-1}\right]\Big|_5^b$$

$$= \lim_{b \to \infty} \left(-\frac{1}{b} + \frac{1}{5}\right)$$

$$= \frac{1}{5}$$

The area is **finite** and it equals $\dfrac{1}{5}$ **unit**^{2}.

(b) Use the shell method.

$$V = \int_5^{\infty} 2\pi x \left(\frac{1}{x^2}\right) dx$$

$$= \lim_{b \to \infty} \int_5^b \frac{2\pi}{x}\, dx$$

$$= \lim_{b \to \infty} 2\pi \ln|x|\Big|_5^b$$

$$= \lim_{b \to \infty} 2\pi(\ln b - \ln 5)$$

$$= +\infty$$

12. Average velocity $= \dfrac{1}{7 - 0} \displaystyle\int_0^7 (t^2 - 7t + 6)\, dt$
(89)

$$= \frac{1}{7}\left[\frac{t^3}{3} - \frac{7t^2}{2} + 6t\right]_0^7$$

$$= \frac{1}{7}\left[\frac{7^3}{3} - \frac{7^3}{2} + 42\right]$$

$$= \frac{7^2}{3} - \frac{7^2}{2} + 6$$

$$= -\frac{13}{6}$$

TEST 32, FORM B

1. For A, note that $n^2 + 1 > n^2$, so $\frac{1}{n^2 + 1} < \frac{1}{n^2}$ for
(127,128) all $n \geq 1$. Since $\sum_{n=1}^{\infty} \frac{1}{n^2}$ is a convergent p-series, $\sum_{n=1}^{\infty} \frac{1}{n^2 + 1}$ converges by the basic comparison test.

Choice B, $\sum_{n=1}^{\infty} \frac{2}{n^2} = 2\sum_{n=1}^{\infty} \frac{1}{n^2}$, is a convergent p-series.

The series in C, $\sum_{n=1}^{\infty} \frac{3n}{n^4} = 3\sum_{n=1}^{\infty} \frac{1}{n^3}$, is also a convergent p-series.

The correct choice is **D.**

2. $\lim\limits_{x \to \infty} \dfrac{x^2 + x^2 \ln x}{1 + x^2}$
(79)

$= \lim\limits_{x \to \infty} \dfrac{2x + \dfrac{x^2}{x} + 2x \ln x}{2x}$

$= \lim\limits_{x \to \infty} \dfrac{2x + x + 2x \ln x}{2x}$

$= \lim\limits_{x \to \infty} \dfrac{2 + 1 + 2 \ln x + 2}{2}$

$= \infty$

The correct choice is **C**.

3.
(118)

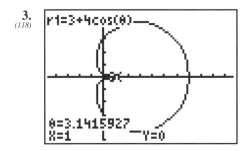

The correct choice is **A**.

4. When terms of the form $x^2 - a^2$ appear in the
(113) integrand, the substitution $x = a \sec \theta$ is useful.
Thus, $x = 3 \sec \theta$ is appropriate for $\int \dfrac{4}{\sqrt{x^2 - 9}}\, dx$
because it simplifies the integral to $\int 4 \sec \theta\, d\theta$.

The correct choice is **B**.

5. $f(x) = x^x$
(31)

$\ln f(x) = x \ln x$

$\dfrac{f'(x)}{f(x)} = \dfrac{x}{x} + \ln x$

$f'(x) = x^x(1 + \ln x)$

$f'(3) = 3^3(1 + \ln 3)$

$f'(3) = \mathbf{27 + 27 \ln 3}$

6. $u^2 = \ln x \quad du = \dfrac{1}{x}\, dx$
(128)

$\displaystyle\int_2^\infty \dfrac{\ln x}{x}\, dx = \int_{\ln 2}^\infty u\, du$

$= \dfrac{u^2}{2}\Big|_{\ln 2}^\infty = \infty$

Since the integral diverges, the series also **diverges**.

7. $\dfrac{2x + 2}{(x^2 + 1)(x - 1)} = \dfrac{Ax + B}{x^2 + 1} + \dfrac{C}{x - 1}$
(126)

$2x + 2 = (Ax + B)(x - 1) + C(x^2 + 1)$

$x = 1: \qquad 4 = 2C$

$\qquad\qquad C = 2$

$x = 0: \qquad 2 = -B + C = -B + 2$

$\qquad\qquad B = 0$

$x = 2: \qquad 6 = 2A(1) + 2(5)$

$\qquad\qquad 2A = -4$

$\qquad\qquad A = -2$

$\displaystyle\int \dfrac{2x + 2}{(x^2 + 1)(x - 1)}\, dx$

$= \displaystyle\int \left(\dfrac{-2x}{x^2 + 1} + \dfrac{2}{x - 1} \right) dx$

$= \mathbf{-\ln |x^2 + 1| + 2 \ln |x - 1| + C}$

8. $\displaystyle\sum_{n=1}^\infty \dfrac{18}{\sqrt[6]{n^5}} = 18 \sum_{n=1}^\infty \dfrac{1}{n^{5/6}}$
(127)

This is a p-series with $p = \frac{5}{6}$. Since $\frac{5}{6} < 1$, the
series **diverges**.

9. $x = 5t - 4 \quad y = 2t^2 + 5$
(119)

$\dfrac{dy}{dt} = 4t \qquad \dfrac{dx}{dt} = 5$

$\dfrac{dy}{dx} = \dfrac{4t}{5}$

$\dfrac{d^2y}{dx^2} = \dfrac{\dfrac{d}{dt}\left(\dfrac{dy}{dx}\right)}{\dfrac{dx}{dt}} = \dfrac{\dfrac{4}{5}}{5} = \dfrac{4}{25}$

The second derivative is positive and independent of
t, which means the curve at $t = 1$ is **concave up**.

10. $\dfrac{dy}{dx} = \dfrac{y}{x}$
(88)

$\dfrac{dy}{y} = \dfrac{dx}{x}$

$\ln |y| = \ln |x| + C$

$|y| = e^{\ln |x| + C}$

$|y| = e^{\ln |x|} e^C$

$|y| = |x| e^c = k|x|$

Since the graph passes through $(1, 6)$, $k = 6$ and
the equation of the curve is $|y| = \mathbf{6|x|}$.

11.
(125)

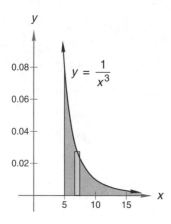

(a) $A = \int_5^\infty \frac{1}{x^3}\, dx$

$= \lim_{b \to \infty} \int_5^b x^{-3}\, dx$

$= \lim_{b \to \infty} \left[\frac{x^{-2}}{-2} \right]_5^b$

$= \lim_{b \to \infty} \left(\frac{b^{-2}}{-2} - \frac{5^{-2}}{-2} \right)$

$= 0 + \frac{1}{50} = \frac{1}{50}$

The area is **finite** and it equals $\dfrac{1}{50}$ **unit**^{2}.

(b) Use the shell method.

$V = \int_5^\infty 2\pi x \left(\frac{1}{x^3} \right) dx$

$= \lim_{b \to \infty} \int_5^b \frac{2\pi}{x^2}\, dx$

$= \lim_{b \to \infty} 2\pi \left. \frac{x^{-1}}{-1} \right|_5^b$

$= \lim_{b \to \infty} 2\pi \left(\frac{1}{5} - \frac{1}{b} \right)$

$= \frac{2}{5}\pi$ **units**^{3}

12.
(89)

Average velocity $= \dfrac{1}{10 - 0} \int_0^{10} (t^2 - 7t + 6)\, dt$

$= \frac{1}{10} \left[\frac{t^3}{3} - \frac{7t^2}{2} + 6t \right]_0^{10}$

$= \frac{1}{10} \left[\frac{1000}{3} - \frac{700}{2} + 60 \right]$

$= \frac{13}{3}$

TEST 33, FORM A

1.
(129)

The graph of $r = 2 \sin (3\theta)$ is a 3-petal rose that completes one loop in $\frac{\pi}{3}$ radians.

Area $= \int_0^{\pi/3} \frac{1}{2}(2 \sin (3\theta))^2\, d\theta$

$= 2 \int_0^{\pi/3} \sin^2 (3\theta)\, d\theta$

The correct choice is **C.**

2.
(130)

Examine the series in A, $\sum_{n=1}^{\infty} \frac{n}{n^n}$, with the root test.

$L = \lim_{n \to \infty} \sqrt[n]{\frac{n}{n^n}} = \lim_{n \to \infty} \frac{\sqrt[n]{n}}{\sqrt[n]{n^n}} = \lim_{n \to \infty} \frac{n^{1/n}}{n}$

$= \frac{1}{\infty} = 0$

Since $L < 1$, the series converges.

For B, use the ratio test.

$L = \lim_{n \to \infty} \dfrac{\dfrac{(n + 1)^2}{(n + 1)!}}{\dfrac{n^2}{n!}}$

$= \lim_{n \to \infty} \frac{(n + 1)^2\, n!}{n^2 (n + 1)!}$

$= \lim_{n \to \infty} \frac{(n + 1)^2}{n^2 (n + 1)}$

$= \lim_{n \to \infty} \frac{n + 1}{n^2} = \lim_{n \to \infty} \frac{1}{2n} = 0$

Since $L < 1$, the series converges.

For C, use the root test.

$L = \lim_{n \to \infty} \sqrt[n]{\frac{2^n}{n^2}} = \lim_{n \to \infty} \frac{\sqrt[n]{2^n}}{\sqrt[n]{n^2}} = \lim_{n \to \infty} \frac{2}{n^{2/n}}$

$= \frac{2}{1} = 2$

Since $L > 1$, the series diverges.

The correct choice is **C.**

3.
(131)

$\int_{-\infty}^{\infty} e^{-|x|}\, dx = \int_{-\infty}^{0} e^{-(-x)}\, dx + \int_0^{\infty} e^{-x}\, dx$

$= \int_{-\infty}^{0} e^x\, dx + \int_0^{\infty} e^{-x}\, dx$

$= \lim_{a \to -\infty} \int_a^0 e^x\, dx + \lim_{b \to \infty} \int_0^b e^{-x}\, dx$

$= \lim_{a \to -\infty} \left. e^x \right|_a^0 + \lim_{b \to \infty} \left. -e^{-x} \right|_0^b$

$= \lim_{a \to -\infty} (1 - e^a)$

$\quad + \lim_{b \to \infty} (-e^{-b} + 1)$

$= 1 - 0 + 0 + 1 = 2$

4.
(131)
$$\int_{-e}^{e} \frac{1}{x}\, dx = \int_{-e}^{0} \frac{1}{x}\, dx + \int_{0}^{e} \frac{1}{x}\, dx$$

$$\int_{0}^{e} \frac{1}{x}\, dx = \lim_{a \to 0^+} \int_{a}^{e} \frac{1}{x}\, dx$$

$$= \lim_{a \to 0^+} \ln x \Big|_{a}^{e}$$

$$= \lim_{a \to 0^+} (1 - \ln a)$$

$$= 1 - (-\infty) = \infty$$

Thus the given integral **diverges**.

5.
(114)
$$L_0^1 = \int_0^1 \sqrt{\left(\frac{dx}{dt}\right)^2 + \left(\frac{dy}{dt}\right)^2}\, dt$$

$$= \int_0^1 \sqrt{(t-1)^2 + (2t^{1/2})^2}\, dt$$

$$= \int_0^1 \sqrt{t^2 - 2t + 1 + 4t}\, dt$$

$$= \int_0^1 (t+1)\, dt$$

$$= \left(\frac{t^2}{2} + t\right)\Big|_0^1 = \frac{3}{2} \text{ units}$$

6.
(38)
$$\int \frac{x^2 + x + 1}{x^2 + 1}\, dx = \int \frac{(x^2 + 1) + x}{x^2 + 1}\, dx$$

$$= \int \left[1 + \frac{x}{x^2 + 1}\right] dx$$

$$= x + \frac{1}{2} \ln (x^2 + 1) + C$$

7.
(111)
The $\lim_{x \to 1} [x + \sin (\pi x)]^{\csc (x-1)}$ is an indeterminate form, 1^∞, so it is easier to work with the natural logarithm of the function.

$$\lim_{x \to 1} \csc (x-1) \ln [x + \sin (\pi x)]$$

$$= \lim_{x \to 1} \frac{\ln [x + \sin (\pi x)]}{\sin (x-1)}$$

$$= \lim_{x \to 1} \frac{\left[\dfrac{1 + \pi \cos (\pi x)}{x + \sin (\pi x)}\right]}{\cos (x-1)}$$

$$= \frac{1 + \pi \cos \pi}{1} = 1 - \pi$$

So the original limit equals $e^{1-\pi}$.

8.
(124)
$$x = \cos y - y$$

$$1 = (-\sin y)\left(\frac{dy}{dx}\right) - \frac{dy}{dx}$$

$$\frac{dy}{dx}(-\sin y - 1) = 1$$

$$\frac{dy}{dx} = \frac{1}{-\sin y - 1}$$

$$\frac{dy}{dx}\Big|_{(1,0)} = \frac{1}{0 - 1} = -1$$

9.
(116)
$$\sum_{n=1}^{3} \frac{5 + 2n}{n^2} = \frac{5 + 2(1)}{1^2} + \frac{5 + 2(2)}{2^2} + \frac{5 + 2(3)}{3^2}$$

$$= 7 + \frac{9}{4} + \frac{11}{9} = 10\frac{17}{36}$$

10.
(123)
$$\vec{f}(t) = \arctan (e^{2t})\, \hat{i} + e^{-(t+2)}\, \hat{j}$$

$$\vec{f}'(t) = \frac{2e^{2t}}{1 + (e^{2t})^2}\, \hat{i} - e^{-(t+2)}\, \hat{j}$$

11. (a)
(121,130)
$$L = \lim_{n \to \infty} \frac{a_{n+1}}{a_n} = \lim_{n \to \infty} \frac{\dfrac{n+2}{n+5}}{\dfrac{n+1}{n+4}}$$

$$= \lim_{n \to \infty} \frac{(n+2)(n+4)}{(n+1)(n+5)}$$

$$= \lim_{n \to \infty} \frac{n^2 + 6n + 8}{n^2 + 6n + 5} = 1$$

The ratio test is **inconclusive**.

(b) $\displaystyle \lim_{n \to \infty} a_n = \lim_{n \to \infty} \frac{n+1}{n+4} = 1$

By the divergence theorem, the series **diverges**.

12.
(129)
Since there is an odd multiple of θ, the rose curve is traced over $(0, \pi)$

$$A = \int_0^\pi \frac{1}{2}[4 \cos (3\theta)]^2\, d\theta$$

$$= \int_0^\pi 8 \cos^2 (3\theta)\, d\theta$$

$$= 8 \int_0^\pi \left[\frac{1}{2} + \frac{1}{2} \cos (6\theta)\right] d\theta$$

$$= 4 \int_0^\pi [1 + \cos (6\theta)]\, d\theta$$

$$= 4\left[\theta + \frac{1}{6} \sin (6\theta)\right]_0^\pi$$

$$= 4[\pi + 0 - (0 + 0)] = 4\pi \text{ units}^2$$

TEST 33, FORM B

1.
(129)
The graph of $r = 2 \cos(3\theta)$ is a 3-petal rose that traces its first complete loop from $\frac{\pi}{6}$ to $\frac{\pi}{2}$.

$$\text{Area} = \int_{\pi/6}^{\pi/2} \frac{1}{2}[2 \cos(3\theta)]^2 \, d\theta$$

$$= 2 \int_{\pi/6}^{\pi/2} \cos^2(3\theta) \, d\theta$$

The correct choice is **C**.

2.
(130)
For A, use the root test.

$$L = \lim_{n \to \infty} \sqrt[n]{\frac{n^3}{n^n}} = \lim_{n \to \infty} \frac{\sqrt[n]{n^3}}{\sqrt[n]{n^n}} = \lim_{n \to \infty} \frac{n^{3/n}}{n}$$

$$= \frac{1}{\infty} = 0$$

Since $L < 1$, the series converges.

For B, use the root test.

$$L = \lim_{n \to \infty} \sqrt[n]{\frac{2^n}{n^2}} = \lim_{n \to \infty} \frac{\sqrt[n]{2^n}}{\sqrt[n]{n^2}} = \lim_{n \to \infty} \frac{2}{n^{2/n}}$$

$$= \frac{2}{1} = 2$$

Since $L > 1$, the series diverges.

For C, use the ratio test.

$$L = \lim_{n \to \infty} \frac{\dfrac{(n+1)^2}{(n+1)!}}{\dfrac{n^2}{n!}} = \lim_{n \to \infty} \frac{(n+1)^2 \, n!}{n^2 (n+1)!}$$

$$= \lim_{n \to \infty} \frac{(n+1)^2}{n^2(n+1)} = \lim_{n \to \infty} \frac{n+1}{n^2}$$

$$= \lim_{n \to \infty} \frac{1}{n} + \frac{1}{n^2} = 0$$

Since $L < 1$, the series converges.

The correct choice is **B**.

3.
(131)
$$\int_{-\infty}^{\infty} e^{-|2x|} \, dx = \int_{-\infty}^{0} e^{-(-2x)} \, dx + \int_{0}^{\infty} e^{-2x} \, dx$$

$$= \int_{-\infty}^{0} e^{2x} \, dx + \int_{0}^{\infty} e^{-2x} \, dx$$

$$= \lim_{a \to -\infty} \int_{a}^{0} e^{2x} \, dx$$

$$+ \lim_{b \to \infty} \int_{0}^{b} e^{-2x} \, dx$$

$$= \lim_{a \to -\infty} \frac{1}{2} e^{2x} \Big|_{a}^{0} + \lim_{b \to \infty} -\frac{1}{2} e^{-2x} \Big|_{0}^{b}$$

$$= \lim_{a \to -\infty} \left(\frac{1}{2} - \frac{e^{2a}}{2} \right)$$

$$+ \lim_{b \to \infty} \left(-\frac{e^{-2b}}{2} + \frac{1}{2} \right)$$

$$= \frac{1}{2} - 0 + 0 + \frac{1}{2} = 1$$

4.
(131)
$$\int_{-\pi}^{\pi} \frac{1}{x} \, dx = \int_{-\pi}^{0} \frac{1}{x} \, dx + \int_{0}^{\pi} \frac{1}{x} \, dx$$

$$\int_{0}^{\pi} \frac{1}{x} \, dx = \lim_{a \to 0^+} \int_{a}^{\pi} \frac{1}{x} \, dx$$

$$= \lim_{u \to 0^+} \ln x \Big|_{a}^{\pi}$$

$$= \lim_{a \to 0^+} \ln \pi - \ln a$$

$$= +\infty$$

Thus the given integral **diverges**.

5.
(114)
$$L_0^4 = \int_0^4 \sqrt{\left(\frac{dx}{dt}\right)^2 + \left(\frac{dy}{dt}\right)^2} \, dt$$

$$= \int_0^4 \sqrt{(t-1)^2 + (2t^{1/2})^2} \, dt$$

$$= \int_0^4 \sqrt{t^2 - 2t + 1 + 4t} \, dt$$

$$= \int_0^4 (t+1) \, dt$$

$$= \frac{t^2}{2} + t \Big|_0^4 = \textbf{12 units}$$

6.
(38)
$$\int \frac{4x^2 + x + 1}{1 + 4x^2} \, dx$$

$$= \int \left[\frac{4x^2 + 1}{4x^2 + 1} + \frac{x}{4x^2 + 1} \right] dx$$

$$= \int \left[1 + \frac{x}{4x^2 + 1} \right] dx$$

$$= x + \frac{1}{8} \ln(4x^2 + 1) + C$$

7.
(111)
The $\lim_{x \to 0} [x + \cos(\pi x)]^{\sec(x - \pi/2)}$ is an indeterminate form, 1^∞, so it is easier to work with the natural logarithm of the function.

$$\lim_{x \to 0} \sec\left(x - \frac{\pi}{2}\right) \ln[x + \cos(\pi x)]$$

$$= \lim_{x \to 0} \frac{\ln[x + \cos(\pi x)]}{\cos\left(x - \dfrac{\pi}{2}\right)}$$

$$= \lim_{x \to 0} \frac{\dfrac{1 - \pi \sin(\pi x)}{x + \cos(\pi x)}}{-\sin\left(x - \dfrac{\pi}{2}\right)}$$

$$= \frac{1 - 0}{-(-1)} = 1$$

Thus the original limit equals e^1, or **e**.

8.
(124)
$$y^2 = \cos x - y$$

$$2y\frac{dy}{dx} = -\sin x - \frac{dy}{dx}$$

$$(2y + 1)\frac{dy}{dx} = -\sin x$$

$$\frac{dy}{dx} = \frac{-\sin x}{2y + 1}$$

$$\frac{dy}{dx}\bigg|_{(1,0)} = \frac{-\sin 1}{2(0) + 1} = \mathbf{-\sin 1}$$

9.
(116)
$$\sum_{n=3}^{5}\frac{4 + n}{n^3} = \frac{4 + 3}{3^3} + \frac{4 + 4}{4^3} + \frac{4 + 5}{5^3}$$

$$= \frac{\mathbf{12{,}319}}{\mathbf{27{,}000}}$$

10.
(123)
$$\vec{f}(t) = \operatorname{arccot}(e^{2t})\,\hat{i} + e^{-(t+2)}\hat{j}$$

$$\vec{f}'(t) = \frac{-2e^{2t}}{1 + (e^{2t})^2}\hat{i} - e^{-(t+2)}\hat{j}$$

11. (a) $L = \lim\limits_{n\to\infty}\dfrac{a_n + 1}{a_n} = \lim\limits_{n\to\infty}\dfrac{\dfrac{1}{(n+1)^2}}{\dfrac{1}{n^2}}$
(121,127)

$$= \lim\limits_{n\to\infty}\frac{n^2}{(n+1)^2}$$

$$= \lim\limits_{n\to\infty}\frac{n^2}{n^2 + 2n + 1} = 1$$

The ratio test is **inconclusive.**

(b) The series $\sum\limits_{n=1}^{\infty}\frac{1}{n^2}$ is a p-series with $p = 2$. Since $p > 1$, this series **converges.**

12. Since there is an odd multiple of θ, the rose curve is
(129) traced over $(0, \pi)$.

$$A = \int_0^\pi \frac{1}{2}(4\sin(3\theta))^2\, d\theta$$

$$= \int_0^\pi 8\sin^2(3\theta)\, d\theta$$

$$= 8\int_0^\pi \left[\frac{1}{2} - \frac{1}{2}\cos(6\theta)\right] d\theta$$

$$= 4\int_0^\pi [1 - \cos(6\theta)]\, d\theta$$

$$= 4\left[\theta - \frac{1}{6}\sin(6\theta)\right]_0^\pi$$

$$= 4[\pi - 0 - (0 - 0)] = \mathbf{4\pi\ units^2}$$

TEST 34, FORM A

1.
(104)
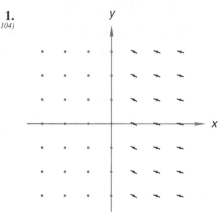

From the graph of the slope field, choice A can be eliminated since $x^2 + y = 1$ is the graph of a parabola. If choice B is solved for y, $y = \frac{4}{x}$, which does not describe the slope field, so B is eliminated. Choice C describes an exponential function defined everywhere. This does not match the slope field. The slope of $\sqrt{x} + y = 2$ is $\frac{dy}{dx} = -\frac{1}{2\sqrt{x}}$, which describes the slope field.

The correct choice is **D.**

2. $F'(x) = \dfrac{d}{dx}\displaystyle\int_0^x \sqrt{\tan t}\, dt = \sqrt{\tan x}$
(98)

$$F'\left(\frac{\pi}{6}\right) = \sqrt{\tan\frac{\pi}{6}} = \sqrt{\frac{1}{\sqrt{3}}} = \mathbf{3^{-1/4}}$$

The correct choice is **A.**

3. $\displaystyle\int_{-1}^{2}\frac{|x|}{x}\, dx = \int_{-1}^{0}\frac{-x}{x}\, dx + \int_{0}^{2}\frac{x}{x}\, dx$
(131)

$$= \lim\limits_{b\to 0^-}\int_{-1}^{b} -1\, dx + \lim\limits_{a\to 0^+}\int_{a}^{2} 1\, dx$$

$$= \lim\limits_{b\to 0^-} -x\bigg|_{-1}^{b} + \lim\limits_{a\to 0^+} x\bigg|_{a}^{2}$$

$$= \lim\limits_{b\to 0^-}(-b - 1) + \lim\limits_{a\to 0^+}(2 - a)$$

$$= -1 + 2 = \mathbf{1}$$

4.
(63)
$$f(x) = x^2 e^{-x}$$
$$f'(x) = -x^2 e^{-x} + 2x e^{-x}$$
$$f'(x) = x(2 - x)e^{-x}$$

Critical numbers: $0, 2$

Check the values of the function at each critical number and endpoint.
$$f(0) = 0$$
$$f(2) = 4e^{-2}$$
$$f(10) = 100e^{-10}$$

The absolute maximum is $\mathbf{4e^{-2}}$.

5. (117)
$$\sum_{n=2}^{\infty} \frac{4^n + 1}{7^n} = \sum_{n=2}^{\infty} \left(\frac{4}{7}\right)^n + \sum_{n=2}^{\infty} \left(\frac{1}{7}\right)^n$$

$$= \left(\frac{4}{7}\right)^2 \sum_{n=0}^{\infty} \left(\frac{4}{7}\right)^n + \left(\frac{1}{7}\right)^2 \sum_{n=0}^{\infty} \left(\frac{1}{7}\right)^n$$

$$= \frac{\left(\frac{4}{7}\right)^2}{\frac{3}{7}} + \frac{\left(\frac{1}{7}\right)^2}{\frac{6}{7}} = \frac{16}{21} + \frac{1}{42}$$

$$= \frac{33}{42} = \frac{11}{14}$$

The correct choice is **A.**

6. (133) $f(x, y) = x^3,\ x_0 = 2,\ y_0 = 1,\ x_1 = 2.3$

$$\Delta x = \frac{2.3 - 2}{1} = 0.3$$

$$y_1 = y_0 + f(x_0, y_0)\,\Delta x$$
$$= 1 + 2^3(0.3)$$
$$= 1 + 2.4 = \textbf{3.4}$$

7. (134) $x = r\cos\theta = 2\cos^2\theta$

$$y = r\sin\theta = 2\cos\theta\sin\theta = \sin(2\theta)$$

$$\frac{dy}{dx} = \frac{2\cos(2\theta)}{(4\cos\theta)(-\sin\theta)}$$

$$\frac{dy}{dx} = -\cot(2\theta)$$

$$\left.\frac{dy}{dx}\right|_{\theta=\frac{\pi}{12}} = -\cot\frac{\pi}{6} = -\sqrt{3}$$

8. (129) The graph of $r = 3 + 3\sin\theta$ is a cardioid.

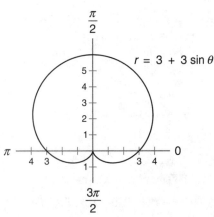

$$A = 2\int_{\pi/2}^{3\pi/2} \frac{1}{2} r^2\, d\theta$$

$$= \int_{\pi/2}^{3\pi/2} (3 + 3\sin\theta)^2\, d\theta$$

9. (78) $v(t) = \sin t + \cos t$

$$v'(t) = \cos t - \sin t$$

$$\cos t - \sin t = 0$$

$$\cos t = \sin t$$

$$\tan t = 1$$

$$t = \frac{\pi}{4}, \frac{5\pi}{4}, \frac{9\pi}{4}, \text{etc.}$$

However, sine and cosine are positive at $\frac{\pi}{4}$ and negative at $\frac{5\pi}{4}$, so the maximum occurs at $\frac{\pi}{4}$.

$$v\left(\frac{\pi}{4}\right) = \sin\left(\frac{\pi}{4}\right) + \cos\left(\frac{\pi}{4}\right) = \frac{\sqrt{2}}{2} + \frac{\sqrt{2}}{2}$$

$$= \sqrt{2}$$

10. (38,64)
$$\int_0^1 \frac{x + 2}{x^2 + 4}\, dx$$

$$= \int_0^1 \frac{x}{x^2 + 4}\, dx + \int_0^1 \frac{2}{x^2 + 4}\, dx$$

$$= \left.\frac{1}{2}\ln\left|x^2 + 4\right|\right|_0^1 + \left.\arctan\left(\frac{x}{2}\right)\right|_0^1$$

$$= \frac{1}{2}(\ln 5 - \ln 4) + \arctan\left(\frac{1}{2}\right) - \arctan 0$$

$$= \frac{1}{2}\ln\left(\frac{5}{4}\right) + \arctan\left(\frac{1}{2}\right)$$

11. (127,128) (a) Use the integral test.

$$\int_1^{\infty} \frac{4x}{x^2 + 1}\, dx = \left.2\ln\left|x^2 + 1\right|\right|_1^{\infty}$$

$$= \infty - \ln 4$$

The integral diverges so $\sum_{n=1}^{\infty} \frac{4n}{n^2 + 1}$ also **diverges.**

(b) The series $\sum_{n=1}^{\infty} \frac{1}{2n} = \frac{1}{2}\sum_{n=1}^{\infty} \frac{1}{n}$ **diverges** since it is $\frac{1}{2}$ times the harmonic series.

(c) $$\sum_{n=1}^{\infty} \left(\frac{4n}{n^2 + 1}\right)\left(\frac{1}{2n}\right) = \sum_{n=1}^{\infty} \frac{2}{n^2 + 1}$$

Note that $\frac{n^2 + 1}{2} > \frac{n^2}{2}$, so $\frac{2}{n^2 + 1} < \frac{2}{n^2}$ for $n \geq 1$. Since $2\sum_{n=1}^{\infty} \frac{1}{n^2}$ is a convergent p-series, $\sum_{n=1}^{\infty} \frac{2}{n^2 + 1}$ **converges** by the basic comparison test.

12. (135) Note that $\sum_{n=1}^{\infty} \left|\frac{\sin n}{n^3}\right| \leq \sum_{n=1}^{\infty} \frac{1}{n^3}$ since $|\sin n| \leq 1$. Since $\sum_{n=1}^{\infty} \frac{1}{n^3}$ is a convergent p-series, $\sum_{n=1}^{\infty} \left|\frac{\sin n}{n^3}\right|$ is absolutely convergent. Therefore, $\sum_{n=1}^{\infty} \frac{\sin n}{n^3}$ must **converge.**

TEST 34, FORM B

1.
(104)

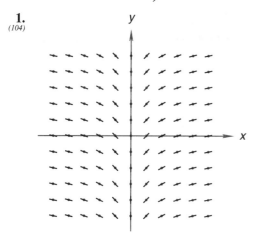

The slope field does not describe a circle (A) or an exponential (D), so these two choices can be eliminated. The graphs of $y = \ln |x| + 1$ (B) and $y = \sqrt{x} + 2$ (C) are similar, but $y = \sqrt{x} + 2$ is not defined for negative x-values.

The correct choice is **B**.

2.
(98)
$$F'(x) = \frac{d}{dx} \int_0^x \sqrt{\tan t} \; dt = \sqrt{\tan x}$$

$$F'\left(\frac{\pi}{4}\right) = \sqrt{\tan \frac{\pi}{4}} = 1$$

The correct choice is **B**.

3.
(131)
$$\int_{-2}^{2} \frac{|x|}{x} \, dx = \int_{-2}^{0} \frac{-x}{x} \, dx + \int_{0}^{2} \frac{x}{x} \, dx$$

$$= \lim_{b \to 0^-} \int_{-2}^{b} -1 \, dx + \lim_{a \to 0^+} \int_{a}^{2} 1 \, dx$$

$$= \lim_{b \to 0^-} -x \Big|_{-2}^{b} + \lim_{a \to 0^+} x \Big|_{a}^{2}$$

$$= \lim_{b \to 0^-} (-b - 2) + \lim_{a \to 0^+} (2 - a)$$

$$= -2 + 2 = \mathbf{0}$$

4.
(63)
$f(x) = x^2 e^{-x}$

$f'(x) = -x^2 e^{-x} + 2x e^{-x}$

$f'(x) = x(2 - x)e^{-x}$

Critical numbers: 0, 2

Check the values of the function at each critical number and endpoint.

$f(-10) = 100 e^{10}$

$f(0) = 0$

$f(2) = 4 e^{-2}$

$f(10) = 100 e^{-10}$

The absolute maximum is $\mathbf{100 e^{10}}$.

5.
(117)
$$\sum_{n=2}^{\infty} \frac{4^n + 1}{3^n} = \sum_{n=2}^{\infty} \left(\frac{4}{3}\right)^n + \sum_{n=2}^{\infty} \left(\frac{1}{3}\right)^n$$

$$= \left(\frac{4}{3}\right)^2 \sum_{n=0}^{\infty} \left(\frac{4}{3}\right)^n + \left(\frac{1}{3}\right)^2 \sum_{n=0}^{\infty} \left(\frac{1}{3}\right)^n$$

Since $\left(\frac{4}{3}\right) > 1$, the series diverges and **the sum is infinite.**

The correct choice is **D**.

6.
(133)
$f(x, y) = x^3, \; x_0 = 2, \; y_0 = 1$

$$\Delta x = \frac{2.3 - 2}{3} = 0.1$$

At $x_1 = 2.1, \; y_1 = 1 + (2)^3(0.1) = 1.8$

At $x_2 = 2.2, \; y_2 = 1.8 + (2.1)^3(0.1) = 2.7261$

At $x_3 = 2.3, \; y_3 = 2.7261 + (2.2)^3(0.1) = \mathbf{3.7909}$

7.
(134)
$x = r \cos \theta = 2 \sin \theta \cos \theta = \sin (2\theta)$

$y = r \sin \theta = 2 \sin^2 \theta$

$$\frac{dy}{dx} = \frac{4 \sin \theta \cos \theta}{2 \cos (2\theta)}$$

$$\frac{dy}{dx} = \tan 2\theta$$

$$\frac{dy}{dx}\Big|_{\theta = \frac{\pi}{3}} = -\sqrt{3}$$

8.
(129)
The graph of $r = 3 + 3 \cos \theta$ is a cardioid.

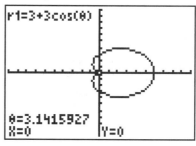

$$A = 2 \int_0^{\pi} \frac{1}{2} r^2 \, d\theta$$

$$= \int_0^{\pi} (3 + 3 \cos \theta)^2 \, d\theta$$

9.
(40)

After graphing $v(x) = 5 \sin x + 3 \cos x$, the `4:maximum` option in the `CALCULATE` menu estimates the maximum velocity to be $\approx$ **5.8310**.

10.
(59)
$$\int_0^1 \frac{x + 2}{x^2 + 4}\, dx$$

$$= \int_0^1 \frac{x}{x^2 + 4}\, dx + \int_0^1 \frac{2}{x^2 + 4}\, dx$$

$$= \frac{1}{2} \ln \left| x^2 + 4 \right| \Big|_0^1 + \arctan \frac{x}{2} \Big|_0^1$$

$$= \frac{1}{2}(\ln 5 - \ln 4) + \arctan \frac{1}{2} - \arctan 0$$

$$= \frac{1}{2} \ln \frac{5}{4} + \arctan \frac{1}{2}$$

11. (a) Use the integral test.
(127,128)
$$\int_1^\infty \frac{4x^3}{x^4 + 1}\, dx = \lim_{b \to \infty} \ln \left| x^4 + 1 \right| \Big|_1^b$$
$$= \infty - \ln 2 = \infty$$

The integral diverges, so $\sum_{n=1}^\infty \frac{4n^3}{n^4 + 1}$ also **diverges.**

(b) The series $\sum_{n=1}^\infty \frac{1}{2n} = \frac{1}{2} \sum_{n=1}^\infty \frac{1}{n}$ **diverges** since it is $\frac{1}{2}$ times the harmonic series.

(c) $$\sum_{n=1}^\infty \left(\frac{9n^2}{n^2 + 4} \right) \left(\frac{8}{3n^2} \right) = \sum_{n=1}^\infty \frac{24}{n^2 + 4}$$

Note that $\frac{n^2 + 4}{24} > \frac{n^2}{24}$ so $\frac{24}{n^2 + 4} < \frac{24}{n^2}$ for $n \geq 1$. Since $24 \sum_{n=1}^\infty \frac{1}{n^2}$ is a convergent p-series, $\sum_{n=1}^\infty \frac{24}{n^2 + 4}$ also **converges** by the basic comparison test.

12. Note that $\sum_{n=1}^\infty \left| \frac{\cos n}{n^3} \right| \leq \sum_{n=1}^\infty \frac{1}{n^3}$ since $\left| \cos n \right| \leq 1$.
(135)
Since $\sum_{n=1}^\infty \frac{1}{n^3}$ is a convergent p-series, $\sum_{n=1}^\infty \left| \frac{\cos n}{n^3} \right|$ is absolutely convergent. Therefore, $\sum_{n=1}^\infty \frac{\cos n}{n^3}$ must **converge.**

TEST 35, FORM A

1. $f'(x) = \left[\dfrac{d}{dx} \displaystyle\int_2^{x^3} \sin t^4\, dt \right] \left[\dfrac{d}{dx}(x^3) \right]$
(136)
$$= (\sin x^{12})(3x^2) = 3x^2 \sin x^{12}$$

The correct choice is **C.**

2. $\displaystyle\int_{-1}^1 f(x)\, dx = \int_{-1}^0 x\, dx + \lim_{a \to 0^+} \int_a^1 x^3\, dx$
(137)

$$= \frac{x^2}{2} \Big|_{-1}^0 + \lim_{a \to 0^+} \frac{x^4}{4} \Big|_a^1$$

$$= -\frac{1}{2} + \frac{1}{4} - \lim_{a \to 0^+} \frac{a^4}{4} = -\frac{1}{4}$$

The correct choice is **A.**

3. The choice of $\delta(\varepsilon)$ must be such that
(103)
$$9 - \varepsilon < 2x - 1 < 9 + \varepsilon$$
$$10 - \varepsilon < 2x < 10 + \varepsilon$$
$$5 - \frac{\varepsilon}{2} < x < 5 + \frac{\varepsilon}{2}$$

So $\delta(\varepsilon) \leq \dfrac{\varepsilon}{2}$.

The correct choice is **C.**

4. $h'(10) = \dfrac{1}{f'(h(10))}$
(92)

$h(10)$ is the solution to $x^3 + 5x + 4 = 10$
$$x^3 + 5x = 6$$

Since this is a cubic, the only solution is $x = 1$ and $h(10) = 1$.

$$h'(10) = \frac{1}{f'(1)}$$
$$= \frac{1}{3(1)^2 + 5}$$
$$= \frac{1}{8}$$

5. $\quad y = t^2 - 4 \quad x = t^3 - 2$
(106)
$$\frac{dy}{dt} = 2t \qquad \frac{dx}{dt} = 3t^2$$
$$\frac{dy}{dx} = \frac{2t}{3t^2} = \frac{2}{3t}$$
$$\frac{dy}{dx} \Big|_{t=5} = \frac{2}{15}$$

6. $\qquad x = v_0 t \cos \theta$
(140)
$$8000 = 1000t \cos \theta$$
$$t = \frac{8}{\cos \theta}$$
$$y = -16t^2 + v_0 t \sin \theta$$
$$0 = -16 \left(\frac{8}{\cos \theta} \right)^2 + 1000 \left(\frac{8}{\cos \theta} \right) \sin \theta$$
$$16 \left(\frac{8}{\cos \theta} \right) = 1000 \sin \theta$$
$$\frac{128}{1000} = \sin \theta \cos \theta$$
$$2 \left(\frac{128}{1000} \right) = \sin (2\theta)$$
$$2\theta = \sin^{-1} \left(\frac{128}{1000} \right)$$
$$\theta = \frac{1}{2} \sin^{-1} \left(\frac{256}{1000} \right)$$

7.
(64)
$$\int \frac{x^2}{x^2 + 4} \, dx = \int \frac{(x^2 + 4) - 4}{x^2 + 4} \, dx$$

$$= \int \left(1 - \frac{4}{x^2 + 4}\right) dx$$

$$= x - \frac{4}{2} \arctan\left(\frac{x}{2}\right) + C$$

$$= x - 2 \arctan\left(\frac{x}{2}\right) + C$$

8.
(109)
$y = x^3; \quad y' = 3x^2$

$$L_2 = \int_1^2 \sqrt{1 + (3x^2)^2} \, dx$$

9.
(118)

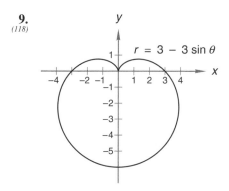

$r = 3 - 3 \sin \theta$

This graph is a **cardioid.**

10.
(75)
Differentiability and continuity are in question only at $x = 1$. The values of the piecewise functions and their first derivatives must match at $x = 1$.

$$\frac{d}{dx}(ax^3 + b) = \frac{d}{dx}[\sin(\pi x)]$$

$$3ax^2 = \pi \cos(\pi x)$$

$$3a = -\pi$$

$$a = \frac{-\pi}{3}$$

$$ax^3 + b = \sin(\pi x)$$

$$\frac{-\pi}{3}(1)^3 + b = \sin \pi$$

$$b = \frac{\pi}{3}$$

11.
(55)

n	$f^{(n)}(x)$	$f^{(n)}(0)$
0	$\cos x$	1
1	$-\sin x$	0
2	$-\cos x$	-1
$\vdots$	$\vdots$	$\vdots$

$$\cos x \approx 1 - \frac{x^2}{2!}$$

$$\cos 0.3 \approx 1 - \frac{0.3^2}{2}$$

$$\cos 0.3 \approx 1 - \frac{0.09}{2}$$

$$\cos 0.3 \approx \mathbf{0.955}$$

12.
(135,138)
$$\sum_{n=1}^{\infty} \left|(-1)^{n+1} \frac{n}{n^2 + 1}\right| = \sum_{n=1}^{\infty} \frac{n}{n^2 + 1}$$

Use the integral test.

$$\int_1^{\infty} \frac{n}{n^2 + 1} = \left[\frac{1}{2} \ln(n^2 + 1)\right]_1^{\infty}$$

$$= \lim_{b \to \infty} \left[\frac{1}{2} \ln(b^2 + 1) - \frac{1}{2} \ln 2\right]$$

$$= \infty$$

The original series does not converge absolutely.

Apply the alternating series test. First, $\sum_{n=1}^{\infty} \frac{n}{n^2 + 1} \geq 0$ for every n. Second, the sequence $\frac{1}{2}$, $\frac{2}{5}$, $\frac{3}{10}$, $\frac{4}{17}$, $\frac{5}{26}$, ... is clearly decreasing. Third, $\lim_{n \to \infty} \frac{n}{n^2 + 1} = 0$. So $\sum_{n=1}^{\infty} (-1)^{n+1} \frac{n}{n^2 + 1}$ satisfies the alternating series test. Therefore, it **converges conditionally.**

TEST 35, FORM B

1.
(103)
The choice of $\delta(\varepsilon)$ must be such that

$$4 - \varepsilon < x - 1 < 4 + \varepsilon$$

$$5 - \varepsilon < x < 5 + \varepsilon$$

So $\delta(\varepsilon) \leq \varepsilon$.

The correct choice is **B.**

2.
(136)
$$f'(x) = \left[\frac{d}{dx} \int_2^{x^4} \cos t^4 \, dt\right]\left[\frac{d}{dx}(x^4)\right]$$

$$= (\cos x^{16})(4x^3) = \mathbf{4x^3 \cos x^{16}}$$

The correct choice is **D.**

3.
(92)
With $f(x) = x^3 + 5x + 4$ note that $f(0) = 4$, so $h(4) = 0$.

$$h'(4) = \frac{1}{f'(h(4))} = \frac{1}{f'(0)} = \frac{1}{3(0)^2 + 5} = \frac{1}{5}$$

4.
(59)
$$\int_{-1}^{1} f(x)\,dx = \int_{-1}^{0} x^2\,dx + \int_{0}^{1} x^3\,dx$$

$$= \left.\frac{x^3}{3}\right|_{-1}^{0} + \left.\frac{x^4}{4}\right|_{0}^{1}$$

$$= \frac{1}{3} + \frac{1}{4} = \frac{7}{12}$$

5.
(106)
$$y = t^2 - 4 \quad x = t^3 - 2$$

$$\frac{dy}{dt} = 2t \qquad \frac{dx}{dt} = 3t^2$$

$$\frac{dy}{dx} = \frac{2t}{3t^2} = \frac{2}{3t}$$

$$\left.\frac{dy}{dx}\right|_{t=3} = \frac{2}{9}$$

6.
(140)
$$x = v_0 t \cos\theta$$

$$7000 = 1000 t \cos\theta$$

$$t = \frac{7}{\cos\theta}$$

$$y = -16t^2 + v_0 t \sin\theta$$

$$0 = -16\left(\frac{7}{\cos\theta}\right)^2 + 1000\left(\frac{7}{\cos\theta}\right)\sin\theta$$

$$16\left(\frac{7}{\cos\theta}\right) = 1000\sin\theta$$

$$\frac{112}{1000} = \sin\theta\cos\theta$$

$$2\left(\frac{112}{1000}\right) = \sin(2\theta)$$

$$2\theta = \sin^{-1}\left(\frac{224}{1000}\right)$$

$$\theta = \frac{1}{2}\sin^{-1}\left(\frac{224}{1000}\right) \approx \mathbf{6.4720°}$$

7.
(64)
$$\int \frac{x^2}{x^2 + 9}\,dx = \int \frac{(x^2 + 9) - 9}{x^2 + 9}\,dx$$

$$= \int \left(1 - \frac{9}{x^2 + 9}\right)dx$$

$$= x - \frac{9}{3}\arctan\left(\frac{x}{3}\right) + C$$

$$= x - 3\arctan\left(\frac{x}{3}\right) + C$$

8.
(109)
$$y = x^3; \quad y' = 3x^2$$

$$L_1^2 = \int_1^2 \sqrt{1 + (3x^2)^2}\,dx$$

Using `fnInt`, this is approximately **7.0825 units.**

9.
(118)
The graph of $r = 3 - 3\cos\theta$ is a **cardioid.**

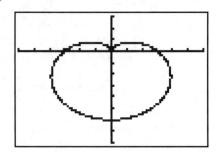

10.
(75)
Continuity and differentiability are in question only at $x = 1$. The values of the piecewise functions and their first derivatives must match at $x = 1$.

$$\frac{d}{dx}(ax^3 + b) = \frac{d}{dx}\left[\cos\left(\frac{\pi}{2}x\right)\right]$$

$$3ax^2 = \frac{-\pi}{2}\sin\left(\frac{\pi}{2}x\right)$$

$$3a = \frac{-\pi}{2}$$

$$a = \frac{-\pi}{6}$$

$$ax^3 + b = \cos\left(\frac{\pi}{2}x\right)$$

$$\frac{-\pi}{6}(1)^3 + b = \cos\frac{\pi}{2}$$

$$b = \frac{\pi}{6}$$

11.
(55)

n	$f^{(n)}(x)$	$f^{(n)}(0)$
0	$\cos x$	1
1	$-\sin x$	0
2	$-\cos x$	-1
3	$\sin x$	0
4	$\cos x$	1
5	$-\sin x$	0
6	$-\cos x$	-1
$\vdots$	$\vdots$	$\vdots$

$$\cos x \approx 1 - \frac{x^2}{2!} + \frac{x^4}{4!} - \frac{x^6}{6!}$$

$$\cos 0.3 \approx 1 - \frac{0.3^2}{2} + \frac{0.3^4}{24} - \frac{0.3^6}{720}$$

$$\cos 0.3 \approx \frac{79{,}666{,}919}{80{,}000{,}000}$$

12.
(135,138)
$$\sum_{n=1}^{\infty}\left|(-1)^n \frac{n}{n^2+1}\right| = \sum_{n=1}^{\infty}\frac{n}{n^2+1}$$

Use the integral test.

$$\int_1^{\infty}\frac{n}{n^2+1} = \left[\frac{1}{2}\ln(n^2+1)\right]_1^{\infty}$$

$$= \lim_{b\to\infty}\left[\frac{1}{2}\ln(b^2+1) - \frac{1}{2}\ln 2\right]$$

$$= \infty$$

So the original series does not converge absolutely.

Apply the alternating series test. First, $\sum_{n=1}^{\infty}\frac{n}{n^2+1} \geq 0$ for every n. Second, the sequence $\frac{1}{2}$, $\frac{2}{5}$, $\frac{3}{10}$, $\frac{4}{17}$, $\frac{5}{26}$, ... is clearly decreasing. Third, $\lim_{n\to\infty}\frac{n}{n^2+1} = 0$. So $\sum_{n=1}^{\infty}(-1)^n\frac{n}{n^2+1}$ satisfies the alternating series test. Therefore, it **converges conditionally.**

TEST 36, FORM A

1.
(55)

n	$f^{(n)}(x)$	$f^{(n)}(0)$
0	e^x	1
1	e^x	1
2	e^x	1
$\vdots$	$\vdots$	$\vdots$

$$e^x = 1 + x + \frac{x^2}{2!} + \frac{x^3}{3!} + \cdots$$

The correct choice is **B.**

2. I. $\lim_{n\to\infty}\frac{1}{3n+2} = 0$
(121,138)

This series converges by the alternating series test.

II. $\lim_{n\to\infty}\frac{n}{3n^2+2} = \lim_{n\to\infty}\frac{1}{6n} = 0$

This series converges by the alternating series test.

III. $\lim_{n\to\infty}\frac{n^2}{3n^2+2} = \lim_{n\to\infty}\frac{1}{3+\frac{2}{n^2}} = \frac{1}{3} \neq 0$

This series diverges by the divergence theorem.

The correct choice is **B.**

3. The series $\sum_{n=0}^{\infty}\frac{(-1)^n x^n}{n!}$ alternates in sign. This
(141) eliminates e^x. The function $\ln(1+x)$ does not expand to produce a factorial denominator. The series for $\sin x$ does not have a value of 1 at $n=0$. However, the function e^{-x} produces the given Taylor series.

The correct choice is **C.**

4.
(117)
$$\sum_{n=1}^{\infty}\frac{2^n-4^n}{3^n} = \sum_{n=1}^{\infty}\left(\frac{2}{3}\right)^n - \sum_{n=1}^{\infty}\left(\frac{4}{3}\right)^n$$

The given geometric series diverges since it is the sum of a convergent series and a **divergent** series.

The correct choice is **D.**

5.
(124)
$$xy + y = 6x$$

$$x\frac{dy}{dx} + y + \frac{dy}{dx} = 6$$

$$2\frac{dy}{dx} + 4 + \frac{dy}{dx} = 6$$

$$3\frac{dy}{dx} = 2$$

$$\frac{dy}{dx} = \frac{2}{3}$$

6. $f(x,y) = x - 4y$, $x_0 = 1$, $y_0 = 2$, $\Delta x = 0.2$
(133)
$$y_n = y_{n-1} + f(x_{n-1}, y_{n-1})\Delta x$$
$$x_1 = 1.2, \; y_1 = 2 + (-7)(0.2) = 2 - 1.4 = 0.6$$
$$x_2 = 1.4, \; y_2 = 0.6 + [1.2 - 4(0.6)](0.2)$$
$$= 0.6 + (-1.2)(0.2) = \mathbf{0.36}$$

7.
(140)
$$x = v_0 t\cos\theta$$
$$20{,}000 = 500t\cos\theta$$
$$t = \frac{40}{\cos\theta}$$
$$y = -16t^2 + v_0 t\sin\theta$$
$$0 = -16\left(\frac{40}{\cos\theta}\right)^2 + 500\left(\frac{40}{\cos\theta}\right)\sin\theta$$
$$16\left(\frac{40}{\cos\theta}\right) = 500\sin\theta$$
$$640 = 500\sin\theta\cos\theta$$
$$\sin\theta\cos\theta = \frac{640}{500}$$
$$\sin(2\theta) = \frac{1280}{500}$$

This is impossible. The sine function never produces a value greater than 1. **The cannonball cannot reach a target 20,000 feet away.**

8.
(71) Use the disk method.

$$V = \pi \int_0^{\pi/4} \sec^2 x \, dx$$

$$= \pi[\tan x]_0^{\pi/4}$$

$$= \pi[1 - 0] = \pi \text{ units}^3$$

9.
(108) $y = x^3 + x - 2;\ y' = 3x^2 + 1$

At $(1, 0)\ y' = 3(1^2) + 1 = 4$. One vector with a slope of 4 is $\langle 1, 4\rangle$. Dividing this vector by its length gives the unit vector $\left\langle \frac{1}{\sqrt{17}}, \frac{4}{\sqrt{17}} \right\rangle$. The other possible answer is $\left\langle -\frac{1}{\sqrt{17}}, -\frac{4}{\sqrt{17}} \right\rangle$.

10.
(129)

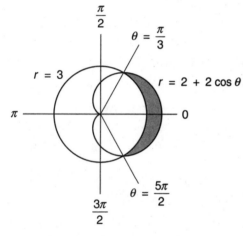

$$A = 2 \int_0^{\pi/3} \frac{1}{2}\left[(2 + 2\cos\theta)^2 - 3^2\right] d\theta$$

$$= \int_0^{\pi/3} (4 + 8\cos\theta + 4\cos^2\theta - 9)\, d\theta$$

$$= \int_0^{\pi/3} \left\{-5 + 8\cos\theta + 4\left[\frac{1}{2} + \frac{1}{2}\cos(2\theta)\right]\right\} d\theta$$

$$= \int_0^{\pi/3} [-3 + 8\cos\theta + 2\cos(2\theta)]\, d\theta$$

$$= [-3\theta + 8\sin\theta + \sin(2\theta)]_0^{\pi/3}$$

$$= -\pi + \frac{8\sqrt{3}}{2} + \frac{\sqrt{3}}{2}$$

$$= \left(\frac{9\sqrt{3}}{2} - \pi\right) \text{units}^2$$

11.
(141)

$$f(x) = \cos x \qquad f\left(\frac{\pi}{6}\right) = \frac{\sqrt{3}}{2}$$

$$f'(x) = -\sin x \qquad f'\left(\frac{\pi}{6}\right) = -\frac{1}{2}$$

$$f''(x) = -\cos x \qquad f''\left(\frac{\pi}{6}\right) = \frac{-\sqrt{3}}{2}$$

$$f'''(x) = \sin x \qquad f'''\left(\frac{\pi}{6}\right) = \frac{1}{2}$$

$$\cos x \approx \frac{\sqrt{3}}{2} - \frac{\frac{1}{2}\left(x - \frac{\pi}{6}\right)}{1!} - \frac{\frac{\sqrt{3}}{2}\left(x - \frac{\pi}{6}\right)^2}{2!}$$

$$+ \frac{\frac{1}{2}\left(x - \frac{\pi}{6}\right)^3}{3!}$$

$$= \frac{\sqrt{3}}{2} - \frac{\left(x - \frac{\pi}{6}\right)}{2} - \frac{\sqrt{3}\left(x - \frac{\pi}{6}\right)^2}{4}$$

$$+ \frac{\left(x - \frac{\pi}{6}\right)^3}{12}$$

12. (a) $\vec{p}(t) = 3\cos\left(\frac{t}{3}\right)\hat{i} + 2\sin\left(\frac{t}{3}\right)\hat{j}$
(142)

$$\vec{p}'(t) = -\sin\left(\frac{t}{3}\right)\hat{i} + \frac{2}{3}\cos\left(\frac{t}{3}\right)\hat{j}$$

$$\vec{p}'(\pi) = -\sin\left(\frac{\pi}{3}\right)\hat{i} + \frac{2}{3}\cos\left(\frac{\pi}{3}\right)\hat{j}$$

$$\vec{p}'(\pi) = -\frac{\sqrt{3}}{2}\hat{i} + \frac{1}{3}\hat{j}$$

(b) $V = \sqrt{\left(-\frac{\sqrt{3}}{2}\right)^2 + \left(\frac{1}{3}\right)^2} = \sqrt{\frac{3}{4} + \frac{1}{9}}$

$$= \sqrt{\frac{31}{36}} = \frac{\sqrt{31}}{6}$$

(c) $\vec{p}''(t) = -\frac{1}{3}\cos\left(\frac{t}{3}\right)\hat{i} - \frac{2}{9}\sin\left(\frac{t}{3}\right)\hat{j}$

$$\vec{p}''(\pi) = -\frac{1}{3}\cos\left(\frac{\pi}{3}\right)\hat{i} - \frac{2}{9}\sin\left(\frac{\pi}{3}\right)\hat{j}$$

$$\vec{p}''(\pi) = -\frac{1}{6}\hat{i} - \frac{\sqrt{3}}{9}\hat{j}$$

TEST 36, FORM B

1.
(55)

n	$f^{(n)}(x)$	$f^{(n)}(0)$
0	e^{-x}	1
1	$-e^{-x}$	-1
2	e^{-x}	1
3	$-e^{-x}$	-1
⋮	⋮	⋮

$$e^{-x} = 1 - x + \frac{x^2}{2!} - \frac{x^3}{3!} + \cdots$$

The correct choice is **C**.

2.   I. $\lim\limits_{n \to \infty} \dfrac{n}{3n + 2} = \dfrac{1}{3} \neq 0$
(121,138)

This series diverges by the divergence theorem.

II. $\lim\limits_{n \to \infty} \dfrac{n}{3n^2 + 2} = \lim\limits_{n \to \infty} \dfrac{1}{6n} = 0$

This series converges by the alternating series test.

III. $\lim\limits_{n \to \infty} \dfrac{n^2}{3n^2 + 2} = \lim\limits_{n \to \infty} \dfrac{1}{3 + \dfrac{2}{n^2}} = \dfrac{1}{3} \neq 0$

This series diverges by the divergence theorem.

The correct choice is **A**.

3.   The series $\sum\limits_{n=0}^{\infty} \dfrac{(-1)^n x^{2n}}{(2n)!}$ alternates in sign. This
(141)   eliminates e^x. The function $\ln(1 + x)$ does not expand to produce a factorial denominator. The series for e^{-x} does not skip any of the positive integer values for x. The series for $\cos x$, however, has the given power series.

The correct choice is **A**.

4. $\sum\limits_{n=1}^{\infty} \dfrac{5^n - 2^n}{3^n} = \sum\limits_{n=1}^{\infty} \left(\dfrac{5}{3}\right)^n - \sum\limits_{n=1}^{\infty} \left(\dfrac{2}{3}\right)^n$
(117)

The given geometric series diverges since it is the sum of a converged series and a divergent series.

The correct answer is **D**.

5.
(124)
$$xy + y = 6x$$
$$x\frac{dy}{dx} + y + \frac{dy}{dx} = 6$$
$$\frac{dy}{dx} + 3 + \frac{dy}{dx} = 6$$
$$2\frac{dy}{dx} = 3$$
$$\frac{dy}{dx} = \frac{3}{2}$$

6. $f(x, y) = x - 4y,\ x_0 = 1,\ y_0 = 2,\ \Delta x = 0.2$
(133) $y_n = y_{n-1} + f(x_{n-1}, y_{n-1})\Delta x$
$x_1 = 1.2,\ y_1 = 2 + (-7)(0.2) = 0.6$
$x_2 = 1.4,\ y_2 = 0.6 + (-1.2)(0.2) = 0.36$
$x_3 = 1.6,\ y_3 = 0.36 + [1.4 - 4(0.36)](0.2)$
$\qquad\qquad = \mathbf{0.352}$

7.
(140)
$$x = v_0 t \cos \theta$$
$$21{,}000 = 700t \cos \theta$$
$$t = \frac{30}{\cos \theta}$$
$$y = -16t^2 + v_0 t \sin \theta$$
$$0 = -16\left(\frac{30}{\cos \theta}\right)^2 + 700\left(\frac{30}{\cos \theta}\right)\sin \theta$$
$$16\left(\frac{30}{\cos \theta}\right) = 700 \sin \theta$$
$$480 = 700 \sin \theta \cos \theta$$
$$\sin \theta \cos \theta = \frac{480}{700}$$
$$\sin(2\theta) = \frac{960}{700}$$

This is impossible. The sine function never produces a value greater than 1. **The cannonball cannot reach a target 21,000 feet away.**

8.   Use the disk method.
(71)

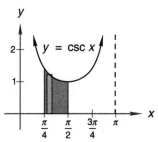

$$V = \pi \int_{\pi/4}^{\pi/2} \csc^2 x \, dx$$
$$= \pi[-\cot x]_{\pi/4}^{\pi/2}$$
$$= \pi \ \mathbf{units^3}$$

9.
(108)
$y = x^3 + x - 2;\ y' = 3x^2 + 1$

At $(2, 8)\ y' = 3(2^2) + 1 = 13$. One vector with a slope of 13 is $\langle 1, 13 \rangle$. Dividing this vector by its length gives the unit vector $\left\langle \frac{1}{\sqrt{170}}, \frac{13}{\sqrt{170}} \right\rangle$. The other possible answer is $\left\langle -\frac{1}{\sqrt{170}}, -\frac{13}{\sqrt{170}} \right\rangle$.

10.
(129)

$$2 + 2 \sin \theta = 3$$

$$\sin \theta = \frac{1}{2}$$

$$\theta = \frac{\pi}{6} \text{ and } \frac{5\pi}{6}$$

$$A = 2 \int_{\pi/6}^{\pi/2} \frac{1}{2} [(2 + 2 \sin \theta)^2 - 3^2]\, d\theta$$

$$= \int_{\pi/6}^{\pi/2} [(2 + 2 \sin \theta)^2 - 9]\, d\theta$$

$$= \int_{\pi/6}^{\pi/2} (4 + 8 \sin \theta + 4 \sin^2 \theta - 9)\, d\theta$$

$$= \int_{\pi/6}^{\pi/2} \left\{ -5 + \sin \theta + 4 \left[\frac{1}{2} - \frac{1}{2} \cos (2\theta) \right] \right\} d\theta$$

$$= \int_{\pi/6}^{\pi/2} [-3 + 8 \sin \theta - 2 \cos (2\theta)]\, d\theta$$

$$= [-3\theta - 8 \cos \theta - \sin (2\theta)]_{\pi/6}^{\pi/2}$$

$$= -\frac{3\pi}{2} + \frac{\pi}{2} + \frac{8\sqrt{3}}{2} + \frac{\sqrt{3}}{2}$$

$$= \left(\frac{9\sqrt{3}}{2} - \pi \right) \text{ units}^2$$

11.
(141)
$f(x) = \sin x$ $f\left(\frac{\pi}{6}\right) = \frac{1}{2}$

$f'(x) = \cos x$ $f'\left(\frac{\pi}{6}\right) = \frac{\sqrt{3}}{2}$

$f''(x) = -\sin x$ $f''\left(\frac{\pi}{6}\right) = -\frac{1}{2}$

$f'''(x) = -\cos x$ $f'''\left(\frac{\pi}{6}\right) = -\frac{\sqrt{3}}{2}$

$$\sin x \approx \frac{1}{2} + \frac{\frac{\sqrt{3}}{2}\left(x - \frac{\pi}{6}\right)}{1!} - \frac{\frac{1}{2}\left(x - \frac{\pi}{6}\right)^2}{2!}$$

$$- \frac{\frac{\sqrt{3}}{2}\left(x - \frac{\pi}{6}\right)^3}{3!}$$

$$= \frac{1}{2} + \frac{\sqrt{3}\left(x - \frac{\pi}{6}\right)}{2} - \frac{\left(x - \frac{\pi}{6}\right)^2}{4}$$

$$- \frac{\sqrt{3}\left(x - \frac{\pi}{6}\right)^3}{12}$$

12.
(142)
(a) $\vec{p}(t) = 3 \sin\left(\frac{t}{3}\right)\hat{i} + 2 \cos\left(\frac{t}{3}\right)\hat{j}$

$\vec{p'}(t) = \cos\left(\frac{t}{3}\right)\hat{i} - \frac{2}{3}\sin\left(\frac{t}{3}\right)\hat{j}$

$\vec{p'}(\pi) = \cos\left(\frac{\pi}{3}\right)\hat{i} - \frac{2}{3}\sin\left(\frac{\pi}{3}\right)\hat{j}$

$\vec{p'}(\pi) = \frac{1}{2}\hat{i} - \frac{\sqrt{3}}{3}\hat{j}$

(b) $V = \sqrt{\left(\frac{1}{2}\right)^2 + \left(\frac{-\sqrt{3}}{3}\right)^2} = \sqrt{\frac{1}{4} + \frac{3}{9}}$

$= \sqrt{\frac{21}{36}} = \frac{\sqrt{21}}{6}$

(c) $\vec{p''}(t) = -\frac{1}{3}\sin\left(\frac{t}{3}\right)\hat{i} - \frac{2}{9}\cos\left(\frac{t}{3}\right)\hat{j}$

$\vec{p''}(\pi) = -\frac{1}{3}\sin\left(\frac{\pi}{3}\right)\hat{i} - \frac{2}{9}\cos\left(\frac{\pi}{3}\right)\hat{j}$

$\vec{p''}(\pi) = -\frac{\sqrt{3}}{6}\hat{i} - \frac{1}{9}\hat{j}$

TEST 37, FORM A

1.
(55)

n	$f^{(n)}(x)$	$f^{(n)}(0)$
0	$\cos x$	1
1	$-\sin x$	0
2	$-\cos x$	-1
3	$\sin x$	0
⋮	⋮	⋮

$$\cos x = 1 - \frac{x^2}{2!} + \frac{x^4}{4!} - \cdots$$

The correct choice is **D.**

2.
(141)

$$\sin t = t - \frac{t^3}{3!} + \frac{t^5}{5!} - \frac{t^7}{7!} + \cdots$$

$$\frac{\sin t}{t} = 1 - \frac{t^2}{3!} + \frac{t^4}{5!} - \frac{t^6}{7!} + \cdots$$

The correct choice is **A**.

3.
(108)

$$|2\hat{i} + 7\hat{j}| = \sqrt{53}$$

$$5\left(\frac{2}{\sqrt{53}}\hat{i} + \frac{7}{\sqrt{53}}\hat{j}\right) = \frac{10}{\sqrt{53}}\hat{i} + \frac{35}{\sqrt{53}}\hat{j}$$

The correct choice is **A**.

4.
(79)

$$\lim_{x \to 0} 6x \csc(7x) = \lim_{x \to 0} \frac{6x}{\sin(7x)} = \frac{6}{7}$$

The correct choice is **B**.

5.
(60)

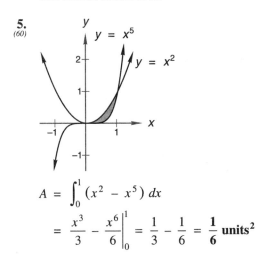

$$A = \int_0^1 (x^2 - x^5)\, dx$$

$$= \frac{x^3}{3} - \frac{x^6}{6}\bigg|_0^1 = \frac{1}{3} - \frac{1}{6} = \frac{1}{6}\ \text{units}^2$$

6. Apply the ratio test.
(145)

$$\lim_{n \to \infty} \left|\frac{(x-1)^{n+1}}{(n+1)^2}\right| \cdot \left|\frac{n^2}{(x-1)^n}\right|$$

$$= \lim_{n \to \infty} |x - 1|\left[\frac{n^2}{(n+1)^2}\right]$$

$$= |x - 1| \lim_{n \to \infty} \frac{n^2}{(n+1)^2}$$

$$= |x - 1|(1)$$

$$= |x - 1|$$

$$|x - 1| < 1$$

$$-1 < x - 1 < 1$$

$$0 < x < 2$$

Check the endpoints.

$$x = 2: \sum_{n=1}^{\infty} \frac{(2-1)^n}{n^2} = \sum_{n=1}^{\infty} \frac{1}{n^2}\ \text{converges}$$

$$x = 0: \sum_{n=1}^{\infty} \frac{(0-1)^n}{n^2} = \sum_{n=1}^{\infty} \frac{(-1)^n}{n^2}\ \text{converges}$$

Thus the interval of convergence is **[0, 2]**.

7. Apply the root test.
(130)

$$\lim_{n \to \infty} \sqrt[n]{\frac{3^n}{n^n}} = \lim_{n \to \infty} \frac{\sqrt[n]{3^n}}{\sqrt[n]{n^n}}$$

$$= \lim_{n \to \infty} \frac{3^{n/n}}{n^{n/n}}$$

$$= \lim_{n \to \infty} \frac{3}{n}$$

$$= 0$$

The series **converges**.

8.
(114)

$$x = 2t \qquad y = t^2$$

$$\frac{dx}{dt} = 2 \qquad \frac{dy}{dt} = 2t$$

$$\text{Arc length} = \int_a^b \sqrt{\left(\frac{dx}{dt}\right)^2 + \left(\frac{dy}{dt}\right)^2}\, dt$$

$$= \int_0^5 \sqrt{4 + 4t^2}\, dt$$

9. Use the shell method.
(94)

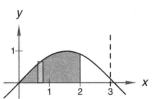

$$2\pi \int_0^2 (3 - x) \sin x\, dx$$

10.
(115,131)

$$\int_0^2 \frac{1}{x^2 - 1}\, dx$$

$$= \int_0^1 \frac{1}{x^2 - 1}\, dx + \int_1^2 \frac{1}{x^2 - 1}\, dx$$

$$\int_0^1 \frac{1}{x^2 - 1}\, dx$$

$$= \lim_{b \to 1^+} \int_0^b \frac{1}{x^2 - 1}\, dx$$

$$= \lim_{b \to 1^+} \int_0^b \frac{1}{(x+1)(x-1)}\, dx$$

$$= \lim_{b \to 1^+} \int_0^b \left[\frac{\frac{1}{2}}{x-1} + \frac{-\frac{1}{2}}{x+1}\right] dx$$

$$= \lim_{b \to 1^+} \left[\frac{1}{2} \ln\left|\frac{x-1}{x+1}\right|\right]_0^b$$

$$= \lim_{b \to 1^+} \left(\frac{1}{2} \ln\left|\frac{b-1}{b+1}\right| - \frac{1}{2} \ln(1)\right) = -\infty.$$

Thus the original integral **diverges**.

11. $e^x \approx 1 + x + \dfrac{x^2}{2!}$
(148)

$e^{t^3} \approx 1 + t^3 + \dfrac{t^6}{2}$

$\displaystyle\int_0^1 e^{t^3}\, dt \approx \int_0^1 \left[1 + t^3 + \dfrac{t^6}{2} \right] dt$

$= \left[t + \dfrac{t^4}{4} + \dfrac{t^7}{14} \right]_0^1$

$= 1 + \dfrac{1}{4} + \dfrac{1}{14} = \dfrac{37}{28}$

12. (a) $\dfrac{1}{1 + x^3} = 1 - (x^3) + (x^3)^2 - (x^3)^3$
(146,147)

$\qquad\qquad + (x^3)^4 - \cdots$

$\qquad = 1 - x^3 + x^6 - x^9 + x^{12} - \cdots$

(b) $\ln(1 + x) = \displaystyle\int \dfrac{1}{1 + x}\, dx$

$= \displaystyle\int \left(1 - x + x^2 - x^3 + x^4 - \cdots \right) dx$

$= C + x - \dfrac{x^2}{2} + \dfrac{x^3}{3} - \dfrac{x^4}{4} + \dfrac{x^5}{5} - \cdots$

At $x = 0$, $\ln(1 + x) = \ln(1) = 0$.

Thus $C = 0$.

$\ln(1 + x)$

$= x - \dfrac{x^2}{2} + \dfrac{x^3}{3} - \dfrac{x^4}{4} + \dfrac{x^5}{5} - \cdots$

TEST 37, FORM B

1. $\cos(-x) = \cos x$
(55)

n	$f^{(n)}(x)$	$f^{(n)}(0)$
0	$\cos(-x)$	1
1	$\sin(-x)$	0
2	$-\cos(-x)$	-1
3	$-\sin(-x)$	0
⋮	⋮	⋮

$\cos(-x) = 1 - \dfrac{x^2}{2!} + \dfrac{x^4}{4!} - \cdots$

The correct choice is **D.**

2. $\cos t = 1 - \dfrac{t^2}{2!} + \dfrac{t^4}{4!} - \dfrac{t^6}{6!} + \cdots$
(141)

$\dfrac{\cos t}{t} = \dfrac{1}{t} - \dfrac{t}{2!} + \dfrac{t^3}{4!} - \dfrac{t^5}{6!} + \cdots$

The correct choice is **D.**

3. $|2\hat{i} + 7\hat{j}| = \sqrt{53}$
(108)

$\dfrac{2}{\sqrt{53}}\hat{i} + \dfrac{7}{\sqrt{53}}\hat{j}$

The correct choice is **C.**

4. $\displaystyle\lim_{x \to 0} 9x \csc(8x)$
(79)

$= \displaystyle\lim_{x \to 0} \dfrac{9x}{\sin(8x)} = \dfrac{9}{8}$

The correct choice is **B.**

5.
(60)

Intersection
X=1   Y=1

$A = \displaystyle\int_0^1 (x^2 - x^7)\, dx$

$= \dfrac{x^3}{3} - \dfrac{x^7}{3} \Big|\, 1! \approx \mathbf{0.2083}$ **units^2**

6. Apply the ratio test.
(145)

$\displaystyle\lim_{n \to \infty} \left| \dfrac{(x - 1)^{n+1}}{(n + 1)} \right| \cdot \left| \dfrac{n}{(x - 1)^n} \right|$

$= \displaystyle\lim_{n \to \infty} |x - 1| \left[\dfrac{n}{n + 1} \right]$

$= |x - 1| \displaystyle\lim_{n \to \infty} \dfrac{n}{n + 1}$

$= |x - 1|(1)$

$= |x - 1|$

$|x - 1| < 1$

$-1 < x - 1 < 2$

$0 < x < 2$

Check the endpoints:

$x = 2$: $\displaystyle\sum_{n=1}^{\infty} \frac{(2-1)^n}{n} = \sum_{n=1}^{\infty} \frac{1}{n}$ diverges

$x = 0$: $\displaystyle\sum_{n=1}^{\infty} \frac{(0-1)^n}{n} = \sum_{n=1}^{\infty} \frac{(-1)^n}{n}$ converges

Thus the interval of convergence is **[0, 2)**.

7.
(130) Apply the root test.

$$\lim_{n\to\infty} \sqrt[n]{\frac{n^n}{3^n}} = \lim_{n\to\infty} \frac{\sqrt[n]{n^n}}{\sqrt[n]{3^n}}$$

$$= \lim_{n\to\infty} \frac{n^{n/n}}{3^{n/n}}$$

$$= \lim_{n\to\infty} \frac{n}{3}$$

$$= \infty$$

The series **diverges**.

8.
(114) $x = 2t \qquad y = t^2$

$\dfrac{dx}{dt} = 2 \qquad \dfrac{dy}{dt} = 2t$

Arc length $= \displaystyle\int_a^b \sqrt{\left(\frac{dx}{dt}\right)^2 + \left(\frac{dy}{dt}\right)^2}\, dt$

$= \displaystyle\int_0^5 \sqrt{4 + 4t^2}\, dt$

fnInt yields **27.8075 units**.

9.
(94) Use the shell method.

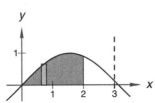

$V = 2\pi \displaystyle\int_0^2 (3-x)\sin x\, dx$

fnInt yields **15.7510 units³**.

10.
(2)

$x \approx -1.4656$

11.
(141) $e^x \approx 1 + x + \dfrac{x^2}{2!} + \dfrac{x^3}{3!}$

$e^{t^3} \approx 1 + t^3 + \dfrac{t^6}{2} + \dfrac{t^9}{6}$

$\displaystyle\int_0^1 e^{t^3}\, dt \approx \int_0^1 \left[1 + t^3 + \frac{t^6}{2} + \frac{t^9}{6}\right] dt$

$\approx \left[t + \dfrac{t^4}{4} + \dfrac{t^7}{14} + \dfrac{t^7}{14} + \dfrac{t^{10}}{60}\right]_0^1$

$\approx 1 + \dfrac{1}{4} + \dfrac{1}{14} + \dfrac{1}{60}$

$\approx \dfrac{281}{210}$

12.
(146,147) (a) $\dfrac{1}{1+x^2} = 1 - (x^2) + (x^2)^2 - (x^2)^3$

$+ (x^2)^4 - \cdots$

$= 1 - x^2 + x^4 - x^6 + x^8 - \cdots$

(b) $\ln(1+x) = \displaystyle\int \frac{1}{1+x}\, dx$

$= \displaystyle\int (1 - x + x^2 - x^3 + x^4 - \cdots)\, dx$

$= C + x - \dfrac{x^2}{2} + \dfrac{x^3}{3} - \dfrac{x^4}{4} + \dfrac{x^5}{5} - \cdots$

At $x = 0$, $\ln(1+x) = \ln(1) = 0$.
Thus $C = 0$.

$\ln(1+x)$

$= x - \dfrac{x^2}{2} + \dfrac{x^3}{3} - \dfrac{x^4}{4} + \dfrac{x^5}{5} - \cdots$

Calculus
Test Masters

Test Forms

Calculus

Testing Schedule

Test to be administered:	Covers material through:	Give after teaching:	
Test 1	Lesson 4	Lesson 8	9 T
Test 2	Lesson 8	Lesson 12	13 Q
Test 3	Lesson 12	Lesson 16	19 T
Test 4	Lesson 16	Lesson 20	23 Q
Test 5	Lesson 20	Lesson 24	27 T
Test 6	Lesson 24	Lesson 28	
Test 7	Lesson 28	Lesson 32	
Test 8	Lesson 32	Lesson 36	
Test 9	Lesson 36	Lesson 40	
Test 10	Lesson 40	Lesson 44	
Test 11	Lesson 44	Lesson 48	
Test 12	Lesson 48	Lesson 52	
Test 13	Lesson 52	Lesson 56	
Test 14	Lesson 56	Lesson 60	
Test 15	Lesson 60	Lesson 64	
Test 16	Lesson 64	Lesson 68	
Test 17	Lesson 68	Lesson 72	
Test 18	Lesson 72	Lesson 76	
Test 19	Lesson 76	Lesson 80	
Test 20	Lesson 80	Lesson 84	
Test 21	Lesson 84	Lesson 88	
Test 22	Lesson 88	Lesson 92	
Test 23	Lesson 92	Lesson 96	
Test 24	Lesson 96	Lesson 100	
Test 25	Lesson 100	Lesson 104	
Test 26	Lesson 104	Lesson 108	
Test 27	Lesson 108	Lesson 112	
Test 28	Lesson 112	Lesson 116	
Test 29	Lesson 116	Lesson 120	
Test 30	Lesson 120	Lesson 124	
Test 31	Lesson 124	Lesson 128	
Test 32	Lesson 128	Lesson 132	
Test 33	Lesson 132	Lesson 136	
Test 34	Lesson 136	Lesson 140	
Test 35	Lesson 140	Lesson 144	
Test 36	Lesson 144	Lesson 148	
Test 37	Lesson 148	Lesson 148	

Test 1, Form A   **SHOW YOUR WORK**   Name: _____

1. Simplify: $(\cos^2 \theta)(\sec \theta)(\tan^2 \theta)(\csc \theta)$

    A. $\sin \theta$ B. $\cos \theta$ C. $\tan \theta$ D. 1

2. Which of the following is a factor of $27a^3 - 8b^6$?

    A. $3a + 2b^2$ B. $9a^2 + 12ab^2 + 4b^4$ C. $9a^2 - 6ab^2 + 4b^4$ D. $3a - 2b^2$

3. The slope-intercept form of the line with slope 7 that goes through the point $(-3, 2)$ is

    A. $y = \dfrac{1}{7}x + \dfrac{17}{7}$ B. $y = 7x + 2$ C. $y = -7x - 19$ D. $y = 7x + 23$

4. Evaluate: $\sin^2 \dfrac{\pi}{3} + \tan \dfrac{\pi}{4}$

5. Evaluate: $\displaystyle\sum_{n=0}^{5} n^2$

6. Solve: $\begin{cases} x^2 + y^2 = 4 \\ x + y = 1 \end{cases}$

7. Simplify: $\dfrac{50!}{46!\,4!}$

8. Write the contrapositive, converse, and inverse of the following conditional statement:

    If $a + b = 5$, then $ab = 4$.

9. Simplify: $\dfrac{1}{1 + \dfrac{1}{1 + \dfrac{1}{2}}}$

10. Write the slope-intercept form of the equation of the line that passes through the point $(5, 3)$ and is parallel to the line $3y = 2x - 3$.

11. State the quadratic formula.

12. (a) Find the coordinates of the intersection points of the graphs of $y = x^2 - 4x + 1$ and $y = x - 3$.

    (b) Find the distance between the points found in (a).

Calculus, Second Edition

1. Simplify: $(\sin^2 \theta)(\sec \theta)(\cot^2 \theta)(\csc \theta)$

    A. $\sin \theta$ B. $\cos \theta$ C. $\tan \theta$ D. $\cot \theta$

2. Which of the following is a factor of $m^6 x^3 + n^3 y^9$?

    A. $m^2 x - ny^3$ B. $m^2 x + ny^3$

    C. $m^4 x^2 + m^2 xny^3 + n^2 y^6$ D. $m^4 x^2 - 2m^2 xny^3 + n^2 y^6$

3. The slope-intercept form of the line with slope 5 that goes through the point (3, 2) is

    A. $y = \dfrac{1}{5}x + \dfrac{7}{5}$ B. $y = 5x - 13$ C. $y = -5x + 17$ D. $y = 5x + 2$

4. Evaluate: $\cos^2 \dfrac{\pi}{3} + \tan \dfrac{\pi}{4}$

5. Evaluate: $\displaystyle\sum_{n=0}^{5} n^3$

6. Solve: $\begin{cases} x^2 + y^2 = 9 \\ x - y = 1 \end{cases}$

7. Simplify: $\dfrac{106!}{104!\ 2!}$

8. Write the contrapositive, converse, and inverse of the following conditional statement:

    If $ab = 4$, then $a + b = 5$.

9. Simplify: $\dfrac{1}{1 + \dfrac{1}{1 + \dfrac{1}{3}}}$

10. Write the slope-intercept form of the equation of the line that passes through the point $(-1, 3)$ and is perpendicular to the line $3y = 2x - 3$.

11. State the quadratic formula.

12. (a) Approximate the coordinates of the intersection points of the graphs of $y = -2x^2 + 6x - 3$ and $y = -x^4 + 4x^2 - 4$ to three decimal places.

    (b) Approximate the distance between the points found in (a) to three decimal places.

Calculus, Second Edition

1. Which of the following functions can be described by the graph to the right?

   A. $y = 2^{-x}$ B. $y = -2^{-x}$

   C. $y = \left(\dfrac{1}{2}\right)^{x}$ D. $y = -2^{x}$

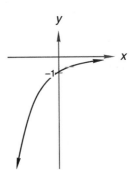

2. Which of the following sets of coordinates cannot lie on the graph of a function?

   A. $\{(0, 0), (1, 1), (2, 2)\}$ B. $\{(0, 1), (1, 2), (2, 3)\}$ C. $\{(0, 1), (1, 1), (2, 1)\}$ D. $\{(0, 1), (0, 2), (0, 3)\}$

3. Which of the following are the coordinates of point P on the unit circle shown?

   A. $(-1, 1)$ B. $\left(-\dfrac{\sqrt{2}}{2}, \dfrac{\sqrt{2}}{2}\right)$

   C. $\left(\dfrac{\sqrt{2}}{2}, \dfrac{\sqrt{2}}{2}\right)$ D. $\left(-\dfrac{\sqrt{3}}{2}, \dfrac{1}{2}\right)$

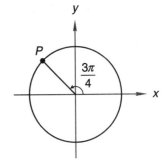

4. Evaluate: $\cot \dfrac{7\pi}{6} \sin -\dfrac{4\pi}{3}$

5. Solve for x in terms of L.

6. Jake has 300 meters of fence and wants to enclose a rectangular region of his dairy farm. Because this region borders an existing stone wall, he has to build only three new sides. Express the area of the region in terms of s, the length of fence that is parallel to the existing stone wall.

7. The monthly revenue in Peggy's Bike Shop varies linearly with the number of bikes sold. When 10 bikes are sold in a month the revenue is $850, and when 16 bikes are sold in a month the revenue is $1180. If Peggy needs a monthly revenue of $2060, how many bikes must she sell per month?

8. Simplify $\dfrac{f(x + h) - f(x)}{h}$ given that $f(x) = -2x + 3$.

9. Find the point of intersection of the graphs of $f(x) = x^2 + 2x - 1$ and $g(x) = x^2 - 5$.

10. Find the domain and range of $y = \sqrt{x + 3}$.

11. Graph the function $y = 7 + 4 \cos\left(x - \dfrac{\pi}{4}\right)$. State the amplitude and period of the function.

12. Develop an identity that relates $\tan^2 \theta$ to $\sec^2 \theta$. (*Hint:* Begin with the identity $\sin^2 \theta + \cos^2 \theta = 1$.)

Calculus, Second Edition

1. Which of the following functions can be described by the graph to the right?

   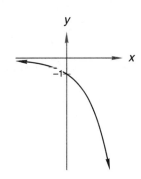

   A. $y = 2^{-x}$ B. $y = -2^{-x}$

   C. $y = \left(\dfrac{1}{2}\right)^x$ D. $y = -2^x$

2. Which of the following sets of coordinates cannot lie on the graph of a function?

   A. $\{(0, 0), (1, 1), (2, 2)\}$ B. $\{(0, 1), (1, 2), (0, 3)\}$ C. $\{(0, 1), (1, 1), (2, 1)\}$ D. $\{(0, 1), (1, 2), (2, 3)\}$

3. Which of the following are the coordinates of point P on the unit circle shown?

   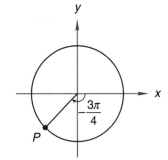

   A. $(-1, -1)$ B. $\left(-\dfrac{\sqrt{2}}{2}, \dfrac{\sqrt{2}}{2}\right)$

   C. $\left(-\dfrac{\sqrt{2}}{2}, -\dfrac{\sqrt{2}}{2}\right)$ D. $\left(-\dfrac{\sqrt{3}}{2}, -\dfrac{1}{2}\right)$

4. Evaluate: $\cos -\dfrac{2\pi}{3} \cot \dfrac{2\pi}{3}$

5. Solve for x in terms of L.

   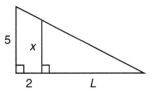

6. Cynthia has 450 yards of fence and wants to enclose a rectangular region of land for her horses. Because this region borders an existing stone wall, she has to build only three new sides. Express the area of the region in terms of s, the length of fence that is parallel to the existing stone wall.

7. The monthly revenue in Paul's Bike Shop varies linearly with the number of bikes sold. When 9 bikes are sold in a month the revenue is \$810, and when 22 bikes are sold in a month the revenue is \$1655. If Paul needs a monthly revenue of \$2500, how many bikes must he sell per month?

8. Simplify $\dfrac{f(x + h) - f(x)}{h}$ given that $f(x) = \dfrac{2}{x}$.

9. Approximate the point of intersection of the graphs of $f(x) = x^2 + 2x - 1$ and $g(x) = -x^3 + x^2 + 1$.

10. Find the domain and range of $y = \sqrt{x - 1}$.

11. Graph the function $y = 3 + 5 \sin\left(x - \dfrac{\pi}{4}\right)$. State the amplitude and period of the function.

12. Develop an identity that relates $\cot^2 \theta$ to $\csc^2 \theta$. (*Hint:* Begin with the identity $\sin^2 \theta + \cos^2 \theta = 1$.)

Calculus, Second Edition

1. Which of the following is the domain of the function $g(x) = \sqrt{x^2 - 1}$?
   A. $\{x \in \mathbb{R} \mid -1 < x < 1\}$
   B. $\{x \in \mathbb{R} \mid -1 \leq x \leq 1\}$
   C. $\{x \in \mathbb{R} \mid x \leq -1 \text{ or } x \geq 1\}$
   D. $\mathbb{R}$

2. Consider the graph of the function f shown to the right. What is $\lim\limits_{x \to 3^+} f(x)$?

   A. 3
   B. -1
   C. 5
   D. The limit does not exist.

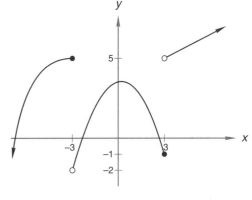

3. According to the rational roots theorem, the possible rational roots of $x^3 - 7x - 6 = 0$ are
   A. $-6, 1$
   B. $\pm 1, \pm 6$
   C. $-7, -6, 1$
   D. $\pm 1, \pm 2, \pm 3, \pm 6$

4. Shown to the right is the graph of the function $y = f(x)$. Sketch the graph of $y = |f(x)|$.

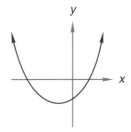

5. Graph: $f(x) = \begin{cases} x + 1 & \text{when } x \leq 0 \\ \ln x & \text{when } x > 0 \end{cases}$

6. The area of a particular rectangle is 12 times the area of a certain square, and the width of the rectangle is three times the length of a side of the square. The perimeter of the rectangle is 30 units greater than the perimeter of the square. Find the dimensions of both the rectangle and the square.

7. Let $f(x) = x^5 - x^4 + 2x^2 - 4x + 3$. Use synthetic division to determine:
   (a) $f(-2)$
   (b) $f(1)$
   (c) $f(-1)$

8. Solve: $\log_x (8 - 2x) = 2$

9. Find the equation of the quadratic function f such that $f(3) = f(-4) = 0$ and $f(0) = 6$.

10. Determine the exact value of $\tan 15°$ using the identity $\tan (A - B) = \dfrac{\tan A - \tan B}{1 + \tan A \tan B}$.

11. Use the remainder theorem to determine the remainder when $x^3 + x^2 - x + 1$ is divided by $x - 2$.

12. Use the key trigonometric identities to develop a formula for $\sin (2t)$.

Calculus, Second Edition

Test 3, Form B   **SHOW YOUR WORK**   Name: _____

1. Which of the following is the domain of the function $g(x) = \sqrt{x^2 - 2x + 1}$?
   A. $\{x \in \mathbb{R} \mid -1 < x < 1\}$ B. $\{x \in \mathbb{R} \mid -1 \le x \le 1\}$
   C. $\{x \in \mathbb{R} \mid x \le -1 \text{ or } x \ge 1\}$ D. $\mathbb{R}$

2. Consider the graph of the function f shown to the right. What is $\lim\limits_{x \to 3^-} f(x)$?

   A. 3   B. −1
   C. 5   D. The limit does not exist.

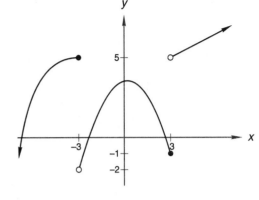

3. According to the rational roots theorem, the possible rational roots of $x^4 - 5x^3 + 8 = 0$ are
   A. $\pm 1, \pm 8$ B. $\pm 1, \pm 2, \pm 4, \pm 8$ C. $1, -5, 8$ D. $\pm 1, \pm\frac{1}{2}, \pm\frac{1}{4}, \pm\frac{1}{8}$

4. Shown to the right is the graph of the function $y = f(x)$. Sketch the graph of $y = |f(x)|$.

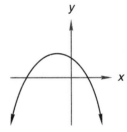

5. Graph: $f(x) = \begin{cases} 1 - x & \text{when } x \le 0 \\ \ln x & \text{when } x > 0 \end{cases}$

6. The area of a particular rectangle is 10 times the area of a certain square, and the width of the rectangle is twice the length of a side of the square. The perimeter of the rectangle is 50 units greater than the perimeter of the square. Find the dimensions of both the rectangle and the square.

7. Let $f(x) = 0.1x^5 - \pi x^3 + \frac{1}{2}x^2 - \sqrt{2}x + 1$. Approximate each of the following to three decimal places.

   (a) $f(\sqrt{31})$ (b) $f\left(-\frac{\pi}{4}\right)$ (c) $f(e)$

8. Solve $\log_x (x + 9) = 2$ for x. Approximate the answer to four decimal places.

9. Find the equation of the quadratic function f such that $f(5) = f(-1) = 0$ and $f(0) = -8$.

10. Determine the exact value of $\tan 75°$ using the identity $\tan (A + B) = \dfrac{\tan A + \tan B}{1 - \tan A \tan B}$.

11. Use the remainder theorem to determine the remainder when $x^3 - x^2 + x + 1$ is divided by $x + 2$.

12. Use the key trigonometric identities to develop a formula for $\cos (2t)$.

Calculus, Second Edition

1. What is $\lim\limits_{x \to 3} \dfrac{x - 3}{x^2 - x - 6}$?

    A. $\dfrac{1}{5}$ B. 1

    C. 0   D. The limit does not exist.

2. What is the domain of $f(x) = 2 \ln (x + 2)$?

    A. $\{x \in \mathbb{R} \mid x \geq -2\}$ B. $\{x \in \mathbb{R} \mid x > -2\}$ C. $\{x \in \mathbb{R} \mid x > 0\}$ D. $\{x \in \mathbb{R} \mid x \geq 0\}$

3. Let $\cos \theta = \dfrac{1}{4}$ with θ in Quadrant I. The value of $\cos (2\theta)$ is

    A. $-\dfrac{3}{4}$ B. $\dfrac{1}{2}$ C. 1   D. $-\dfrac{7}{8}$

4. Let $f(x) = x(x - 2)(x + 4)(x - 6)$. Which of the following is true?

    A. f is positive over the interval $(-4, 0)$.   B. f has a root at $x = 3$.

    C. f is negative over the interval $(-\infty, -4)$.   D. f is positive over the interval $(0, 2)$.

5. Sketch the graphs of $y = \sin^{-1} x$, $y = \cos^{-1} x$, and $y = \tan^{-1} x$ on separate sets of axes. Clearly indicate all endpoints and asymptotes.

6. The sum of two integers L and M is 503, and L is 19 less than $2M$. Find L and M.

7. Let $f(x) = 5x^2 + 7$. Evaluate $\lim\limits_{h \to 0} \dfrac{f(x + h) - f(x)}{h}$.

8. Solve: $25^{3x - 2} = 5^{2x}$

9. (a) Write $\log (2^3 7^5)$ in terms of $\log 2$ and $\log 7$.

    (b) Write $\ln \dfrac{x^4}{y^8}$ in terms of $\ln x$ and $\ln y$.

10. Show on a number line the values of $y \in \mathbb{R}$ for which $|y - 5| < 0.01$.

11. Solve: $\sin^2 x + 2 \cos x - 2 = 0$ $(0 \leq x < 2\pi)$

12. Graph: $f(x) = |x^2 - 4| + 6$

                       Calculus, Second Edition

1. Which of the following best approximates $\displaystyle\lim_{x\to 5} \frac{x+6}{x^2-4x+7}$?

   A. 0.11   B. 0.863

   C. 0.917   D. The limit does not exist.

2. What is the domain of $f(x) = 4\ln(x-3)$?

   A. $\{x \in \mathbb{R} \mid x \ge 3\}$ B. $\{x \in \mathbb{R} \mid x < 3\}$ C. $\{x \in \mathbb{R} \mid x > 0\}$ D. $\{x \in \mathbb{R} \mid x > 3\}$

3. Let $\sin\theta = \dfrac{1}{3}$ with θ in Quadrant I. The value of $\sin(2\theta)$ is

   A. $\dfrac{2}{3}$ B. 0   C. $\dfrac{4\sqrt{2}}{9}$ D. $\dfrac{2\sqrt{2}}{9}$

4. Let $f(x) = 2x(x-1)(x+5)(x-4)$. Which of the following is true?

   A. f is positive over the interval $(-5, 0)$.   B. f has a root at $x = -1$.

   C. f is positive over the interval $(-\infty, -5)$.   D. f is positive over the interval $(1, 4)$.

5. Sketch the graphs of $y = \sin^{-1} x$, $y = \cos^{-1} x$, and $y = \tan^{-1} x$ on separate sets of axes. Clearly indicate all endpoints and asymptotes.

6. The sum of two integers L and M is 643, and L is 8 more than $4M$. Find L and M.

7. Let $f(x) = 4x^2 - 9$. Evaluate $\displaystyle\lim_{h\to 0} \frac{f(x+h)-f(x)}{h}$.

8. Approximate the solution of $7^{3x-2} = 13^{x+1}$ to three decimal places.

9. (a) Write $\ln(x^5 y^6)$ in terms of $\ln x$ and $\ln y$.

   (b) Write $\log\dfrac{3^2}{5^7}$ in terms of $\log 3$ and $\log 5$.

10. Show on a number line the values of $x \in \mathbb{R}$ for which $|x-3| < 0.5$.

11. Solve: $\cos^2 x + 2\sin x - 2 = 0$ $(0 \le x < 2\pi)$

12. Graph: $f(x) = |x^2 - 5| + 3$

Calculus, Second Edition

1. What is $\lim\limits_{x \to 2} \dfrac{x + 7}{x^2 + 5x - 14}$?

    A. 0

    C. $+\infty$

    B. $-\infty$

    D. The limit does not exist.

2. What solution(s) does the equation $\sin x = \cos x$ have $(0 \le x < 2\pi)$?

    A. $\dfrac{\pi}{4}$

    B. $\dfrac{\pi}{4}, \dfrac{3\pi}{4}$

    C. $\dfrac{\pi}{4}, \dfrac{5\pi}{4}$

    D. There are no solutions.

3. Which of the following is **not** equal to $\cos (2x)$?

    A. $\cos^2 x - \sin^2 x$ B. $2 \cos^2 x - 1$ C. $2 \sin^2 x - 1$ D. $\cot (2x) \sin (2x)$

4. What is $\lim\limits_{x \to \infty} \dfrac{-x^5 + 14x^3 - 2}{6x^4 + 10x^2 - 1}$?

    A. 0

    B. $-\dfrac{1}{6}$

    C. ∞

    D. $-\infty$

5. Which of the following equals $\log_7 20$?

    A. $\dfrac{\log_5 7}{\log_5 20}$ B. $\ln \dfrac{20}{7}$ C. $\dfrac{\log_{10} 20}{\log_{10} 7}$ D. 7^{20}

6. The intensity of a light source measured at a point P varies inversely as the square of the distance from P to the light source. If the intensity measured at a point 5 meters from the light source is 15, what would be the intensity measured at a point 10 meters from the light source?

7. Solve: $-3 \log 2 - \log (x + 1) = -\log \dfrac{1}{3}$

8. Let $f(x) = x^2 + 2x$ and $g(x) = x - 1$. Find $(f \circ g)(x)$ and $(g \circ f)(x)$.

9. Determine the intervals on which the function $y = x^2 + 7x - 30$ is decreasing.

10. Evaluate: $\cos^{-1} -\dfrac{1}{2}$

11. Let $f(x) = x^3 + 1$ and $g(x) = \sqrt{x^2 - 16}$. Determine the domain of $\dfrac{f}{g}(x)$.

12. Use the definition of the derivative to find $\dfrac{dy}{dx}$ where $y = 3x^2$.

Calculus, Second Edition

1. What is $\lim\limits_{x \to 3} \dfrac{2}{2x^2 - 12x + 18}$?

    A. 0   B. $-\infty$

    C. $+\infty$ D. The limit does not exist.

2. What solution(s) does the equation $\sin x = -\cos x$ have $(0 \le x < 2\pi)$?

    A. $\dfrac{3\pi}{4}$ B. $\dfrac{3\pi}{4}, \dfrac{7\pi}{4}$

    C. $\dfrac{\pi}{4}, \dfrac{5\pi}{4}$ D. There are no solutions.

3. Which of the following is nearest to the slope of the curve $y = 2^x$ at $x = 1.75$?

    A. 0.8074   B. 1.75   C. 2.3315   D. 3.3636

4. What is $\lim\limits_{x \to \infty} \dfrac{x^5 - 14x^3 + 2}{6x^4 + 10x^2 - 1}$?

    A. 0   B. $-\dfrac{1}{6}$ C. ∞ D. $-\infty$

5. Which of the following is closest to $\log_3 17$?

    A. 0.3878   B. 2.8332   C. 1.2304   D. 2.5789

6. The intensity of a light source measured at a point P varies inversely as the square of the distance from P to the light source. If the intensity measured at a point 4 feet from the light source is 27, what would be the intensity measured at a point 11 feet from the light source?

7. Use a graphing calculator to graph the set of all points (x, y) that satisfy the equation $\frac{x^2}{16} + \frac{y^2}{25} = 1$. State the two functions that must be graphed.

8. Let $f(x) = x^2 - 3x$ and $g(x) = x + 4$. Find $(f \circ g)(x)$ and $(g \circ f)(x)$.

9. Determine the intervals on which the function $y = \left| x^2 - 16 \right|$ is decreasing.

10. Evaluate: $\sin^{-1} -\dfrac{1}{2}$

11. Let $f(x) = \sqrt{x^2 - 4}$ and $g(x) = x^3 - 27$. Determine the domain of $\dfrac{g}{f}(x)$.

12. Use the definition of the derivative to find $\dfrac{dy}{dx}$ where $y = \dfrac{3}{x}$.

Calculus, Second Edition

1. The coefficient of x^5y^3 in the expansion of $(x + 4y)^8$ is

   A. 56   B. 64   C. 3584   D. 65,536

2. Which of the following is the equation of the function whose graph is identical to the graph of $y = x^2$ except that it is shifted 5 units to the right and 3 units down?

   A. $y = x^2 + 10x + 22$ B. $y = x^2 - 10x + 22$

   C. $y = x^2 - 10x + 28$ D. $y = x^2 + 10x + 28$

3. Which of the following is the graph of $y = \dfrac{1}{(x + 3)^2}$?

   A.   B.   C.   D.

4. What is $\lim\limits_{x \to \infty} \dfrac{3x^2}{5x^3 - 4x + 1}$?

   A. $+\infty$ B. $\dfrac{3}{5}$

   C. 0   D. The limit does not exist.

5. Find the exact values of the x-intercepts of $y = x^2 - 20x + 14$.

6. Solve: $\sin(3\theta) = -\dfrac{1}{2}$ $(0 \le \theta < 2\pi)$

7. Express the distance from the point $(5, 6)$ to a point (x, y) on the graph of $y = x^3$ as a function of x.

8. Show that $(1 - \sin^2 x)\sec^2 x - \cos^2 x = \sin^2 x$ for all values of x for which both sides of the equation are defined.

9. Let $f(x) = \dfrac{1}{\sqrt[4]{x^3}}$. Find $f'(x)$.

10. Identify and graph the conic section whose equation is $4x^2 + 9y^2 + 16x - 54y + 61 = 0$.

11. Let $f(x) = x^2$ and $g(x) = \sqrt{x}$.

    (a) Determine the domain of $f \circ g$.

    (b) Determine the domain of $g \circ f$.

12. Use the definition of the derivative to find $f'(x)$ given that $f(x) = 8x - 5$.

Calculus, Second Edition

1. The coefficient of $x^{10}y^5$ in the expansion of $(2x - y)^{15}$ is

   A. -1024 B. -3003 C. 3003 D. $-3,075,072$

2. Which of the following is the equation of the function whose graph is identical to the graph of $y = x^2$ except that it is shifted 5 units to the left and 3 units up?

   A. $y = x^2 + 10x + 22$ B. $y = x^2 - 10x + 22$

   C. $y = x^2 - 10x + 28$ D. $y = x^2 + 10x + 28$

3. Which of the following is the graph of $y = \dfrac{-1}{(x - 3)^2}$?

   A.   B.   C.   D.

4. What is $\lim\limits_{x \to \infty} \dfrac{-3x^4}{5x^3 + 4x - 1}$?

   A. $-\infty$

   B. $-\dfrac{3}{5}$

   C. 0

   D. The limit does not exist.

5. Approximate the real zero(s) of the polynomial $y = x^3 - 20x^2 + 14x - 8$.

6. Solve: $\tan(3\theta) = -1$ $(0 \le \theta < 2\pi)$

7. Express the distance from the point $(1, 4)$ to a point (x, y) on the graph of $y = x^4$ as a function of x.

8. Show that $(1 - \cos^2 x)\csc^2 x - \sin^2 x = \cos^2 x$ for all values of x for which both sides of the equation are defined.

9. Let $f(x) = \dfrac{1}{\sqrt[3]{x^2}}$. Find $f'(x)$.

10. Identify and graph the conic section whose equation is $4x^2 - 9y^2 + 16x + 54y - 101 = 0$. Write two equations that can be used to graph the conic section on a graphing calculator.

11. Let $f(x) = e^x$ and $g(x) = \ln x$.
    (a) Determine the domain of $f \circ g$.
    (b) Determine the domain of $g \circ f$.

12. Use the definition of the derivative to find $f'(x)$ given that $f(x) = 16x + 7$.

Calculus, Second Edition

1. The slope of the line tangent to $y = x^{1/3}$ at $x = 8$ is

   A. 2   B. $\dfrac{1}{12}$ C. $\dfrac{1}{6}$ D. $\dfrac{4}{3}$

2. What is $\displaystyle\lim_{h \to 0} \dfrac{\ln(2 + h) - \ln 2}{h}$?

   A. $\ln 2$ B. $\dfrac{1}{2}$

   C. 0   D. The limit does not exist.

3. Let $f(x) = \cos x$. Then $f'''\left(\dfrac{\pi}{6}\right)$ equals

   A. $-\dfrac{1}{2}$ B. $-\dfrac{\sqrt{3}}{2}$ C. $\dfrac{\sqrt{3}}{2}$ D. $\dfrac{1}{2}$

4. Let $y = \dfrac{2}{x^3} + 3e^x + 4\cos x$. What is $\dfrac{dy}{dx}$?

   A. $\dfrac{2}{3x^2} + 3e^x - 4\sin x$ B. $-\dfrac{6}{x^4} + 3xe^{x-1} + 4\sin x$

   C. $-\dfrac{6}{x^4} + 3e^x - 4\sin x$ D. $-\dfrac{6}{x^4} + 3e^x + 4\sin x$

5. What is $\displaystyle\lim_{x \to -3^+} \dfrac{x^2 + x - 6}{x^3 + 3x^2}$?

   A. $-\dfrac{5}{9}$ B. $+\infty$

   C. 0   D. The limit does not exist.

6. The amount of money in Nathan's bank account was decreasing at an exponential rate. If the account contained $2000 on the first day of the month and only $500 on the twenty-first day of the month, how much did it contain on the thirty-first day of the month?

7. Sketch the graph of $y = x^{1/3} - 2$.

8. Determine $\sin^2 x$ given that $\cos(2x) = \dfrac{1}{4}$.

9. Sketch the graph of $y = \dfrac{x - 5}{(x - 7)(x - 1)(x - 11)}$. Clearly indicate all x-intercepts and asymptotes.

10. Find all real values x such that $\log(x - 4) = 2\log 2 + \log(x - 3) - \log x$.

11. Suppose $f(x) = q(x)(x - 7) - 17$ where $f(x)$ and $q(x)$ are polynomials. Determine the value of $f(7)$.

12. Use the definition of the derivative to find $\dfrac{d}{dx}\sqrt{x}$.

Calculus, Second Edition

1. Which of the following is the best approximation of the slope of the line tangent to $y = 4 \sin x$ at $x = \dfrac{11\pi}{32}$?

    A. 0.0698   B. 1.0799   C. 1.8856   D. 3.5277

2. What is $\lim\limits_{h \to 0} \dfrac{e^{2+h} - e^2}{h}$?

    A. e^2 B. $2e$

    C. 0   D. The limit does not exist.

3. Let $f(x) = \sin x$. Then $f'''\left(\dfrac{\pi}{6}\right)$ equals

    A. $-\dfrac{1}{2}$ B. $-\dfrac{\sqrt{3}}{2}$ C. $\dfrac{\sqrt{3}}{2}$ D. $\dfrac{1}{2}$

4. Let $y = -\dfrac{2}{x^4} + 6e^x - 5 \sin x$. What is $\dfrac{dy}{dx}$?

    A. $\dfrac{8}{x^5} + 6xe^{x-1} - 5 \cos x$ B. $\dfrac{8}{x^5} + 6e^x - 5 \cos x$

    C. $\dfrac{8}{x^5} + 6e^x + 5 \cos x$ D. $-\dfrac{2}{4x^3} + 6e^x - 5 \cos x$

5. What is $\lim\limits_{x \to -5^-} \dfrac{x^2 + 4x - 5}{x^4 + 5x^3}$?

    A. 0   B. $+\infty$

    C. 0.048   D. The limit does not exist.

6. The amount of money in Natasha's bank account was decreasing at an exponential rate. If the account contained $3000 on the first day of the month and only $200 on the eighteenth day of the month, how much did it contain on the thirtieth day of the month?

7. Sketch the graph of $f(x) = x^{2/3} + 12$.

8. Determine $\cos^2 x$ given that $\cos(2x) = -\dfrac{1}{6}$.

9. Sketch the graph of $y = \dfrac{(x - 3)(x + 5)}{(x - 7)(x + 1)(x - 2)}$. Clearly indicate all x-intercepts and asymptotes.

10. Approximate all real values x such that $2 \ln 2 - 2 \ln (x + 2) = \ln (x - 5)$.

11. Suppose $f(x) = q(x)(x - 4) + 29$ where $f(x)$ and $q(x)$ are polynomials. Determine the value of $f(4)$.

12. Use the definition of the derivative to find $\dfrac{d}{dx}(x^{-2})$.

1. An equation of the line tangent to $y = x^4 + 7$ at $x = 3$ is

   A. $y = 36x - 20$ B. $y = 108x - 236$ C. $y = 88x - 176$ D. $y = 108x + 88$

2. Let $f(x) = x^{10} + 2x$ and $g(x) = \sqrt{x}$. Then $(f \circ g)(-4)$ equals

   A. 1028   B. $\sqrt{1{,}048{,}568}$

   C. 1020   D. The value does not exist.

3. The vertical asymptotes of the function $f(x) = \dfrac{x^3 - 3x^2 + 2x}{x^4 + x^3 - 6x^2}$ are

   A. $x = 0$ B. $x = 0, \ x = -3$

   C. $x = 0, \ x = 2, \ x = -3$ D. There are no vertical asymptotes.

4. Which of the following is an antiderivative of $7x^6$?

   A. $42x^5$ B. $\dfrac{1}{7}x^7 - 19$ C. $7x^6 + 2$ D. $x^7 + 12$

5. If $y = x^3 \ln x$, then dy equals

   A. $x^2 \, dx$ B. $3x^2 \ln x \, dx$ C. $3x \, dx$ D. $(x^2 + 3x^2 \ln x) \, dx$

6. Equal-sized squares are cut from the corners of a 12- by 12-inch sheet of tin. The resulting flaps are folded up to form a box with no top. Assuming the length of the sides of the squares that were cut away is x, write an expression for the volume of the box in terms of x.

7. Given that $\sin A = \dfrac{1}{2}$, $\sin B = \dfrac{1}{4}$, $\cos A = \dfrac{\sqrt{3}}{2}$, and $\cos B = \dfrac{\sqrt{15}}{4}$, determine $\cos (A - B)$.

8. Let $f(x) = e^x(x^3 + 7x^2 + 1)$. Find $f''(x)$.

9. Identify and graph the conic section whose general equation is $x^2 - y^2 + 2y - 5 = 0$.

10. Solve: $\csc x = 2 \ \ (0 \le x < 2\pi)$

11. Let $f(x) = 12(x - 3)(x - 7)$.

    (a) State the zeros and asymptotes of the graph of f.

    (b) State the zeros and asymptotes of the graph of $\dfrac{1}{f}$.

12. Sketch the graph of $y = \sec x$ for x between 0 and 2π. Clearly indicate all zeros and asymptotes.

         Calculus, Second Edition

1. An equation of the line tangent to $y = x^7 - 76$ at $x = 2$ is

    A. $y = 32x - 12$ B. $y = 448x + 52$ C. $y = 52x - 52$ D. $y = 448x - 844$

2. Let $f(x) = x^{10} + 2x$ and $g(x) = \sqrt{x}$. Then $(g \circ f)(-4)$ equals

    A. 1028   B. $\sqrt{1,048,568}$

    C. $\sqrt{1,048,576}$ D. The value does not exist.

3. The zeros of the function $f(x) = \dfrac{x^3 - 3x^2 + 2x}{x^4 + x^3 - 6x^2}$ are

    A. $x = 1$ B. $x = 0,\ x = -3$

    C. $x = 0,\ x = 2,\ x = 1$ D. There are no zeros.

4. Which of the following is an antiderivative of $5x^4$?

    A. $5x^5 + 1$ B. $20x^3$ C. $x^5 - 17$ D. $\dfrac{1}{5}x^5 + 44$

5. If $y = x^2 e^x$, then dy equals

    A. $(x^2 e^x + 2xe^x)\, dx$ B. $2xe^x\, dx$ C. $x^2 e^x\, dx$ D. $(x^3 e^{x-1} + 2xe^x)\, dx$

6. Equal-sized squares are cut from the corners of a 9- by 14-inch sheet of aluminum. The resulting flaps are folded up to form a box with no top. Assuming the length of the sides of the squares that were cut away is x, write an expression for the volume of the box in terms of x.

7. Given that $\sin A = \dfrac{4}{5}$, $\sin B = \dfrac{\sqrt{3}}{2}$, $\cos A = \dfrac{3}{5}$, and $\cos B = \dfrac{1}{2}$, determine $\sin(A - B)$.

8. Let $f(x) = e^x(x^4 - 3x^3 + 4)$. Find $f''(x)$.

9. Identify and graph the conic section whose general equation is $x^2 - 4x + 4y^2 - 5 = 0$.

10. Solve: $\sec x = 2$ $(0 \le x < 2\pi)$

11. Let $f(x) = \dfrac{2x(x - 2)(x - 6)}{(x + 4)}$.

    (a) State the zeros and asymptotes of the graph of f.

    (b) State the zeros and asymptotes of the graph of $\dfrac{1}{f}$.

12. Sketch the graph of $y = \cot x$ for x between 0 and 2π. Clearly indicate all zeros and asymptotes.

Calculus, Second Edition

1. An antiderivative of $3 \sin t$ is

   A. $3 \cos t + 5$ B. $3 \sin t + 2$ C. $-3 \cos t + 10$ D. $\cos (3t)$

2. Which of the following is a possible graph of the function $y = -2x^3 + ax^2 + bx + c$, where a, b, and c are real numbers?

   A.   B.   C.   D.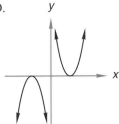

3. Which of the following equals $\int 2x^3 \, dx$?

   A. $2x^4 + C$ B. $8x^4 + C$ C. $6x^2 + C$ D. $\dfrac{1}{2}x^4 + C$

4. The critical numbers of the function $y = \dfrac{1}{4}x^4 + 2x^3 + 4x^2$ are

   A. $-4, -2, 0$ B. $0, 2, 4$ C. $0, 1, 2$ D. $-8, -6, 0$

5. What is $\lim\limits_{t \to \infty} \dfrac{5t^2 + 8t + 1}{2 - 6t - 3t^2}$?

   A. $\dfrac{5}{2}$ B. 0 C. $-\dfrac{5}{3}$ D. $+\infty$

6. Find the critical numbers of $y = x^4 + 4x^3 - 20x^2 + 21$. State whether each represents a local maximum, a local minimum, or neither.

7. Let $y^3 + 7y = e^x$. Determine $\dfrac{dy}{dx}$.

8. Determine the slope of the line tangent to the graph of $f(x) = x \cos x$ at $x = 0$.

9. Identify the conic section whose equation is $x^2 + 4y^2 + 4x - 24y + 36 = 0$. Sketch the graph of this conic section.

10. Solve for b: $\log_b 121 = 2$

11. Sketch the graph of $y = x(x - 1)(x + 1)(x - 2)^2$. Clearly indicate the behavior of the graph near the points where the graph touches or crosses the x-axis.

12. (a) Let $f(x) = 5x^3 + 10x^2 + 6x - 9$. Describe the behavior of the graph as x approaches $\pm\infty$.

    (b) What would the description be if the function were $f(x) = 5x^6 + 10x^2 + 6x - 9$?

Calculus, Second Edition

1. An antiderivative of $3 \cos t$ is

   A. $3 \cos t + 5$ B. $3 \sin t + 2$ C. $-3 \sin t + 10$ D. $\sin 3t$

2. Which of the following is a possible graph of the function $y = 5x^4 + ax^2 + bx + c$, where a, b, and c are real numbers?

   A. y B. y C. y D. y

3. Which of the following equals $\int 5 \sqrt{t}\ dt$?

   A. $\dfrac{5}{2}t^2 + C$ B. $5t + C$ C. $\dfrac{5}{2}t^{-1/2} + C$ D. $\dfrac{10}{3}t^{3/2} + C$

4. The critical numbers of the function $y = 5x^{2/3} + x^{5/3}$ are

   A. $-2, 0$ B. -2

   C. $1, 5$ D. There are no critical numbers.

5. What is $\displaystyle\lim_{t \to \infty} \dfrac{4t^3 - 7t^2 + 1}{8t^4 + 21}$?

   A. $\dfrac{1}{2}$ B. 0 C. $\dfrac{1}{21}$ D. $+\infty$

6. Find the critical numbers of $y = x^4 + 4x^3 - 2x^2 - 12x + 4$. State whether each represents a local maximum, a local minimum, or neither.

7. Let $2xy + y^2 = \sin x$. Determine $\dfrac{dy}{dx}$.

8. Approximate the slope of the line tangent to the graph of $f(x) = x \cos x$ at $x = -1$.

9. Identify the conic section whose equation is $x^2 + 4x - y^2 + 2y = 0$. Sketch the graph of this conic section.

10. Approximate $\log_7 9$ accurate to three decimal places.

11. Sketch the graph of $y = \dfrac{x(x + 1)}{(x - 1)(x - 2)(x - 3)}$. Clearly indicate the zeros and asymptotes of the graph.

12. (a) Let $f(x) = -x^6 + 8x^5 - 10x^3 + 17$. Describe the behavior of the graph as x approaches $\pm\infty$.

    (b) What would the description be if the function were $f(x) = -x^7 + 8x^5 - 10x^3 + 17$?

Calculus, Second Edition

1. $\int (5 \cos x - 6x - \sqrt{x} + 7)\, dx$ equals

    A. $-5 \sin x - 6 - \frac{1}{2}x^{-1/2} + C$

    B. $-5 \sin x - 3x^2 - \frac{2}{3}x^{3/2} + 7x + C$

    C. $5 \sin x - 3x^2 - \frac{2}{3}x^{3/2} + 7x + C$

    D. $5 \sin x - 6 - \frac{1}{2}x^{-1/2} + C$

2. Let $y = \cos^3 x$. Then $\dfrac{dy}{dx}$ equals

    A. $3 \cos^2 x$ B. $-3 \cos^2 x \sin x$ C. $-3 \sin^2 x \cos x$ D. $\dfrac{\cos^4 x}{4}$

3. A particle is moving along the number line so that its distance (in meters) from the origin at any time t (in seconds) is given by $s(t) = 8t^2 + \ln t$. The velocity of the particle at $t = 1$ second is

    A. $8 \dfrac{m}{s}$ B. $9 \dfrac{m}{s}$ C. $17 \dfrac{m}{s}$ D. $\dfrac{11}{3} \dfrac{m}{s}$

4. Let $f(x) = x^3 + 5 \ln |x|$. Then $f''(2)$ equals

    A. $8 + 5 \ln 2$ B. 14.5   C. 13.25   D. 10.75

5. Let $f(x) = \dfrac{7}{x}$. Then $\int f(x)\, dx$ equals

    A. $-\dfrac{7}{x^2} + C$ B. $7 \ln |x| + C$ C. $7x + C$ D. $\dfrac{7}{x} + C$

6. Find the point-slope form of the equation of the line normal to the graph of $y = 3 \sin (2x)$ at $x = \dfrac{\pi}{8}$.

7. Simplify: $(\tan^2 \theta + 1)(1 - \cos^2 \theta)$

8. Let $f(x) = x^2 e^x$. Find the critical numbers of f.

9. Find $\dfrac{dA}{dt}$ where $A = 4\pi r^2$ and both A and r are functions of t.

10. Evaluate: $\displaystyle\lim_{x \to 2} \dfrac{x^2 + 6x - 16}{x^2 - 2x}$

11. Use a left sum to approximate the area under $y = x^2 + 1$ on the interval $[1, 5]$ using 4 subintervals.

12. A railroad engine is moving along a straight stretch of track. The distance from the engine to the terminal at time t is given by the function $s(t) = t^2 - 2t$, where s is in kilometers and t is in minutes. Find the velocity of the engine when $t = 0$, $t = 1$, and $t = 2$.

Calculus, Second Edition

1. $\int (5 \sin x - 2x - \sqrt{x} + 7)\, dx$ equals

   A. $-5 \cos x - 2 - \dfrac{1}{2}x^{-1/2} + C$ B. $5 \cos x - x^2 - \dfrac{2}{3}x^{3/2} + 7x + C$

   C. $5 \cos x - x^2 - \dfrac{2}{3}x^{3/2} + 7x + C$ D. $5 \cos x - 2 - \dfrac{1}{2}x^{-1/2} + C$

2. Let $y = \sin^3 x$. Then $\dfrac{dy}{dx}$ equals

   A. $3 \sin^2 x$ B. $-3 \sin^2 x \cos x$ C. $3 \sin^2 x \cos x$ D. $\dfrac{\sin^4 x}{4}$

3. A particle is moving along the number line so that its distance (in meters) from the origin at any time t (in seconds) is given by $s(t) = 8t^3 + \ln t$. The velocity of the particle at $t = 1$ second is

   A. $8\ \dfrac{\text{m}}{\text{s}}$ B. $9\ \dfrac{\text{m}}{\text{s}}$ C. $17\ \dfrac{\text{m}}{\text{s}}$ D. $25\ \dfrac{\text{m}}{\text{s}}$

4. Let $f(x) = x^3 + 7 \ln |x|$. Then $f''(2)$ equals
   A. $8 + 7 \ln 2$ B. 10.25 C. 13.75 D. 15.5

5. Let $f(x) = \dfrac{4}{x}$. Then $\int f(x)\, dx$ equals

   A. $4 \ln |x| + C$ B. $-\dfrac{4}{x^2} + C$ C. $4x + C$ D. $\dfrac{4}{x} + C$

6. Find the point-slope form of the equation of the line normal to the graph of $y = 5 \cos (2x)$ at $x = \dfrac{\pi}{12}$.

7. Simplify: $(\sec^2 \theta - 1)(1 - \sin^2 \theta)$

8. Let $f(x) = x^3 e^{1-x^2}$. Approximate the maximum value of f over the interval $[0, 3]$.

9. Find $\dfrac{dV}{dt}$ where $V = \dfrac{4}{3}\pi r^3$ and both V and r are functions of t.

10. Evaluate: $\lim\limits_{x \to -6} \dfrac{x^2 + 7x + 6}{x^2 + 4x - 12}$

11. Use a right sum to approximate the area under $y = x^2 + 1$ on the interval $[1, 5]$ using 4 subintervals.

12. A muon moves along a straight path with velocity $v(t) = t^3 - 5t^2 + 6t + 165,000$, where t is time in seconds and v is in kilometers per second. Find the acceleration of the muon when $t = 0$, $t = 0.5$, and $t = 2.75$.

Calculus, Second Edition

1. Let $y = \cos u$ and $u = 7x^2$. Then $\dfrac{dy}{dx}$ equals

   A. $-\sin(7x^2)$ B. $\cos(14x)$ C. $14x \sin(7x^2)$ D. $-14x \sin(7x^2)$

2. If $f(x) = \dfrac{x^2 + 1}{e^x + 2}$, then $f'(x)$ equals

   A. $\dfrac{2x(e^x + 2) - (x^2 + 1)e^x}{(e^x + 2)^2}$ B. $\dfrac{2x}{e^x}$

   C. $\dfrac{2x(e^x + 2) + (x^2 + 1)e^x}{(e^x + 2)^2}$ D. $\dfrac{(x^2 + 1)e^x - 2x(e^x + 2)}{(e^x + 2)^2}$

3. What is $\lim\limits_{x \to 1} \dfrac{4x - 4}{x^2 - 2x + 1}$?

   A. 0   B. 2   C. 1   D. The limit does not exist.

4. Which of the following equals $\sin^{-1} -\dfrac{\sqrt{3}}{2}$?

   A. $240°$ B. $-60°$ C. $60°$ D. $120°$

5. The graph of a function f is shown to the right. Which of the following is the graph of $g(x) = f(x - 3) + 2$?

   A. 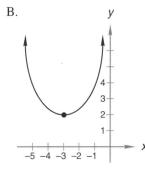   B.   y   C. y   D. y

           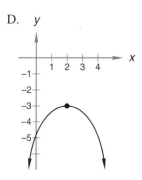

6. Use the definition $f'(a) = \lim\limits_{x \to a} \dfrac{f(x) - f(a)}{x - a}$ to find $f'(4)$ where $f(x) = 7x^2$.

7. If $s = 2 \ln v$ and $v = \dfrac{e^t}{t}$, what is $\dfrac{ds}{dt}$?   8. Integrate: $\displaystyle\int \left(\dfrac{3}{x} + e^x\right) dx$

9. Find $f'(1)$ where $f(x) = (x^3 + 2x) \ln x$.

10. Sketch the graph of $y = \dfrac{(x^2 + 4)(x - 1)^2}{x^2(x + 3)(x - 2)^2}$. Clearly indicate all zeros and asymptotes.

11. Graph $y = \sin x$ for $-2\pi \le x \le 2\pi$. On the same set of axes, graph $y = \csc x$.

12. Find the exact area under $y = x^2$ on the interval $[0, 2]$ by using an infinite number of circumscribed rectangles. (*Hint:* $1^2 + 2^2 + 3^2 + \cdots + n^2 = \frac{n(n + 1)(2n + 1)}{6}$.)

Calculus, Second Edition

Test 11, Form B   **SHOW YOUR WORK**   **Name:** _____

1. Let $y = \sin u$ and $u = 5x^2$. Then $\dfrac{dy}{dx}$ equals

   A. $\cos (5x^2)$ B. $\sin (10x)$ C. $10x \cos (5x^2)$ D. $-10x \cos (5x^2)$

2. If $f(x) = \dfrac{\sin x + 1}{e^x + 2}$, then $f'(x)$ equals

   A. $\dfrac{(\sin x + 1)e^x - (e^x + 2) \cos x}{(e^x + 2)^2}$

   B. $\dfrac{(e^x + 2) \cos x - (\sin x + 1)e^x}{(e^x + 2)^2}$

   C. $\dfrac{(e^x + 2)(-\cos x) - (\sin x + 1)e^x}{(e^x + 2)^2}$

   D. $\dfrac{\cos x}{e^x}$

3. What is $\lim\limits_{x \to 2} \dfrac{4x - 8}{x^2 - 4x + 4}$?

   A. 1   B. ∞ C. 0   D. The limit does not exist.

4. Which of the following equals $\cos^{-1} -\dfrac{\sqrt{3}}{2}$?

   A. 210°   B. 30°   C. 150°   D. –30°

5. The graph of a function f is shown to the right. Which of the following is the graph of $g(x) = f(x - 2) + 3$?

A.

B.

C.

D.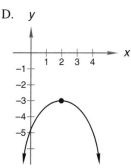

6. Use the definition $f'(a) = \lim\limits_{x \to a} \dfrac{f(x) - f(a)}{x - a}$ to find $f'(3)$ where $f(x) = 5x^2$.

7. If $u = \dfrac{v}{e^v}$ and $v = 3 \ln t$, what is $\dfrac{du}{dt}$?

8. Integrate: $\displaystyle\int \left(\dfrac{6}{x} - e^x \right) dx$

9. Approximate $f'(1.44)$ to three decimal places where $f(x) = (x^4 + 2x^3 - 3x) \ln x$.

10. Sketch the graph of $y = \dfrac{(x^2 + 1)(x + 1)^2}{x^2(x - 3)^2 (x + 2)}$. Clearly indicate all zeros and asymptotes.

11. Graph $y = \cos x$ for $-2\pi \le x \le 2\pi$. On the same set of axes, graph $y = \sec x$.

12. Find the exact area under $y = x^2$ on the interval [0, 2] by using an infinite number of circumscribed rectangles. (*Hint:* $1^2 + 2^2 + 3^2 + \cdots + n^2 = \frac{n(n + 1)(2n + 1)}{6}$.)

Calculus, Second Edition

Test 12, Form A   **SHOW YOUR WORK**   Name: _____

1. The derivative of $x^2 \tan x$ equals

   A. $2x \sec^2 x$

   C. $x^2 \sec x \tan x + 2x \tan x$

   B. $2x \tan x + x^2 \sec^2 x$

   D. $2x \sec x \tan x + \dfrac{x^3}{3} \tan x$

2. Which of the following values is **not** in the domain of the function $y = \arcsin x$?

   A. 0   B. −1   C. $\dfrac{\pi}{4}$ D. π

3. The indefinite integral $\displaystyle\int \left(\dfrac{1}{u^{1/3}} + 5u^3 - 1 + 3 \sin u \right) du$ equals

   A. $\dfrac{3}{4}u^{4/3} + \dfrac{5u^4}{4} - u + 3 \cos u + C$

   B. $\dfrac{3}{2}u^{2/3} + 15u^2 - 3 \cos u + C$

   C. $\dfrac{3}{2}u^{2/3} + \dfrac{5u^4}{4} - u + 3 \cos u + C$

   D. $\dfrac{3}{2}u^{2/3} + \dfrac{5u^4}{4} - u - 3 \cos u + C$

4. What is the area of the shaded region in the figure to the right?

   A. 12   B. $\dfrac{34}{5}$

   C. $\dfrac{27}{4}$ D. 9

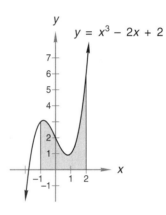

$y = x^3 - 2x + 2$

5. Which of the following is a solution of $\log_3 (x - 5) + \log_3 (x + 3) = 2$?

   A. −4   B. 7

   C. 5   D. 6

6. The critical numbers of $f(x) = 2x^3 + 3x^2 + 4$ are −1 and 0. Use a rough sketch of f to find the local maximum and local minimum values of f.

7. Find the slope of the line tangent to the curve $x^2 + y^2 = 1$ at the point $\left(-\dfrac{\sqrt{2}}{2}, \dfrac{\sqrt{2}}{2} \right)$.

8. A particle moves along a straight line so that its position at time t is given by the equation $s(t) = 5t^3 - 3t^2 + 10$ where s is in feet and t is in minutes. Find the velocity of the particle at time $t = 2$ minutes.

9. An 8-foot ladder leans against a vertical wall. The base of the ladder is pulled away from the wall at a rate of 1 foot per second. How fast is the top of the ladder sliding down the wall when the base of the ladder is 5 feet away from the wall?

10. The volume of a spherical balloon is increasing at a rate of 1 cm³/s. What is the rate at which the diameter of the balloon is increasing when the diameter is 12 cm?

11. To the right is a sketch of the graph of f'. Sketch the graph of f.

12. Find the derivative of $\cot x$ with respect to x using the derivatives of $\sin x$ and $\cos x$.

Calculus, Second Edition

1. The derivative of $x^3 \sec x$ equals

   A. $3x^2 \sec x \tan x$

   B. $3x^2 \sec x + x^3 \sec^2 x$

   C. $x^3 \sec x \tan x + 3x^2 \sec x$

   D. $x^3 \sec x \tan x + \dfrac{x^4}{4} \sec x$

2. Which of the following values is **not** in the range of the function $y = \arcsin x$?

   A. π B. -1 C. $\dfrac{\pi}{4}$ D. 0

3. The indefinite integral $\displaystyle\int \left(\dfrac{1}{u^{2/3}} - 4u^3 + u - 3 \cos u \right) du$ equals

   A. $-\dfrac{2}{3}u^{-5/3} - 12u^2 + 1 + 3 \sin u + C$

   B. $3u^{1/3} - u^4 + \dfrac{1}{2}u^2 - 3 \sin u + C$

   C. $3u^{1/3} - u^4 + \dfrac{1}{2}u^2 + 3 \sin u + C$

   D. $\dfrac{3}{2}u^{2/3} - \dfrac{u^4}{4} + \dfrac{1}{2}u^2 + 3 \sin u + C$

4. Which of the following is closest to the area of the shaded region in the figure to the right?

   A. 4.3639   B. 7.8891

   C. 10.8005   D. 5.3639

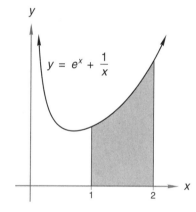

$y = e^x + \dfrac{1}{x}$

5. Which of the following is an approximation of $\log_5 120$ accurate to three decimal places?

   A. 0.336   B. 2.975

   C. 3   D. 4.787

6. Let $f(x) = \dfrac{3x^2 + 2x + 1}{x}$ for $x > 0$. Approximate the coordinates of the relative minimum point of the graph of f.

7. Approximate the slope of the line tangent to the curve $y = e^x \sin x$ at $x = \pi$.

8. A particle moves along a straight line so that its velocity in meters per second at time t seconds is given by the equation $v(t) = 3t^4 - 2t^2 + 7$. Find the acceleration of the particle at time $t = 1.5$ seconds.

9. An 11-foot ladder leans against a vertical wall. The base of the ladder is pulled away from the wall at a rate of 2 feet per second. How fast is the top of the ladder sliding down the wall when the base of the ladder is 8 feet away from the wall?

10. The volume of a spherical balloon is increasing at a rate of 2 cm^3/s. What is the rate at which the diameter of the balloon is increasing when the diameter is 10 cm?

11. To the right is a sketch of the graph of f'. Sketch the graph of f.

12. Find the derivative of $\tan x$ with respect to x using the derivatives of $\sin x$ and $\cos x$.

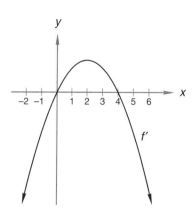

f'

Calculus, Second Edition

Test 13, Form A   **SHOW YOUR WORK**   Name: _____

1. Let $f(x) = \dfrac{x-1}{x+1}$ for all $x \neq -1$. Then $f'(1)$ equals

   A. -1 B. $-\dfrac{1}{2}$ C. 0 D. $\dfrac{1}{2}$

2. The indefinite integral $\displaystyle\int 3x^2 e^{x^3}\, dx$ equals

   A. $e^{x^3} + C$ B. $e^{3x^2} + C$ C. $3x^2 e^{x^3} + C$ D. None of these

3. The value of $\displaystyle\lim_{x\to\pi} \dfrac{\sin x - \sin \pi}{x - \pi}$ is

   A. 0 B. $\dfrac{1}{2}$ C. -1 D. 1

4. The area of the region between the graph of $y = 3x^2 + 2x$ and the x-axis from $x = 1$ to $x = 3$ is
   A. 36 B. 34 C. 31 D. 28

5. Which of the following equals $\dfrac{d}{dx}(\tan x + \sec x)$?

   A. $\sec x + \tan x$ B. $(\sec x)(1 + \tan x)$ C. $(\sec x)(1 + \sec x)$ D. $(\sec x)(\sec x + \tan x)$

6. Find the coordinates of any points of inflection of the graph of $f(x) = \dfrac{1}{3}x^3 - \dfrac{1}{2}x^2 + 3$.

7. Determine the domain of the function $f(x) = \dfrac{\sqrt{x-5}}{x}$.

8. Find y' given $y = e^{x^2+1} \sin(x^3 - 4)$.

9. Evaluate: $\displaystyle\lim_{n\to\infty} \dfrac{1 + 3n^2}{n^2 + 1000}$

10. Find y' given $y = (x^3 + 1)^{15}$.

11. Suppose g is a function such that $g'(1) = 0$, $g'(x) > 0$ when x lies in the interval $(-1, 1)$, and $g'(x) < 0$ when x lies in the interval $(1, 3)$. Sketch the graph of g for values of x near $x = 1$. Indicate any special characteristics of g at $x = 1$.

12. Dertia wants to enclose a rectangular plot of land that adjoins a barn's wall. If she has only 50 feet of fence, what should the dimensions of the rectangular plot be so that the enclosed area is maximized?

Calculus, Second Edition

1. Let $f(x) = \dfrac{x-2}{x+2}$ for all $x \neq -2$. Then $f'(1)$ equals

     A. 4   B. $-\dfrac{1}{3}$ C. $\dfrac{4}{9}$ D. 1

2. The indefinite integral $\displaystyle\int 4x^3 e^{x^4}\, dx$ equals

     A. $e^{4x^3} + C$ B. $e^{x^4} + C$ C. $4x^3 e^{x^4} + C$ D. None of these

3. The value of $\displaystyle\lim_{x \to \pi} \dfrac{\cos x - \cos \pi}{x - \pi}$ is

     A. 0   B. $\dfrac{1}{2}$ C. -1 D. 1

4. The area of the region between the graph of $y = 3x^2 - 2x$ and the x-axis from $x = 0.75$ to $x = 2.25$ is best approximated by

     A. 15.469   B. 10.688   C. 5.344   D. 6.469

5. Which of the following equals $\dfrac{d}{dx}(\tan x - \sec x)$?

     A. $\sec x - \tan x$ B. $(\sec x)(\sec x - \tan x)$ C. $(\sec x)(1 - \sec x)$ D. $(\sec x)(1 - \tan x)$

6. Find the coordinates of any points of inflection of the graph of $f(x) = x^3 - x^2 + \dfrac{1}{3}$.

7. Determine the domain of the function $f(x) = \dfrac{\sqrt{x+3}}{x}$.

8. Find y' given $y = (x^3 + 1)^{15} \cos(x^2 - 3)$.

9. Evaluate: $\displaystyle\lim_{n \to \infty} \dfrac{1 - 3n^2}{n^2 + 1000}$

10. Find y' given $y = e^{\tan x} + 1$.

11. Suppose g is a function such that $g'(2) = 0$, $g' < 0$ when x lies in the interval $(0, 2)$, and $g' > 0$ when x lies in the interval $(2, 4)$. Sketch the graph of g for values of x near $x = 2$. Indicate any special characteristics of g at $x = 2$.

12. David wants to enclose a rectangular plot of land that adjoins a barn's wall. If he has only 21 meters of fence, what should the dimensions of the rectangular plot be so that the enclosed area is maximized?

Calculus, Second Edition

1. Let $g(x) = \dfrac{x(x-2)^2(x+3)}{(x^2+2)(x-4)(x+5)^2}$. Which of the following statements about g must be true?

   I. The graph of g has a hole at $x = 2$.
   II. The graph of g is positive on the interval $(0, 2)$.
   III. The graph of g has a vertical asymptote at $x = -5$.

   A. I only   B. III only   C. I and III only   D. II and III only

2. If the radius of a sphere is increasing at a rate of 2 inches per second, how fast is the volume increasing when the radius is 10 inches?

   A. $800\pi \dfrac{\text{in.}^3}{\text{s}}$ B. $800 \dfrac{\text{in.}^3}{\text{s}}$ C. $3200\pi \dfrac{\text{in.}^3}{\text{s}}$ D. $80\pi \dfrac{\text{in.}^3}{\text{s}}$

3. The area of the region between the graph of $y = 8x^3 + 5x$ and the x-axis from $x = 1$ to $x = 3$ is

   A. 100   B. 140   C. 160   D. 180

4. Which of the following integrals could be used to evaluate $\displaystyle\lim_{n\to\infty} \frac{3}{n} \sum_{i=1}^{n} \ln(x_i)$?

   A. $\dfrac{3}{n} \displaystyle\int_1^n \ln x \, dx$ B. $\displaystyle\int_1^3 \ln x \, dx$ C. $\displaystyle\int_1^4 \ln x \, dx$ D. $\displaystyle\int_1^4 \frac{1}{x} \, dx$

5. The position of a particle on the x-axis at time t (in seconds) is given by $x(t) = t^3 - 4t^2 - 12t + 15$. The acceleration of the particle at $t = 2$ seconds is

   A. $-17 \dfrac{\text{units}}{\text{s}^2}$ B. $4 \dfrac{\text{units}}{\text{s}^2}$ C. $-16 \dfrac{\text{units}}{\text{s}^2}$ D. $6 \dfrac{\text{units}}{\text{s}^2}$

6. A ball is thrown vertically upward from the top of a 150-foot building. Its height above the ground at time t is given by $h(t) = 150 + 7t - 16t^2$ where h is in feet and t is in seconds. Determine the time at which the ball reaches its maximum height.

7. Integrate: $\displaystyle\int (\sec^2 x)(\sec x \tan x) \, dx$

8. Let $f(x) = e^{2x} \ln(3x)$. Determine $f'(x)$.

9. Describe the concavity of the graph of $y = x^2 \ln x$ at $x = 1$.

10. Find the equation of the line normal to the graph of $y = \dfrac{\sin x}{x^2 + 1}$ at $x = 0$.

11. (a) Find the Maclaurin series for $f(x) = \ln(1 + x)$.
    (b) Use the first three terms of this series to approximate the value of $\ln 2$.

12. (a) Find the exact area under $y = x^2$ on the interval $[0, 4]$ by writing and evaluating a definite integral.
    (b) Find the exact area under $y = x^2$ on the interval $[0, 4]$ by summing the areas of an infinite number of left rectangles. (*Hint:* $1^2 + 2^2 + 3^2 + \cdots + (n-1)^2 = \frac{n(n-1)(2n-1)}{6}$.)

Calculus, Second Edition

1. Let $g(x) = \dfrac{(x + 2)^2(x^2 + 3)}{x(x + 2)(x - 1)(x + 5)^2}$. Which of the following statements about g must be true?

   I. The graph of g has a hole at $x = -2$.
   II. The graph of g is positive on the interval $(0, 1)$.
   III. The graph of g has a vertical asymptote at $x = 1$.

   A. I only   B. III only   C. I and II only   D. I and III only

2. If the radius of a sphere is increasing at a rate of 3 centimeters per second, how fast is the volume increasing when the radius is 9 centimeters?

   A. $108\pi \ \dfrac{\text{cm}^3}{\text{s}}$ B. $972\pi \ \dfrac{\text{cm}^3}{\text{s}}$ C. $486\pi \ \dfrac{\text{cm}^3}{\text{s}}$ D. $972 \ \dfrac{\text{cm}^3}{\text{s}}$

3. The best approximation for the area of the region between the graph of $y = 2.7x^2 + 3.4x$ and the x-axis from $x = 1.35$ to $x = 3.46$ is

   A. 50.1753   B. 50.5649   C. 52.3187   D. 53.6109

4. Which of the following integrals could be used to evaluate $\displaystyle\lim_{n \to \infty} \frac{2}{n} \sum_{i=1}^{n} \ln (x_i)$?

   A. $\displaystyle\int_0^2 \frac{1}{x} \, dx$ B. $\displaystyle\int_1^3 \ln x \, dx$ C. $\displaystyle\int_1^4 \ln x \, dx$ D. $\displaystyle\frac{2}{n} \int_1^n \ln x \, dx$

5. The position of a particle moving along the x-axis at time t (in seconds) is given by $x(t) = t^3 + 5t^2 - 21t + 10$. The acceleration of the particle at $t = 3.1$ seconds is

   A. $28.6 \ \dfrac{\text{units}}{\text{s}^2}$ B. $6 \ \dfrac{\text{units}}{\text{s}^2}$ C. $38.83 \ \dfrac{\text{units}}{\text{s}^2}$ D. $10 \ \dfrac{\text{units}}{\text{s}^2}$

6. A ball is thrown vertically upward from the top of a 250-foot building. Its height above the ground at time t is given by $h(t) = 250 + 17t - 16t^2$ where h is in feet and t is in seconds. Determine the time at which the ball reaches its maximum height.

7. Integrate: $\displaystyle\int \cos^6 (3t) \sin (3t) \, dt$

8. Let $f(x) = e^{3x} \ln (2x)$. Determine $f'(x)$.

9. Describe the concavity of the graph of $y = x^2 e^x$ at $x = -1.62$.

10. Find an approximation of the line normal to the graph of $y = \dfrac{\sin x}{x^2 + 1}$ at $x = \pi$.

11. (a) Find the Maclaurin series for $f(x) = \ln (1 + x)$.
    (b) Use the first three terms of this series to approximate the value of $\ln 1.15$.

12. (a) Find the exact area under $y = x^2$ on the interval $[0, 4]$ by writing and evaluating a definite integral.
    (b) Find the exact area under $y = x^2$ on the interval $[0, 4]$ by summing the areas of an infinite number of right rectangles. (*Hint:* $1^2 + 2^2 + 3^2 + \cdots + n^2 = \frac{n(n + 1)(2n + 1)}{6}$.)

     Calculus, Second Edition

1. The area of the region bounded by the graphs of $f(x) = 2 - x^2$ and $g(x) = x$ is

   A. $\dfrac{9}{2}$ B. $\dfrac{27}{16}$ C. $\dfrac{1}{2}$ D. $\dfrac{11}{2}$

2. Which of the following properties of the definite integral is/are true?

   I. $\displaystyle\int_a^b k\, f(x)\, dx = k\int_a^b f(x)\, dx$ where k is a constant

   II. $\displaystyle\int_a^b x\, f(x)\, dx = x\int_a^b f(x)\, dx$

   III. $\displaystyle\int_a^b f(x)\, dx = \int_a^c f(x)\, dx + \int_c^b f(x)\, dx$

   A. I and III only   B. II only   C. I only   D. I, II, and III

3. A point moves on the x-axis in such a way that its velocity at time t $(t > 0)$ is given by $v(t) = \frac{\ln t}{t}$. The value of t that maximizes the velocity is

   A. 1   B. $e^{1/2}$ C. e D. $e^{3/2}$

4. Which of the following is the Maclaurin series for e^x?

   A. $1 - x + \dfrac{x^2}{2} - \dfrac{x^3}{3} + \dfrac{x^4}{4} + \cdots$ B. $1 + x + \dfrac{x^2}{2} + \dfrac{x^3}{3} + \dfrac{x^4}{4} + \cdots$

   C. $1 + x + \dfrac{x^2}{2!} + \dfrac{x^3}{3!} + \dfrac{x^4}{4!} + \cdots$ D. $1 - x + \dfrac{x^2}{2!} + \dfrac{x^3}{3!} + \dfrac{x^4}{4!} + \cdots$

5. Integrate: $\displaystyle\int x^2 e^{x^3}\, dx$

   A. $\dfrac{1}{3}e^{x^3} + C$ B. $3e^{x^3} + C$ C. $\dfrac{1}{3}(x^3 + e^{x^3} + C)$ D. $e^{x^3}(3x^4 + 2x) + C$

6. Determine the area of the region completely enclosed by the graph of $y = 9x - x^3$ and the x-axis.

7. Let $y = \cos(\cos^2 x)$. Find $\dfrac{dy}{dx}$.

8. Let $f(x) = x^7 + 2$. Find $f^{-1}(x)$.

9. A rectangle is to be inscribed in a circle whose radius is 2 units. Find the dimensions that maximize the area of this rectangle.

10. Find the slope of the line tangent to the ellipse $\dfrac{x^2}{9} + \dfrac{y^2}{16} = 1$ at the point $(3, 0)$.

11. The graph of the derivative of f is shown to the right. Sketch the graph of f.

12. Let $g(x) = x^3 + 6x + 10$.
    (a) State the interval(s) over which g is increasing.
    (b) State the interval(s) over which g is concave down.

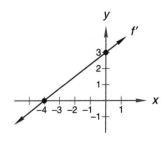

Calculus, Second Edition

Test 15, Form B   **SHOW YOUR WORK**   Name: _____

1. The area of the region bounded by the graphs of $f(x) = -2 + x^2$ and $g(x) = -x$ is

   A. $\dfrac{27}{16}$ B. $\dfrac{9}{2}$ C. $\dfrac{11}{2}$ D. $\dfrac{1}{2}$

2. Which of the following properties of the definite integral is/are true?

   I. $\displaystyle\int_a^b x f(x)\, dx = x \int_a^b f(x)\, dx$

   II. $\displaystyle\int_a^c f(x)\, dx + \int_c^b f(x)\, dx = \int_a^b f(x)\, dx$

   III. $\displaystyle\int_a^b k f(x)\, dx = k \int_a^b f(x)\, dx$ where k is a constant

   A. III only   B. I only   C. II and III only   D. I, II, and III

3. A point moves on the x-axis in such a way that its velocity at time t $(t > 0)$ is given by $v(t) = \frac{\ln t}{t}$. The value of t that maximizes the velocity is approximately

   A. 1   B. 1.648   C. 2.718   D. 4.482

4. Which of the following is the Maclaurin series for e^x?

   A. $1 - x + \dfrac{x^2}{2} - \dfrac{x^3}{3} + \dfrac{x^4}{4} + \cdots$

   B. $1 + x + \dfrac{x^2}{2} + \dfrac{x^3}{3} + \dfrac{x^4}{4} + \cdots$

   C. $1 + x + \dfrac{x^2}{2!} + \dfrac{x^3}{3!} + \dfrac{x^4}{4!} + \cdots$

   D. $1 - x + \dfrac{x^2}{2!} - \dfrac{x^3}{3!} + \dfrac{x^4}{4!} + \cdots$

5. Integrate: $\displaystyle\int x \cos(2x^2)\, dx$

   A. $4\sin(2x^2) + C$ B. $4x \sin(2x^2) + C$ C. $-\dfrac{1}{4}\sin(2x^2) + C$ D. $\dfrac{1}{4}\sin(2x^2) + C$

6. Approximate the area of the region bounded by the graph of $y = xe^{-x}$ and the x-axis over the interval $[-0.7, 2.4]$.

7. Let $y = \sin(\sin^2 x)$. Find $\dfrac{dy}{dx}$.

8. Let $f(x) = x^9 + 10$. Find $f^{-1}(x)$.

9. A rectangle is to be inscribed in a circle whose radius is 3 units. Find the dimensions that maximize the area of this rectangle.

10. Approximate the slope of the line tangent to the ellipse $\dfrac{x^2}{9} + \dfrac{y^2}{16} = 1$ at the point $\left(1, -\dfrac{8\sqrt{2}}{3}\right)$.

11. The graph of the derivative of f is shown to the right. Sketch the graph of f.

12. Let $g(x) = x^3 + 6x + 10$.

    (a) State the interval(s) over which g is increasing.

    (b) State the interval(s) over which g is concave down.

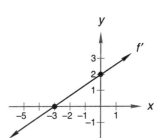

Calculus, Second Edition

1. An equation of the line tangent to the graph of $y = \arcsin x$ at the origin is

    A. $\pi x - 2y = 0$ B. $x - y = 0$ C. $x - 2y = 0$ D. $y = 0$

2. The minimum value of $f(x) = 2x^3 - 3x^2 - 12x + 1$ on the interval $[-3, 3]$ is

    A. 8   B. -8 C. -19 D. -44

3. The definite integral $\int_0^1 \dfrac{1}{x^2 + 1}\, dx$ equals

    A. $\dfrac{\pi}{4}$ B. $\dfrac{\pi}{2}$ C. $\ln 2$ D. $-\dfrac{1}{2}$

4. Let $\int_1^3 f(x)\, dx = 5$ and $\int_1^6 f(x)\, dx = 9$. Then $\int_3^6 2f(x)\, dx$ equals

    A. 4   B. 8   C. 28   D. -4

5. Shown is the graph of f''. Which of the following could be the graph of f?

    A.   B.   C.   D.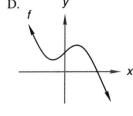

6. A variable force of $F(x) = 2x$ newtons is applied to an object in the direction it moves the object where x is measured in meters. Find the work done by the force as the object moves from $x = 2$ m to $x = 4$ m.

7. Suppose $f(x) = ae^x + b$. Given that $f'(0) = 2$ and $f(0) = 7$, find a and b.

8. Find the area between the graphs of $y = 5e^x$ and $y = 6e^x$ from $x = \ln 5$ to $x = \ln 6$.

9. Integrate: $\displaystyle\int \dfrac{2x - 3}{x^2 - 3x}\, dx$

10. Let $g(x) = \dfrac{e^{2x} + x}{\sin x - e^x} + \sec x$. Determine $g'(0)$.

11. Let R be the region in the first quadrant bounded by the graphs of $y = \frac{7}{x}$ and the x-axis over the interval $[1, c]$ where $c > 1$.

    (a) Sketch R.

    (b) Find the value of c such that the area of R is 21 square units.

12. Suppose f is a function that is continuous on the closed interval $[-1, 4]$, with $f(-1) = 7$ and $f(4) = 10$. In addition, f' and f'' have the properties listed in the table to the right. Sketch a possible graph of f and find where f attains its maximum and minimum values on the interval $[-1, 4]$.

x	$-1 < x < 2$	$x = 2$	$2 < x < 4$
$f'(x)$	negative	undefined	positive
$f''(x)$	negative	undefined	negative

Calculus, Second Edition

1. An equation of the line tangent to the graph of $y = \arctan x$ at the origin is

   A. $\pi x - 2y = 0$ B. $x + y = 0$ C. $x - 2y = 0$ D. $y = x$

2. The minimum value of $f(x) = 2x^3 + 3x^2 - 12x - 4$ on the interval $[-3.14, 3.14]$ is

   A. 16   B. 1.3405   C. -11   D. -4

3. The definite integral $\int_0^1 \dfrac{1}{\sqrt{1 - x^2}}\, dx$ equals

   A. $\dfrac{\pi}{2}$ B. $\dfrac{\pi}{4}$ C. -2 D. $-\dfrac{1}{2}$

4. Let $\int_{-1}^2 f(x)\, dx = 4$ and $\int_{-1}^7 f(x)\, dx = 11$. Then $\int_2^7 2f(x)\, dx$ equals

   A. 15   B. 7   C. 14   D. -14

5. Shown is the graph of f''. Which of the following could be the graph of f?

   A.   B.   C.   D.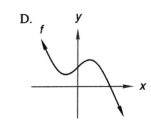

6. A variable force of $F(x) = \frac{1}{3}x^3 + x^2$ newtons is applied to an object in the direction it moves the object where x is measured in meters. Approximate the work done by the force as the object moves from $x = 1.2$ m to $x = 3.7$ m.

7. Suppose $f(x) = ae^x + b$. Given that $f'(1) = 2$ and $f(2) = 7$, approximate a and b.

8. Approximate the area between the graphs of $y = 3^x$ and $y = -3^{-x}$ from $x = -2$ to $x = 2$.

9. Integrate: $\displaystyle\int \dfrac{3x^2 + 6x}{x^3 + 3x^2 - 5}\, dx$

10. Let $g(x) = \dfrac{e^{2x} - x}{\sin x + e^x} - \tan x$. Determine $g'(0)$.

11. Let R be the region in the first quadrant bounded by the graphs of $y = \frac{7}{x}$ and the x-axis over the interval $[2, c]$ where $c > 2$.

    (a) Sketch R.

    (b) Find the value of c such that the area of R is 28 square units.

12. Suppose f is a function that is continuous on the closed interval $[-1, 4]$, with $f(-1) = 7$ and $f(4) = 5$. In addition, f' and f'' have the properties listed in the table to the right. Sketch a possible graph of f and find where f attains its maximum and minimum values on the interval $[-1, 4]$.

x	$-1 < x < 2$	$x = 2$	$2 < x < 4$
$f'(x)$	positive	undefined	negative
$f''(x)$	positive	undefined	positive

Calculus, Second Edition

1. Which of the following statements is true about the function $f(x) = x + \sin x$?
   A. The graph of f is symmetric about the y-axis.   B. The graph of f is symmetric about the x-axis.
   C. The graph of f is symmetric about the origin.   D. None of these.

2. Which of the following definite integrals is equivalent to $\int_0^{\pi/4} [\cos (2x)] e^{\sin (2x)} \, dx$?

   A. $\dfrac{1}{2} \int_0^1 e^u \, du$ B. $\int_0^1 -e^u \, du$ C. $\int_0^1 e^u \, du$ D. $\dfrac{1}{2} \int_0^{\pi/4} e^u \, du$

3. The minimum value of the function $f(x) = x^3 - 6x^2 + 9x$ on the interval $[-1, 5]$ is
   A. 0   B. –16   C. 4   D. None of these

4. The slope of the line tangent to the graph of $y = \arctan (x^2)$ at $x = 1$ is

   A. $\dfrac{\pi}{4}$ B. 0   C. 1   D. 2

5. Which of the following functions is even?
   A. $y = x^8 - x^4 + 16x$ B. $y = x \cos x$
   C. $y = x + e^x$ D. $y = e^{x^4}$

6. Integrate over y to find the area completely enclosed by the graphs of $x = y^2 - 2$ and $y = x$.

7. Find the Maclaurin series for $f(x) = e^{-x}$.

8. An airplane is flying in a horizontal straight-line path. The speed of the airplane is 200 meters per second, and its altitude is 1000 meters. What is the rate of change of the angle of elevation θ with respect to the reference point P when L is 2000 meters?

9. Integrate: $\displaystyle\int \dfrac{8 \cos (2x)}{\sqrt{8 + \sin (2x)}} \, dx$

10. Find $f'(0)$ given $f(x) = \dfrac{x^2 + 1}{\sin (2x) + \tan x + 3}$.

11. A ball is thrown downward with a velocity of 20 meters per second from the top of a building that is 160 meters tall.
    (a) Develop velocity and position functions for the ball. (Acceleration due to gravity is 9.8 m/s² downward.)
    (b) How long will it take the ball to hit the ground?

12. Let $f(x) = 7x + 6$.
    (a) Find an equation for f^{-1}.
    (b) Evaluate: $(f \circ f^{-1})(x)$
    (c) Graph f and f^{-1} on the same set of axes.

Calculus, Second Edition

1. Which of the following statements is true about the function $f(x) = x^2 \cos x$?

    A. The graph of f is symmetric about the y-axis.   B. The graph of f is symmetric about the x-axis.

    C. The graph of f is symmetric about the origin.   D. None of these.

2. Which of the following definite integrals is equivalent to $\int_0^{\pi/8} \sec^2(2x)\, e^{\tan(2x)}\, dx$?

    A. $\int_0^1 e^u\, du$ B. $\int_0^1 -e^u\, du$ C. $\frac{1}{2}\int_0^1 e^u\, du$ D. $\frac{1}{2}\int_0^{\pi/4} e^u\, du$

3. The minimum value of the function $f(x) = x^3 - 5x^2 + 8x$ on the interval $\left[\dfrac{3}{2}, 5\right]$ is

    A. 0   B. 4   C. −14   D. None of these

4. The slope of the line tangent to the graph of $y = \sin^{-1}(x^2)$ at $x = 0.25$ is closest to

    A. 0.5625   B. 0.0625   C. 1.0328   D. 0.5010

5. Which of the following functions is odd?

    A. $y = x^8 - x^4 + 16x$ B. $y = x \cos x$

    C. $y = x + e^x$ D. $y = e^{x^4}$

6. Find the area completely enclosed by the graphs of $x = 3 - y^2$ and $y = \dfrac{1}{2}x$.

7. Find the Maclaurin series for $f(x) = e^{-x}$.

8. An airplane is flying in a horizontal straight-line path. The speed of the airplane is 150 meters per second, and its altitude is 1000 meters. What is the rate of change of the angle of elevation θ with respect to the reference point P when L is 1000 meters?

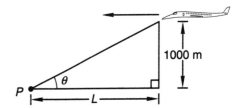

9. Integrate: $\displaystyle\int \frac{9 \sin(3x)}{\sqrt{9 - \cos(3x)}}\, dx$

10. Find $f'(0)$ given $f(x) = \dfrac{x^3 - 1}{\sin x + \tan(2x) - 4}$.

11. A ball is thrown downward with a velocity of 30 meters per second from the top of a building that is 220 meters tall.

    (a) Develop velocity and position functions for the ball. (Acceleration due to gravity is 9.8 m/s² downward.)

    (b) How long will it take the ball to hit the ground?

12. Let $f(x) = \dfrac{x - 6}{7}$.

    (a) Find an equation for f^{-1}.

    (b) Evaluate: $(f \circ f^{-1})(x)$

    (c) Graph f and f^{-1} on the same set of axes.

Calculus, Second Edition

1. Let R be the region bounded by $y = x^2 + 2$, the x-axis, $x = 0$, and $x = 4$. Which of the following represents the volume of the solid formed when R is revolved about the x-axis?

   A. $\displaystyle\int_0^4 \pi(x^2 + 2)^2 \, dx$　　　B. $\displaystyle\int_0^4 \pi(x^2 + 2) \, dx$　　　C. $\displaystyle\int_0^4 2\pi(x^3 + 2x) \, dx$　　　D. $\displaystyle\int_2^{18} \pi(y^2 + 2)^2 \, dy$

2. If $y = \log_6 x - \log_4 x + 5\log_7 x$, then y' equals

   A. $\dfrac{1}{x \ln 6} - \dfrac{1}{x \ln 4} + \dfrac{5}{x \ln 7}$

   B. $\dfrac{\ln 6}{x} - \dfrac{\ln 4}{x} + \dfrac{5 \ln 7}{x}$

   C. $\dfrac{6}{\ln x} - \dfrac{4}{\ln x} + \dfrac{35}{\ln x}$

   D. $37x$

3. Which of the following limits is undefined?

   A. $\displaystyle\lim_{x \to 2} \dfrac{x^3 - 8}{x - 2}$　　　B. $\displaystyle\lim_{x \to 0^-} \dfrac{|x|}{x}$　　　C. $\displaystyle\lim_{x \to 0+} x \sin x$　　　D. $\displaystyle\lim_{x \to 0} \dfrac{1}{x}$

4. Given that $\displaystyle\lim_{x \to 2} f(x) = L$, $\displaystyle\lim_{x \to 2} g(x) = M$, and $\displaystyle\lim_{x \to 2} h(x) = 2$, what is $\displaystyle\lim_{x \to 2} \dfrac{f(x) + g(x)h(x)}{h(x)}$?

   A. $\dfrac{L + M}{2}$　　　B. $\dfrac{L}{2} + M$　　　C. $\dfrac{L}{M} + 2$　　　D. The limit is undefined.

5. The area under the curve $y = x^2$ from $x = 0$ to $x = 4$ is

   A. 4 units^2　　　B. 16 units^2　　　C. $\dfrac{64}{3}$ units^2　　　D. 64 units^2

6. Integrate: $\displaystyle\int x \cos(2x) \, dx$

7. Find the volume of the solid formed by revolving the region bounded by $y = -2x + 3$ and the coordinate axes about the x-axis.

8. Differentiate $f(x) = 2.7^x + 4^x + e^{x^2}$ with respect to x.

9. Integrate: $\displaystyle\int \dfrac{1}{x^2 + 4} \, dx$

10. Determine the exact value of $\displaystyle\int_0^3 x\sqrt{x^2 + 1} \, dx$.

11. A rectangle is inscribed between the graph of $y = 4 - x^2$ and the x-axis as shown.

    (a) Express the area of the rectangle in terms of x, the x-coordinate of the upper right-hand corner of the rectangle.

    (b) Find the exact area of the largest possible rectangle that can be inscribed in this fashion.

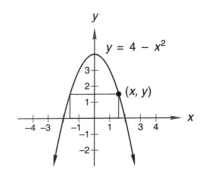

12. Let $f(x) = |x| + 3$ and $h(x) = -|x| + 3$.

    (a) Graph the functions f and h.

    (b) Suppose g is a function such that $f(x) \le g(x) \le h(x)$ for all x near 0. Find $\displaystyle\lim_{x \to 0} g(x)$.

Calculus, Second Edition

1. Let R be the region bounded by $y = \ln x$, the x-axis, $x = 1$, and $x = 5$. Which of the following represents the volume of the solid generated when R is revolved about the x-axis?

    A. $\displaystyle\int_1^5 \ln x \, dx$
    B. $\displaystyle\int_1^5 \pi(\ln x)^2 \, dx$
    C. $\displaystyle\int_1^5 2\pi x \ln x \, dx$
    D. $\displaystyle\int_1^5 \pi(\ln x) \, dx$

2. If $y = \log_6 x + 5 \log_4 x - \log_7 x$, then y' equals

    A. $\dfrac{1}{x \ln 6} + \dfrac{1}{5x \ln 4} - \dfrac{1}{x \ln 7}$

    B. $\dfrac{\ln 6}{x} + \dfrac{5 \ln 4}{x} - \dfrac{\ln 7}{x}$

    C. $\dfrac{6}{\ln x} + \dfrac{20}{\ln x} - \dfrac{7}{\ln x}$

    D. $\dfrac{1}{x \ln 6} + \dfrac{5}{x \ln 4} - \dfrac{1}{x \ln 7}$

3. Which of the following limits is undefined?

    A. $\displaystyle\lim_{x \to 2} \dfrac{x^3 - 8}{x - 2}$
    B. $\displaystyle\lim_{x \to 0^-} \dfrac{|x|}{x}$
    C. $\displaystyle\lim_{x \to 0} \sin \dfrac{1}{x}$
    D. $\displaystyle\lim_{x \to \infty} \dfrac{1}{x}$

4. Given that $\displaystyle\lim_{x \to 3} f(x) = L$, $\displaystyle\lim_{x \to 3} g(x) = M$, and $\displaystyle\lim_{x \to 3} h(x) = 4$, what is $\displaystyle\lim_{x \to 3} \dfrac{f(x) - g(x)h(x)}{h(x)}$?

    A. $\dfrac{L - M}{4}$
    B. $\dfrac{L}{M} - 4$
    C. $\dfrac{L}{4} - M$
    D. The limit is not defined.

5. The area under the curve $y = x^3 - 2x + 4$ from $x = -1.5$ to $x = 2.25$ is best approximated by

    A. 17.3291 units^2 B. 5.3291 units^2 C. 17.1093 units^2 D. 7.2656 units^2

6. Integrate: $\displaystyle\int x \sin(2x) \, dx$

7. Find the exact volume of the solid formed by revolving the region bounded by $y = -2x + 3$ and the coordinate axes about the x-axis.

8. Approximate $f'(3)$ given $f(x) = 2.7^x + 4^x + e^{x^2}$.

9. Integrate: $\displaystyle\int \dfrac{1}{\sqrt{4 - x^2}} \, dx$

10. Evaluate: $\displaystyle\int_0^3 x e^{x^2 + 1} \, dx$

11. A rectangle is inscribed between the graph of $y = 4 - x^4$ and the x-axis as shown.

    (a) Express the area of the rectangle in terms of x, the x-coordinate of the upper right-hand corner of the rectangle.

    (b) Approximate the area of the largest possible rectangle that can be inscribed in this fashion.

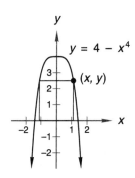

12. Let $f(x) = |x| + 3$, $g(x) = x \sin \dfrac{1}{x} + 3$, and $h(x) = -|x| + 3$.

    (a) Graph the functions f, g, and h in the same window of a graphing calculator. Copy these graphs to your paper.

    (b) Find $\displaystyle\lim_{x \to 0} g(x)$.

Calculus, Second Edition

1. The indefinite integral $\int \sin^3 x \cos^3 x \, dx$ equals

   A. $\dfrac{\sin^4 x}{4} - \dfrac{\sin^6 x}{6} + C$ B. $\dfrac{\cos^4 x}{4} - \dfrac{\cos^6 x}{6} + C$ C. $-\dfrac{\cos^4 x}{4} + C$ D. $\dfrac{\sin^4 x}{4} + C$

2. Let $f(x) = \begin{cases} ax^2 & \text{when } x \le 2 \\ bx & \text{when } x > 2. \end{cases}$

   Which of the following pairs of a and b will make f continuous over the set of all real numbers?

   A. $a = 1, b = 1$ B. $a = \sqrt{2}, b = 2$ C. $a = -2, b = -1$ D. $a = \dfrac{5}{6}, b = \dfrac{5}{3}$

3. Which of the following equals $\int \log_2 x \, dx$?

   A. $x \log_2 x - x + C$

   B. $\dfrac{x}{\ln 2}(\log_2 x - 1) + C$

   C. $\dfrac{1}{\ln 2}(x \ln x - x) + C$

   D. $\ln 2 \, (x \ln x - x) + C$

4. Let $xy + y^2 = x + 1$. Then $\dfrac{dy}{dx}$ at the point (2, 1) equals

   A. 3   B. 0   C. –1   D. 1

5. The area between $y = 3^x$, the x-axis, $x = 0$, and $x = 5$ is

   A. 243 units^2 B. 242 units^2 C. $\dfrac{242}{\ln 3} \text{ units}^2$ D. $\dfrac{243}{\log_3 5} \text{ units}^2$

6. Let R be the region bounded by $y = x^3 + 1$, the x-axis, $x = 0$, and $x = 1$. Find the volume of the solid formed when R is rotated around the x-axis.

7. Find the slope of the line tangent to the graph of $y = 3^{x^2 + 1} + \ln (x^3 + 1)$ at the point (0, 3).

8. The shaded region represents a vertical end of a trough that is 10 meters long. The trough is filled with a fluid whose weight density is 1000 N/m³. Find the force the fluid exerts against the end of the trough.

9. Integrate: $\displaystyle\int \dfrac{x - 2}{\sqrt{x}} \, dx$

10. Find the critical numbers for the function $g(x) = x(\ln x)^3$.

11. From the top of a 10.5-meter-tall tower, an object is thrown straight up with an initial velocity of 49 meters per second.

    (a) Develop equations that describe the height and velocity of the object as functions of time t.

    (b) How long does it take the ball to reach its highest point?

    (c) Find the maximum height of the ball.

12. Explain why the following statement is not true:

    If f is a function such that $\displaystyle\lim_{x \to 1^-} f(x) = \lim_{x \to 1^+} f(x)$, then f is continuous at $x = 1$.

1. The indefinite integral $\int \sin^3 x \cos^4 x \, dx$ equals

   A. $\dfrac{\sin^7 x}{7} - \dfrac{\sin^5 x}{5} + C$ B. $\dfrac{\cos^7 x}{7} - \dfrac{\cos^5 x}{5} + C$ C. $-\dfrac{\cos^5 x}{5} + C$ D. $\dfrac{\sin^4 x}{4} + C$

2. Let $f(x) = \begin{cases} ax & \text{when } x \le 2 \\ bx^2 & \text{when } x > 2. \end{cases}$

   Which of the following pairs of a and b will make f continuous over the set of all real numbers?

   A. $a = \sqrt{2}, \ b = \dfrac{1}{\sqrt{2}}$ B. $a = 2, \ b = 2$ C. $a = -1, \ b = 5$ D. $a = -5, \ b = 1$

3. Which of the following is equal to $\int 4^x \, dx$?

   A. $\dfrac{4^{x+1}}{x+1} + C$ B. $\dfrac{4^x}{\ln 4} + C$ C. $4^x \ln 4 + C$ D. $x \ln 4 + C$

4. Let $2xy - y^2 = 1 - x$. Then $\dfrac{dy}{dx}$ at the point $(1, 2)$ equals

   A. $\dfrac{1}{2}$ B. 0 C. -1 D. $\dfrac{5}{2}$

5. The area between $y = \log_4 x$, the x-axis, $x = 1$, and $x = 4$ is closest to
   A. 1.8360 units^2 B. 2.9115 units^2 C. 0.3933 units^2 D. 2.5452 units^2

6. Let R be the region bounded by $y = x^3 + 1$, the x-axis, $x = 0$, and $x = 7$. Find the volume of the solid formed when R is rotated around the x-axis.

7. Approximate the slope of the line tangent to the graph of $y = 3^{x^2+1} + \ln(x^3 + 1)$ at $x = 2$.

8. The shaded region represents a vertical end of a trough that is 8 meters long. The trough is filled with gasoline whose weight density is 6468 N/m³. Find the total force the gasoline exerts against one end of the trough.

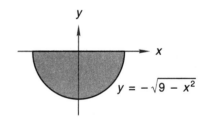

9. Integrate: $\displaystyle\int \dfrac{x+3}{\sqrt{x}} \, dx$

10. Use a graphing calculator to approximate the minimum value of the function $g(x) = x^2(\ln x)^3$.

11. From the top of a 100-meter-tall building, an object is thrown straight up with an initial velocity of 20 meters per second.
    (a) Develop equations that describe the height and velocity of the object as functions of time t.
    (b) How long does it take the ball to reach its highest point?
    (c) Approximate the maximum height of the ball.

12. Explain why the following statement is not true:

    If f is a function such that $\displaystyle\lim_{x \to 1^-} f(x) = \lim_{x \to 1^+} f(x)$, then f is continuous at $x = 1$.

Calculus, Second Edition

1. Let $f(x) = 2 + |x - 5|$. Then $f'(5)$ equals

   A. 2 B. 1

   C. -1 D. The derivative does not exist.

2. Let $f(x) = \dfrac{x^2 - x - 2}{x - 1}$. Which of the following most completely describes the asymptotes of f?

   A. $x = 1$ B. $y = x$ C. $x = 1$ and $y = 1$ D. $x = 1$ and $y = x$

3. Let $g(x)$ be a function continuous for all x with a relative maximum at $(-1, 4)$ and a relative minimum at $(3, -2)$. Which of the following statements must be true?

   A. The graph of g has a horizontal asymptote.

   B. The graph of g has a horizontal tangent line at $x = 3$.

   C. The graph of g must cross the x-axis between $x = -1$ and $x = 3$.

   D. The graph of g must have a point of inflection between $x = -1$ and $x = 3$.

4. What is $\displaystyle\lim_{x \to \infty} \dfrac{x^2 + \cos x}{x^2 + 5}$?

   A. 0 B. $\dfrac{1}{5}$ C. 1 D. ∞

5. The area of the region bounded by $y = \dfrac{3}{1 + x^2}$ and the x-axis from $x = 0$ to $x = 1$ is

   A. $\dfrac{3\pi}{4}$ units^2 B. $\dfrac{\pi}{4}$ unit^2 C. $\dfrac{3}{2}$ units^2 D. None of these

6. Integrate: $\displaystyle\int \cos^3 x \, dx$

7. Evaluate: $\displaystyle\lim_{x \to 0} \dfrac{e^{2x} - 1}{\tan x}$

8. Sketch the graph of $y = \dfrac{(x - 2)(x + 1)}{x - 3}$. Clearly indicate all zeros and asymptotes.

9. Evaluate: $\displaystyle\int_0^{\pi/2} \dfrac{\cos x}{\sqrt{\sin x + 3}} \, dx$

10. Find the slope of the line normal to the graph of $y = \log_2 x$ at $x = 3$.

11. A particle moves along the x-axis so that its acceleration is given by $a(t) = 6t - 4$. The particle's velocity is 1 at $t = 1$, and its position is 3 at $t = 0$.

    (a) Develop the equations that express the particle's position and velocity as functions of t.

    (b) Determine the values of t for which the velocity is increasing.

12. A rectangular tank having a depth of 2 meters, a width of 4 meters, and a length of 7 meters is completely filled with water, which has a weight density of 9800 N/m^3.

    (a) Find the force the water exerts against one of the vertical 4-by-2-meter ends of the tank.

    (b) Find the work done in pumping all the water out of the top of the tank.

Calculus, Second Edition

1. Let $f(x) = 5 + |x - 2|$. Then $f'(5)$ equals

   A. 8   B. 1

   C. –1   D. The derivative does not exist.

2. Let $f(x) = \dfrac{x^2 - x - 2}{x^2 - 1}$. Which of the following most completely describes the asymptotes of f?

   A. $x = 1$ B. $y = x$ C. $x = 1$ and $y = 1$ D. $x = 1$ and $y = x$

3. Let $g(x)$ be a function continuous for all x with a relative minimum at $(-4, -2)$ and a relative maximum at $(3, 3)$. Which one of the following statements must be true?

   A. The graph of g has a horizontal asymptote.

   B. The graph of g has a horizontal tangent line at $x = 3$.

   C. The graph of g must have a point of inflection between $x = -4$ and $x = 3$.

   D. The graph of g must cross the x-axis between $x = -4$ and $x = 3$.

4. What is $\displaystyle\lim_{x \to \infty} \dfrac{x - \cos x}{x^2 + 5x + 6}$?

   A. 0   B. $\dfrac{1}{6}$ C. 1   D. ∞

5. The area of the region bounded by $y = \dfrac{3 \ln x}{1 + x^2}$ and the x-axis from $x = 1.2$ to $x = 3.9$ is approximately

   A. 26.3641 units^2 B. 0.4059 unit^2 C. 0.9346 unit^2 D. None of these

6. Integrate: $\displaystyle\int \sin^3 x \, dx$

7. Evaluate: $\displaystyle\lim_{x \to 0} \dfrac{\sin x}{e^{2x} - 1}$

8. Sketch the graph of $y = \dfrac{(x + 3)(x + 1)}{x - 1}$. Clearly indicate all zeros and asymptotes.

9. Evaluate: $\displaystyle\int_0^{\pi/2} \dfrac{3 - \sin x}{\sqrt{\cos x + 3x}} \, dx$

10. Find the slope of the line normal to the graph of $y = -\log_4 x$ at $x = 5$.

11. A particle moves along the x-axis so that its acceleration is given by $a(t) = 8t - 7$. The particle's velocity is 1 at $t = 1$, and its position is –5 at $t = 0$.

    (a) Develop the equations that express the particle's position and velocity as functions of t.

    (b) Determine the values of t for which the velocity is increasing.

12. A rectangular tank having a depth of 3 meters, a width of 5 meters, and a length of 8 meters is completely filled with water, which has a weight density of 9800 N/m^3.

    (a) Find the force the water exerts against one of the vertical 5-by-3-meter ends of the tank.

    (b) Find the work done in pumping all the water out of the top of the tank.

Calculus, Second Edition

1. Let $f(x) = \begin{cases} ax^2 & \text{when } x \leq 1 \\ bx + 3 & \text{when } x > 1. \end{cases}$

Which of the following pairs of a and b will make f both continuous and differentiable everywhere?

A. $a = -3, b = -6$ B. $a = 0, b = -3$ C. $a = 2, b = 1$ D. $a = 3, b = -3$

2. What is $\lim\limits_{x \to 0} \dfrac{6x^2}{3 \sin (4x)}$?

A. 0   B. 1   C. 2   D. ∞

3. Which of the following functions is even?

A. $f(x) = \sin \cos x$ B. $f(x) = \sin (x^3)$ C. $f(x) = |x + 2|$ D. $f(x) = (x + 1)^2$

4. Which of the following functions is continuous at $x = 0$ but not differentiable at $x = 0$?

A. $y = \dfrac{|x|}{x}$ B. $y = \dfrac{x - 2}{x^2}$ C. $y = x^{2/3} + 5$ D. $y = 5x^2$

5. Find the area of the region in the first quadrant bounded by $f(x) = xe^x$, $g(x) = e^x$, and the y-axis.

6. A spring with a spring constant of 2.5 newtons per meter is stretched from $x = 1$ meter to $x = 4$ meters. Find the work done on the spring.

7. Use logarithmic differentiation to find y' given $y = x^{2 \sin x}$.

8. Integrate: $\displaystyle\int 4 \cos^2 x \, dx$

9. Differentiate: $y = x^2 e^{x + 3}$

10. Evaluate: $\lim\limits_{x \to 2} \dfrac{x^3 - x^2 - x - 2}{x - 2}$

11. Let R be the region in the first quadrant between $y = x^2$ and the x-axis over $[0, 1]$.

(a) Find the volume of the solid formed by revolving R about the x-axis.

(b) Find the volume of the solid formed by revolving R about the y-axis.

12. Let $f(x) = \dfrac{2x + 4}{x^2 - 5x + 4}$.

(a) Write the equations of all the asymptotes of the graph of the function.

(b) Sketch the graph of the function.

Calculus, Second Edition

Test 21, Form B   **SHOW YOUR WORK**   Name: _____

1. Let $f(x) = \begin{cases} ax + 3 & \text{when } x \leq 1 \\ bx^2 & \text{when } x > 1. \end{cases}$

   Which of the following pairs of a and b will make f both continuous and differentiable everywhere?

   A. $a = -3,\ b = 0$ B. $a = -6,\ b = -3$ C. $a = 1,\ b = 2$ D. $a = -3,\ b = 3$

2. What is $\lim\limits_{x \to 0} \dfrac{6x}{3 \sin (4x)}$?

   A. 0 B. 1 C. $\dfrac{1}{2}$ D. ∞

3. Which of the following functions is odd?

   A. $f(x) = \sin \cos x$ B. $f(x) = \sin (x^3)$ C. $f(x) = |x + 2|$ D. $f(x) = (x + 1)^2$

4. Which of the following functions is both continuous at $x = 0$ and differentiable at $x = 0$?

   A. $y = \dfrac{|x|}{x}$ B. $y = \dfrac{x - 2}{x^2}$ C. $y = x^{2/3} + 5$ D. $y = 5x^2$

5. Find the area of the region in the first quadrant bounded by $f(x) = x^2 e^x$, $g(x) = e^x$, and the y-axis.

6. A spring with a spring constant of 2.5 newtons per meter is stretched from $x = 2$ meters to $x = 4$ meters. Find the work done on the spring.

7. Use logarithmic differentiation to find y' given $y = x^{2 \cos x}$.

8. Integrate: $\displaystyle \int 4 \sin^2 x \, dx$

9. Differentiate: $y = x^3 e^{2x}$

10. Evaluate: $\lim\limits_{x \to 2} \dfrac{x^4 - x^3 - x - 6}{x - 2}$

11. Let R be the region in the first quadrant between $y = x^3$ and the x-axis over $[0, 1]$.
    (a) Approximate the volume of the solid formed by revolving R about the x-axis.
    (b) Approximate the volume of the solid formed by revolving R about the y-axis.

12. Let $f(x) = \dfrac{2x + 4}{x^2 - 7x + 6}$.
    (a) Write the equations of all the asymptotes of the graph of the function.
    (b) Sketch the graph of the function, using your graphing calculator as a guide.

Calculus, Second Edition

1. Let $f(x) = \cos x$ and $g(x) = x^5 + x^3 + 3x$. If $\int_0^k (fg)(x)\, dx = 12$, then $\int_{-k}^k (fg)(x)\, dx$ equals

   A. -12 B. 0 C. 12 D. 24

2. What is $\lim_{x \to 1} \dfrac{x^5 - 1}{x - 1}$?

   A. 1 B. 5

   C. ∞ D. The limit does not exist.

3. Let $y = x^{\ln x}$. Then $\dfrac{dy}{dx}$ equals

   A. $\dfrac{2 \ln x}{x}$ B. $\dfrac{2x^{\ln x} \ln x}{x}$ C. $\dfrac{2x^{\ln x}}{x}$ D. $(\ln x)x^{\ln x - 1}$

4. The function $f(x) = x^{2/3}$ does not satisfy the conditions of the Mean Value Theorem over the interval $[-8, 8]$ because

   A. $f(0)$ is not defined.   B. $f'(-1)$ does not exist.

   C. $f'(0)$ does not exist.   D. $f(x)$ is not defined for $x < 0$.

5. Given $\dfrac{dy}{dx} = 9y^4$ and $y = 1$ when $x = 0$, determine the value of y when $x = \dfrac{1}{3}$.

6. Integrate: $\displaystyle\int \dfrac{9 + x}{1 + x^2}\, dx$

7. Find a general solution to the differential equation $x^2\, dx + 3y\, dy = 0$.

8. Find the critical numbers for the function $f(x) = \dfrac{x^2 - 3x - 4}{x + 2}$.

9. Simplify: $\displaystyle\lim_{h \to 0} \dfrac{\sin(x + h) - \sin(x)}{h}$

10. Let $f(x) = 3 \cos x$. Find the number c in the interval $\left[\dfrac{\pi}{2}, \dfrac{3\pi}{2}\right]$ guaranteed by Rolle's theorem.

11. Let R be the region bounded by the x-axis and the graph of $y = e^x$ on the interval $[0, 1]$. Find the volume of the solid formed when R is revolved about the y-axis.

12. Mallory wishes to open a savings account in which her money will be compounded continuously so that the rate of increase of money will be exponential. If the annual interest rate is 8%, how much money should Mallory invest now if she wants the account to contain $10,000 after 10 years?

       Calculus, Second Edition

1. Let $f(x) = \cos x$ and $g(x) = x^4 + x^2$. If $\int_0^k (fg)(x)\, dx = 12$, then $\int_{-k}^k (fg)(x)\, dx$ equals

   A. -12 B. 0 C. 12 D. 24

2. What is $\lim\limits_{x \to 1} \dfrac{x^3 - 1}{x - 1}$?

   A. 1 B. 3

   C. ∞ D. The limit does not exist.

3. Let $y = x^{e^x}$. Then $\dfrac{dy}{dx}$ equals

   A. $x^{e^x} e^x \left(\ln x + \dfrac{1}{x} \right)$ B. $\dfrac{x^{e^x} e^x \ln x}{x}$ C. $e^x x^{e^x - 1}$ D. $e^x x^{e^x - 1}$

4. The function $f(x) = x^{3/2}$ does not satisfy the conditions of the Mean Value Theorem over the interval $[-8, 8]$ because

   A. $f(0)$ is not defined.   B. $f'(1)$ does not exist.

   C. $f(x)$ is not continuous at $x = 1$.   D. $f(x)$ is not defined for $x < 0$.

5. Given $\dfrac{dy}{dx} = 8y^5$ and $y = 1$ when $x = \dfrac{1}{2}$, determine the value of y when $x = -\dfrac{1}{4}$.

6. Integrate: $\displaystyle\int \dfrac{7 + 2x}{1 + x^2}\, dx$

7. Find a general solution to the differential equation $x^2\, dx - 3y^2\, dy = 0$.

8. Find the critical numbers for the function $f(x) = \dfrac{x^2 - 3x + 5}{x - 4}$.

9. Simplify: $\lim\limits_{h \to 0} \dfrac{\cos(x + h) - \cos(x)}{h}$

10. Let $f(x) = 3\cos(2x)$. Find the number c in the interval $\left[\dfrac{\pi}{4}, \dfrac{3\pi}{4} \right]$ guaranteed by Rolle's theorem.

11. Let R be the region bounded by the x-axis and the graph of $y = e^x$ on the interval $[1, 2]$. Find the volume of the solid formed when R is revolved about the y-axis.

12. Lucas wishes to open a savings account in which his money will be compounded continuously so that the rate of increase of money will be exponential. If the annual interest rate is 8%, how much money should Lucas invest now if he wants the account to contain \$20,000 after 10 years?

Calculus, Second Edition

1. A particle moves along the x-axis so that its position at any time t is $x(t) = 8t - 3t^2$. The total distance traveled by the particle between $t = 1$ and $t = 2$ is

   A. 1   B. $\dfrac{4}{3}$ C. $\dfrac{5}{3}$ D. 2

2. The average value of the function $g(x) = \sqrt{x}$ over the interval $[0, 2]$ is

   A. $\dfrac{4}{3}\sqrt{2}$ B. $\dfrac{1}{2}\sqrt{2}$ C. $\dfrac{2}{3}\sqrt{2}$ D. 1

3. What is $\lim\limits_{x \to (\pi/2)^-} (\tan x - \sec x)$?

   A. $-\infty$ B. 0   C. 1   D. ∞

4. The exact value of $\displaystyle\int_{-\pi}^{\pi} \cos^2 (2x)\, dx$ is

   A. 0   B. $\dfrac{\pi}{2}$ C. π D. 2π

5. Let $\tan (xy) = x$. Determine $\dfrac{dy}{dx}$.

6. The Mean Value Theorem for Integrals states that every continuous function on a specified interval attains its average value at a point c on that interval. Let $f(x) = 3x^2 - 12x + 10$. Find the value c on the interval $[0, 5]$ guaranteed by the Mean Value Theorem for Integrals.

7. Find the volume of the solid formed when the region bounded by $y = 2^x$, $y = 2x$, and the y-axis from $x = 0$ to $x = 1$ is revolved about the y-axis.

8. Find the general solution of the differential equation $\dfrac{dy}{dx} = 7y^2$.

9. Let $f(x) = x^3 + x - 1$. Find the slope of the graph of the inverse of f at the point $(-1, 0)$.

10. Evaluate: $\lim\limits_{x \to \infty} e^{-x} \ln (x^5)$

11. Let R be the region in the first quadrant bounded by $y = \sqrt{6x + 4}$, $y = 2x$, and the y-axis.
    (a) Find the area of R.
    (b) Set up, but **do not integrate,** an integral expression in terms of a single variable that could be used to find the volume of the solid generated by revolving R about the x-axis.
    (c) Set up, but **do not integrate,** an integral expression in terms of a single variable that could be used to find the volume of the solid generated by revolving R about the y-axis.

12. A particle moves along the x-axis so that its acceleration at any time t is given by $a(t) = 6t - 17$. At time $t = 2$, the velocity of the particle is 10.
    (a) Find an expression for the velocity, $v(t)$, of the particle at any time t.
    (b) Find the average velocity of the particle over the interval of time $[0, 3]$.

Calculus, Second Edition

Test 23, Form B   **SHOW YOUR WORK**   Name: _____

1. The value of $\int_{-\pi}^{\pi} \sin^2(2x)\, dx$ is exactly

   A. 0   B. $\dfrac{\pi}{2}$ C. π D. 2π

2. The average value of the function $g(x) = \sqrt[3]{x}$ over the interval $[0, 2]$ is exactly

   A. $\dfrac{3}{8}\sqrt[3]{2}$ B. $\dfrac{3}{4}\sqrt[3]{2}$ C. $\dfrac{1}{2}\sqrt{2}$ D. 1

3. What is $\lim\limits_{x \to 0^+} (\cot x - \csc x)$?

   A. $-\infty$ B. 0   C. 1   D. ∞

4. A particle moves along the x-axis so that its position at any time t is $x(t) = 7t - 2t^2$. Find the total distance traveled by the particle between $t = 1$ and $t = 2$.

5. Let $\tan(xy) = y$. Determine $\dfrac{dy}{dx}$.

6. The Mean Value Theorem for Integrals states that every continuous function on a specified interval attains its average value at a point c on that interval. Let $f(x) = 3x^2 - 12x + 10$. Find the value c on the interval $[1, 5]$ guaranteed by the Mean Value Theorem for Integrals.

7. Find the volume of the solid formed when the region bounded by $y = 3^x$, $y = 3x$, and the y-axis from $x = 0$ to $x = 1$ is revolved about the x-axis.

8. Find the general solution of the differential equation $\dfrac{dy}{dx} = -9y^{-2}$.

9. Let $f(x) = x^3 + 4x - 7$. Find the slope of the graph of the inverse of f at the point $(-7, 0)$.

10. Evaluate: $\lim\limits_{x \to \infty} e^{-x} \ln\left(x^7\right)$

11. Let R be the region in the first quadrant bounded by $y = \sqrt{6x + 3}$, $y = 3x$, and the y-axis.
    (a) Approximate the area of R.
    (b) Approximate the volume of the solid generated by revolving R about the x-axis.
    (c) Approximate the volume of the solid generated by revolving R about the y-axis.

12. A particle moves along the x-axis so that its acceleration at any time t is given by $a(t) = 6t - 17$. At time $t = 2$, the velocity of the particle is 3.
    (a) Find an expression for the velocity, $v(t)$, of the particle at any time t.
    (b) Find the average velocity of the particle over the interval of time $[0, 3]$.

Calculus, Second Edition

1. Let $f(x) = x^3 + x$. If g is the inverse of f, then $g'(2)$ equals

   A. $\dfrac{1}{13}$ B. $\dfrac{1}{4}$ C. 4   D. 13

2. Which of the following is equal to $\displaystyle\int_{-3}^{3} |x + 2|\, dx$?

   A. 9   B. 12   C. 13   D. 14

3. What is $\displaystyle\lim_{x \to 0} x \csc x$?

   A. $-\infty$ B. -1 C. 1   D. $+\infty$

4. Let f be a continuous function for all real numbers. Assume the maximum value of f is 8 and the minimum value of f is -12. Which of the following statements must be true?

   A. The maximum value of $|f(x)|$ is 8.   B. The minimum value of $f(|x|)$ is 0.
   C. The maximum value of $|f(x)|$ is 12.   D. The minimum value of $f(|x|)$ is -12.

5. The general solution of the differential equation $\dfrac{dy}{dx} = \dfrac{1 - 2x}{2y}$ is a family of

   A. Circles   B. Ellipses   C. Hyperbolas   D. Parabolas

6. A particle moves along the x-axis so that its velocity at time t, $t > 0$, is given by $v(t) = \frac{t-2}{t}$. What value does the particle's acceleration approach as t gets large?

7. Integrate: $\displaystyle\int \dfrac{2}{\sqrt{1 - x}}\, dx$

8. Illustrate the Mean Value Theorem by finding a number c in $[1, 3]$ such that $f'(c) = \frac{f(3) - f(1)}{3 - 1}$ where $f(x) = 3x^2 + 4x - 1$.

9. Let R be the region bounded by $y = x^3$ and the x-axis on the interval $[0, 1]$. Find the volume of the solid formed when R is rotated about the line $x = 1$.

10. Find the interval(s) on which the graph of $y = \dfrac{1}{3}x^3 - 5x^2 + 21x - 3$ is concave down.

11. Let $f(x) = x^3 + 4x^2 - 21x$.
    (a) Find the roots of this polynomial function.
    (b) Use Newton's method with $x_1 = 2$ to approximate the largest root of the polynomial by calculating x_2. Compare your results to those in (a).

12. (a) Approximate $\displaystyle\int_{1}^{4} x^3\, dx$ using the trapezoidal rule with $n = 3$ subdivisions.

    (b) Find the exact area under the curve of $f(x) = x^3$ on the interval $[1, 4]$. Compare this value to the answer in (a).

Calculus, Second Edition

1. Let $f(x) = x^3 + 2x$. If g is the inverse of f, then $g'(3)$ equals

   A. $\dfrac{1}{5}$ B. $\dfrac{1}{33}$ C. $\dfrac{1}{29}$ D. 33

2. The general solution of the differential equation $\dfrac{dy}{dx} = \dfrac{1 + 2x}{2y}$ is a family of

   A. Circles   B. Ellipses   C. Hyperbolas   D. Parabolas

3. What is $\lim\limits_{x \to 0} x^{-3} \sin x$?

   A. $-\infty$ B. -1 C. 1 D. $+\infty$

4. Let f be a continuous function for all real numbers. Assume the maximum value of f is -8 and the minimum value of f is -12. Which of the following statements must be true?

   A. The maximum value of $|f(x)|$ is 8.   B. The minimum value of $f(|x|)$ is 0.
   C. The maximum value of $|f(x)|$ is 12.   D. The minimum value of $f(|x|)$ is -12.

5. Evaluate: $\displaystyle\int_{-3}^{3} |x - 2|\, dx$

6. A particle moves along the x-axis so that its velocity at time t, $t > 0$, is given by $v(t) = \dfrac{t}{t-2}$. What value does the particle's acceleration approach as t gets large?

7. Integrate: $\displaystyle\int \dfrac{2}{\sqrt{1+x}}\, dx$

8. Illustrate the Mean Value Theorem by finding a number c in $[1, 3]$ such that $f'(c) = \dfrac{f(3) - f(1)}{3 - 1}$ where $f(x) = x^2 + 8x - 1$.

9. Let R be the region bounded by $y = x^3$ and the x-axis on the interval $[0, 1]$. Approximate the volume of the solid formed when R is rotated about the line $x = 2$.

10. Find the interval(s) on which the graph of $y = \dfrac{1}{3}x^3 - 5x^2 + 21x - 3$ is concave up.

11. Let $f(x) = x^3 + 4x^2 - 21x + 15$.

    (a) Approximate the roots of this polynomial function.
    (b) Use Newton's method with $x_1 = 4$ to approximate the largest root of the polynomial by calculating x_2 and x_3. Compare your results to those in (a).

12. (a) Approximate $\displaystyle\int_{1}^{4} x^3\, dx$ using the trapezoidal rule with $n = 3$ subdivisions.

    (b) Find the exact area under the curve of $f(x) = x^3$ on the interval $[1, 4]$. Compare this value to the answer in (a).
    (c) Find the number of subdivisions that are required in the trapezoidal rule to approximate $\displaystyle\int_{1}^{4} x^3\, dx$ with an error less than 0.001.

Calculus, Second Edition

Test 25, Form A   **SHOW YOUR WORK**   Name: _____

1. The base of a solid is the region in the first quadrant bounded by $x^2 = 4y$, $y = 2$, and the y-axis. Every vertical cross section of the solid perpendicular to the y-axis is a square. The volume of this solid is

   A. 8 units^3 B. 16 units^3 C. 32 units^3 D. 64 units^3

2. Let $f(x) = \left| \cos x - \dfrac{1}{2} \right|$. The maximum value attained by f is

   A. $\dfrac{1}{2}$ B. 1   C. $\dfrac{3}{2}$ D. $\dfrac{\pi}{2}$

3. Let $F(x) = \displaystyle\int_1^x e^{-t^2}\, dt$. Then $F'(x)$ equals

   A. $2xe^{-x^2}$ B. $-2xe^{-x^2}$ C. e^{-x^2} D. $\dfrac{e^{-x^2+1}}{-x^2+1} - e$

4. Use differentials to approximate $\sqrt[4]{78}$. Remember $\sqrt[4]{81} = 3$.

   A. $3 - \dfrac{13}{450}$ B. $3 - \dfrac{7}{250}$ C. $3 - \dfrac{1}{36}$ D. $3 + \dfrac{1}{72}$

5. Let f be a function such that $f' > 0$ for all real values of x. Which of the following statements must be true?

   A. $f(x) > 0$ for all values of x.   B. $f(x_1) > f(x_2)$ for every x_1 and x_2 where $x_1 > x_2$.

   C. f is concave upward everywhere.   D. f is concave downward everywhere.

6. Integrate: $\displaystyle\int \tan^3 x\, dx$

7. Use the trapezoidal rule with $n = 4$ subdivisions to approximate $\displaystyle\int_0^2 (x^2 + 1)\, dx$.

8. Let $f(x) = x^3 + 7x - 1$. Using $x_1 = 0$, determine x_2, the first value given by Newton's method.

9. Evaluate: $\displaystyle\lim_{x \to 0} 5x \csc(2x)$

10. Find the volume of the solid formed when the region between $y = \sec x$ and the x-axis on the interval $\left[0, \frac{\pi}{4}\right]$ is revolved around the x-axis.

11. Suppose $f(x) = x^3 + 3x$ and f^{-1} is the inverse function of f.
    (a) Determine $f^{-1}(4)$.
    (b) Determine $(f^{-1})'(4)$.

12. The height of a right circular cone is increasing at a rate of 8 cm/s, and the radius of the circular base is decreasing at a rate of 2 cm/s. Find the rate at which the volume of the cone is changing when the height of the cone is 12 cm and the radius of the base is 3 cm.

Calculus, Second Edition

1. The base of a solid is the region in the first quadrant bounded by $-x^2 = 4y$, $y = -2$, and the y-axis. Every vertical cross section of the solid perpendicular to the y-axis is a square. The volume of this solid is

   A. 8 units^3 B. 16 units^3 C. 32 units^3 D. 64 units^3

2. Let $f(x) = \left| \sin(3x) - \dfrac{1}{2} \right|$. The maximum value attained by f is

   A. $\dfrac{1}{2}$ B. 1   C. $\dfrac{3}{2}$ D. $\dfrac{\pi}{2}$

3. Let $F(u) = \displaystyle\int_1^u e^{-x^2}\, dx$. Then $F'(u)$ equals

   A. $2ue^{-u^2}$ B. $-2ue^{-u^2}$ C. e^{-u^2} D. $\dfrac{e^{-u^2+1}}{-u^2+1} - e$

4. Use differentials to approximate $\sqrt[4]{78}$. Remember $\sqrt[4]{81} = 3$.

   A. $3 + \dfrac{1}{36}$ B. $3 - \dfrac{1}{78}$ C. $3 - \dfrac{1}{36}$ D. $3 - \dfrac{4}{81}$

5. Let f be a function such that $f'' < 0$ for all real values of x. Which of the following statements must be true?
   A. $f(x) > 0$ for all values of x.   B. $f(x_1) > f(x_2)$ for every x_1 and x_2 where $x_1 > x_2$.
   C. f is concave upward everywhere.   D. f is concave downward everywhere.

6. Integrate: $\displaystyle\int \cot^3 x \, dx$

7. Use the trapezoidal rule with $n = 6$ subdivisions to approximate $\displaystyle\int_0^2 \dfrac{1}{\sqrt{x^2 + 1}}\, dx$.

8. Let $f(x) = x^3 + 7x - 1$. Use Newton's method to approximate the real root of f accurate to eight decimal places.

9. Evaluate: $\displaystyle\lim_{x \to 0} \pi x \csc(2x)$

10. Find the volume of the solid formed when the region between $y = \sec x$ and the x-axis on the interval $[0, \frac{\pi}{12}]$ is revolved around the x-axis.

11. Suppose $f(x) = x^5 + 2x$ and f^{-1} is the inverse function of f.
    (a) Determine $f^{-1}(3)$.
    (b) Determine $(f^{-1})'(3)$.

12. The height of a right circular cone is increasing at a rate of 6 cm/s, and the radius of the circular base is decreasing at a rate of 1 cm/s. Find the rate at which the volume of the cone is changing when the height of the cone is 12 cm and the radius of the base is 3 cm.

Calculus, Second Edition

1. The velocity of a particle moving along a straight line at time t is given by $v(t) = \frac{1}{3}t^3 - \frac{7}{2}t^2 + 12t$ for $t > 0$. The time(s) at which the acceleration of the particle is zero is/are

   A. $t = 0$ B. $t = 3$ C. $t = 1$ and $t = 3$ D. $t = 3$ and $t = 4$

2. What is $\lim\limits_{x \to 0} \dfrac{5x}{\sin (6x)}$?

   A. 0   B. $\dfrac{5}{6}$ C. $\dfrac{6}{5}$ D. 5

3. What is $\lim\limits_{x \to \infty} x^4 e^{-x}$?

   A. $-\infty$ B. 0   C. 24   D. $+\infty$

4. Let R be the region bounded by $y = x$, $y = 0$, and $x = 2$. Find the volume of the solid formed by revolving R about the line $y = 3$.

5. Evaluate: $\displaystyle\int_0^5 |x - 3|\, dx$

6. Integrate: $\displaystyle\int \pi \sec^2 x\, e^{\tan x}\, dx$

7. Function f is continuous on the interval $[1, 8]$. Also, $f(1) = 5$, $f(4) = 9$, and $f(8) = 6$. Moreover, f' and f'' satisfy the properties given in the chart. Sketch the graph of f.

	$1 < x < 4$	$x = 4$	$4 < x < 8$
f'	positive	undefined	negative
f''	positive	undefined	positive

8. Integrate: $\displaystyle\int \sin^3 x\, dx$

9. Let $f(x) = \dfrac{d}{dx} \displaystyle\int_5^x (\cos t)e^{t+2}\, dt$. Find $f(0)$.

10. Draw a slope field for the differential equation $\dfrac{dy}{dx} = x$.

11. Given that the derivative of $\ln x$ with respect to x is $\frac{1}{x}$, use implicit differentiation to prove that the derivative of e^x with respect to x is e^x.

12. Use the definition of the derivative and the fact that $\lim\limits_{h \to 0} \frac{\cos h - 1}{h} = 0$ to prove that the derivative of $\sin x$ with respect to x is $\cos x$.

Calculus, Second Edition

1. What is $\lim\limits_{x \to 0} \dfrac{7x}{\sin (8x)}$?

   A. 0   B. 0.875   C. 1.1429   D. 7

2. What is $\lim\limits_{x \to \infty} x^{-4} e^x$?

   A. $-\infty$ B. 0   C. 24   D. $+\infty$

3. The velocity of a particle moving along a straight line at time t is given by $v(t) = t^3 - 7t^2 + 12t$ for $t > 0$. Approximate the times at which the acceleration of the particle is zero.

4. Let R be the region bounded by $y = x$, $y = 0$, and $x = 2$. Find the volume of the solid formed by revolving R about the line $y = 4$.

5. Evaluate: $\displaystyle\int_0^8 |2x - 3| \, dx$

6. Integrate: $\displaystyle\int 3 \sec x \tan x \, e^{\sec x} \, dx$

7. Function f is continuous on the interval $[1, 8]$. Also, $f(1) = 5$, $f(4) = 9$, and $f(8) = 12$. Moreover, f' and f'' satisfy the properties given in the chart. Sketch the graph of f.

	$1 < x < 4$	$x = 4$	$4 < x < 8$
f'	positive	zero	positive
f''	positive	zero	negative

8. Integrate: $\displaystyle\int \cos^3 x \, dx$

9. Let $f(x) = \dfrac{d}{dx} \displaystyle\int_5^x \sin\left(t + \dfrac{\pi}{4}\right) e^{t+2} \, dt$. Find $f(0)$.

10. Draw a slope field for the differential equation $\dfrac{dy}{dx} = y$.

11. Given that the derivative of $\ln x$ with respect to x is $\frac{1}{x}$, use implicit differentiation to prove that the derivative of e^x with respect to x is e^x.

12. Use the definition of the derivative and the fact that $\lim\limits_{h \to 0} \dfrac{\cos h - 1}{h} = 0$ to prove that the derivative of $\sin x$ with respect to x is $\cos x$.

Calculus, Second Edition

Test 27, Form A   **SHOW YOUR WORK**   Name: _____

1. Which of the following vectors equals $3\langle 4, -1\rangle - 2\langle -2, -3\rangle$?

   A. $\langle 8, 3\rangle$ B. $16\hat{i} + 3\hat{j}$ C. $\langle 16, -3\rangle$ D. $3\hat{i} - 3\hat{j}$

2. Which of the following sequences converge(s)?

   I. $a_n = \dfrac{5 - 3n + n^2}{n^3}$ II. $a_n = \dfrac{n^3}{3^n}$ III. $a_n = \dfrac{3^n}{2^n}$

   A. I only   B. II only   C. III only   D. I and II only

3. What is $\lim\limits_{x \to \infty} \left(1 + \dfrac{1}{x}\right)^{5x}$?

   A. ∞ B. e^5 C. $5e$ D. $e^{1/5}$

4. The rectangular form of the polar equation $r = \cos\theta$ is

   A. $x^2 + y^2 = x$ B. $x^2 + y^2 = y$ C. $x^2 + y^2 = 1$ D. $x^2 - y^2 = y$

5. The function $y = x^2 - 2$ has two real zeros. Using Newton's method with $x_1 = \frac{3}{2}$, determine the value of x_2, the second approximation of the zero of the function.

6. Find the average value of the function $f(x) = \dfrac{1}{x}$ on the interval $[1, e]$.

7. Integrate: $\displaystyle\int e^x \sin x \, dx$

8. Find a unit vector parallel to the line tangent to the curve $y = 7x^2 - 2x + 1$ at the point $(1, 6)$.

9. Find the Maclaurin series for the function $g(x) = \ln(x + 1)$.

10. Use an epsilon-delta proof to show that $\lim\limits_{x \to 2} (2x + 3) = 7$.

11. Let $f(x) = \dfrac{3}{2}x^{2/3} + 3x^{1/3}$ on the interval $[-8, 8]$.

    (a) Determine the absolute maximum and absolute minimum values of f on the interval $[-8, 8]$.
    (b) Determine the intervals on which f is concave upward.

12. A particle moves in the Cartesian plane according to the parametric equations $x = 3t$ and $y = t^2 + 1$.

    (a) Eliminate the parameter and express the parametric equations in rectangular form.
    (b) Sketch the graph of the path of the particle.

Calculus, Second Edition

1. Which of the following vectors equals $-2\langle 4, -1 \rangle + 3\langle -1, -3 \rangle$?

   A. $\langle -11, -11 \rangle$ B. $4\hat{i} - 3\hat{j}$ C. $\langle -6, -12 \rangle$ D. $-11\hat{i} - 7\hat{j}$

2. Which of the following sequences converge(s)?

   I. $a_n = \dfrac{5 - 3n + n^2}{n^3}$ II. $a_n = \dfrac{3^n}{n^4}$ III. $a_n = \dfrac{3^n}{2^n}$

   A. I only   B. II only   C. III only   D. I and II only

3. What is $\displaystyle\lim_{x \to \infty} \left(1 + \dfrac{1}{x} \right)^{8x}$?

   A. ∞ B. e^8 C. $8e$ D. $e^{1/8}$

4. The rectangular form of the polar equation $r = \sin\theta$ is

   A. $x^2 + y^2 = x$ B. $x^2 + y^2 = y$ C. $x^2 + y^2 = 1$ D. $x^2 - y^2 = y$

5. The function $y = x^2 - 2$ has two real zeros. Using Newton's method with $x_1 = 1.5$, determine the value of x_3, the third approximation of the zero of the function.

6. Find the average value of the function $f(x) = \dfrac{1}{x}$ on the interval $[1, e]$.

7. Integrate: $\displaystyle\int e^x \cos x \, dx$

8. Find a unit vector parallel to the line tangent to the curve $y = 7x^2 - 12x + 1$ at the point $(2, 5)$.

9. Use the first three nonzero terms of the Maclaurin series for the function $g(x) = \ln(1 + x)$ to approximate $\ln 1.3$.

10. Use an epsilon-delta proof to show that $\displaystyle\lim_{x \to 5} (3x + 1) = 16$.

11. Let $f(x) = \dfrac{3}{2}x^{2/3} + 3x^{1/3}$ on the interval $[-8, 0]$.

    (a) Determine the absolute maximum and absolute minimum values of f on the interval $[-8, 0]$.

    (b) Determine the intervals on which f is concave upward.

12. A particle moves in the Cartesian plane according to the parametric equations $x = 3t$ and $y = t^3 + 1$.

    (a) Eliminate the parameter and express the parametric equations in rectangular form.

    (b) Sketch the graph of the path of the particle.

Calculus, Second Edition

1. The length of the curve $y = \ln(\sec x)$ from $x = 0$ to $x = 1$ may be expressed by the integral

   A. $\displaystyle\int_0^1 \sec x \; dx$ B. $\displaystyle\int_0^1 \sec x \tan x \; dx$

   C. $\displaystyle\int_0^1 \sqrt{1 + [\ln(\sec x)]^2} \; dx$ D. $\displaystyle\int_0^1 \sqrt{1 + (\sec^2 x \tan^2 x)} \; dx$

2. A unit vector normal to the line tangent to $y = 3x^2 - 8x + 4$ at the point $(2, 0)$ is

   A. $\langle 1, 4 \rangle$ B. $\langle 4, -1 \rangle$ C. $\left\langle \frac{1}{\sqrt{17}}, \frac{4}{\sqrt{17}} \right\rangle$ D. $\left\langle -\frac{4}{\sqrt{17}}, \frac{1}{\sqrt{17}} \right\rangle$

3. What is $\displaystyle\lim_{x \to 0^+} x^x$?

   A. 0   B. $\dfrac{1}{e}$ C. 1   D. e

4. The graph of the parametric equations $x = 3 \sin t$ and $y = 4 \cos t$ is a(n)

   A. Parabola   B. Circle   C. Ellipse   D. Hyperbola

5. Which of the following is equivalent to $\displaystyle\int_0^1 \sin^3 \frac{\pi}{2} x \cos \frac{\pi}{2} x \; dx$?

   A. $\dfrac{\pi}{2} \displaystyle\int_0^1 \sin^3 u \; du$ B. $\dfrac{2}{\pi} \displaystyle\int_0^{\pi/2} \sin^3 u \; du$ C. $\dfrac{2}{\pi} \displaystyle\int_0^1 u^3 \; du$ D. $\dfrac{2}{\pi} \displaystyle\int_0^{\pi/2} u^3 \; du$

6. Find $\dfrac{dy}{dx}$ given $x = 5 \sin t$ and $y = 7 \cos t$.

7. Write the polar form of the rectangular equation $x^2 + y^2 - 2x + 4y = 0$.

8. Evaluate: $\displaystyle\lim_{x \to 0^+} \left(\frac{1}{x^2} - \frac{1}{\sin x} \right)$

9. Use the equation of the line tangent to $2xy - 4x^2 + y^2 = 20$ at the point $(1, 4)$ to approximate the value of y in $2xy - 4x^2 + y^2 = 20$ when $x = 1.1$.

10. Let R be the region beneath the curve $y = \frac{1}{x^2 - 1}$ on the interval $[2, 4]$. Determine the volume of the solid formed when R is revolved around the y-axis.

11. (a) Find the generator of the sequence whose first few terms are $\dfrac{3}{2}, \dfrac{9}{10}, \dfrac{27}{50},$ and $\dfrac{81}{250}$.

    (b) Determine whether this sequence converges or diverges. If it converges, state its limit.

12. Find the arc length of the function $f(x) = \dfrac{1}{2} x^2$ on the interval from $x = 0$ to $x = 1$.

    Note: $\displaystyle\int \sec^3 x \; dx = \frac{\sec x \tan x}{2} + \frac{1}{2} \ln |\sec x + \tan x| + C$

Calculus, Second Edition

1. The length of the curve $y = \ln(\csc x)$ from $x = 0$ to $x = 1$ may be expressed by the integral

   A. $\displaystyle\int_0^1 \csc x \, dx$

   B. $\displaystyle\int_0^1 \csc x \cot x \, dx$

   C. $\displaystyle\int_0^1 \sqrt{1 + [\ln(\csc x)]^2} \, dx$

   D. $\displaystyle\int_0^1 \sqrt{1 + (\csc^2 x \cot^2 x)} \, dx$

2. A unit vector normal to the line tangent to $y = x^2 - 4x + 4$ at the point (4, 4) is

   A. $\langle 1, 4 \rangle$ B. $\langle 4, -1 \rangle$ C. $\left\langle \frac{1}{\sqrt{17}}, \frac{4}{\sqrt{17}} \right\rangle$ D. $\left\langle -\frac{4}{\sqrt{17}}, \frac{1}{\sqrt{17}} \right\rangle$

3. What is $\displaystyle\lim_{x \to 0^+} x^{2x}$?

   A. 0   B. $\dfrac{1}{e}$ C. 1   D. e

4. The graph of the parametric equations $x = 3 \sin t$ and $y = 3 \cos t$ is a(n)

   A. Parabola   B. Circle   C. Ellipse   D. Hyperbola

5. Which of the following is equivalent to $\displaystyle\int_0^1 \cos^3 \frac{\pi}{2}x \sin \frac{\pi}{2}x \, dx$?

   A. $-\dfrac{\pi}{2} \displaystyle\int_0^1 \sin^3 u \, du$ B. $\dfrac{2}{\pi} \displaystyle\int_0^{\pi/2} \sin^3 u \, du$ C. $-\dfrac{2}{\pi} \displaystyle\int_1^0 u^3 \, du$ D. $\dfrac{2}{\pi} \displaystyle\int_{\pi/2}^{\theta} u^3 \, du$

6. Approximate $\dfrac{dy}{dx}$ at $t = \dfrac{\pi}{6}$ given $x = 5 \sin t$ and $y = 7 \cos t$.

7. Write the polar form of the rectangular equation $x^2 + y^2 + 3x - 5y = 0$.

8. Evaluate: $\displaystyle\lim_{x \to 0^+} \left(\frac{1}{x} - \frac{1}{2 \sin x} \right)$

9. Use the equation of the line tangent to $2xy - 4x^2 + y^2 = 20$ at the point (1, 4) to approximate the value of y in $2xy - 4x^2 + y^2 = 20$ when $x = 0.9$.

10. Let R be the region beneath the curve $y = \frac{1}{x^2 + 1}$ on the interval [2, 4]. Determine the volume of the solid formed when R is revolved around the y-axis.

11. (a) Find the generator of the sequence whose first few terms are $\dfrac{9}{10}, \dfrac{27}{50}, \dfrac{81}{250}$, and $\dfrac{243}{1250}$.

    (b) Determine whether this sequence converges or diverges. If it converges, state its limit.

12. Approximate the arc length of the function $f(x) = \dfrac{1}{2}x^3$ on the interval from $x = 0$ to $x = 1$.

Calculus, Second Edition

1. The third partial sum of $\displaystyle\sum_{n=1}^{\infty} \frac{3}{2^n}$ is

    A. $\dfrac{3}{8}$ B. $\dfrac{3}{2}$ C. $\dfrac{15}{8}$ D. $\dfrac{21}{8}$

2. Which of the following statements is/are true about the graph of the polar equation $r = 4\cos\theta$?

    I. It is a circle with radius 4.

    II. It is a circle with center at the point (2, 0) in the Cartesian plane.

    III. It is tangent to the x-axis.

    A. I only   B. II only   C. II and III only   D. I and III only

3. Evaluate: $\displaystyle\int_{-1}^{1} \frac{dx}{x^2 + 5x + 6}$

    A. $\ln\dfrac{3}{2}$ B. $\ln\dfrac{1}{4}$ C. $\ln 6$ D. $\dfrac{9}{4}$

4. To which of the following differential equations could the given slope field correspond?

    A. $\dfrac{dy}{dx} = y^2$ B. $\dfrac{dy}{dx} = x^2 y^2$

    C. $\dfrac{dy}{dx} = x + y$ D. $\dfrac{dy}{dx} = x^2 + y$

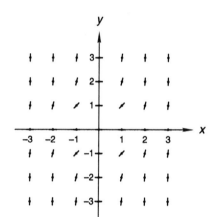

5. Suppose f is a function defined for all real values of x such that $|f(x)| = -f(x)$. Which of the following statements must be true?

    A. f is an odd function.

    B. f is an even function.

    C. $f(x) \le 0$ for all values of x.

    D. f is continuous for all real values of x.

6. Evaluate: $\displaystyle\int_0^1 (4 - x^2)^{-3/2}\, dx$

7. A swimming pool has the shape of an ellipse with the equation $\frac{x^2}{16} + \frac{y^2}{64} = 1$. Every vertical cross section of the pool perpendicular to the ground and parallel to the x-axis is a square. Find the volume of the pool.

8. Evaluate: $\displaystyle\lim_{x \to 0^+} (e^x - 1)^x$

9. Let $x = t - t^2$ and $y = \sqrt{2t + 5}$. Evaluate $\dfrac{dy}{dx}$ at $t = 2$.

10. Determine whether the sequence $a_n = \left(\dfrac{n + 3}{n}\right)^n$ converges or diverges. If it converges, state its limit.

11. A particle moves along the x-axis so that its velocity at time t $(0 < t < 4)$ is given by $v(t) = \dfrac{1}{\sqrt{16 - t^2}}$.

    (a) At what time t is the particle at rest?

    (b) Determine the acceleration of the particle at time $t = 1$.

12. A curve is given parametrically by the equations $x = 3t - t^3$ and $y = 3t^2$. Find the length of the curve from $t = 0$ to $t = 2$.

Calculus, Second Edition

1. The fourth partial sum of $\displaystyle\sum_{n=1}^{\infty} \frac{3}{2^n}$ is

    A. $\dfrac{3}{16}$ B. $\dfrac{3}{8}$ C. $\dfrac{45}{16}$ D. $\dfrac{21}{16}$

2. Which of the following statements is/are true about the graph of the polar equation $r = 4 \sin \theta$?
    I. It is a circle with radius 4.
    II. It is a circle with center at the point (0, 2) in the Cartesian plane.
    III. It is tangent to the x-axis.
    A. I only   B. II only   C. II and III only   D. I and III only

3. Integrate: $\displaystyle\int \frac{dx}{x^2 + 5x + 6}$

    A. $\ln \dfrac{|x + 2|}{|x + 3|} + C$ B. $\ln (x^2 + 5x + 6) + C$

    C. $\ln |(x + 3)(x + 2)| + C$ D. $\dfrac{x + 3}{x + 2} + C$

4. Suppose f is a function defined for all real values of x such that $|f(x)| = f(x)$. Which of the following statements must be true?
    A. f is an odd function.   B. $f(x) \geq 0$ for all values of x.
    C. f is an even function.   D. f is continuous for all real values of x.

5. To which of the following differential equations could the given slope field correspond?

    A. $\dfrac{dy}{dx} = x^2$ B. $\dfrac{dy}{dx} = \sqrt{x + y}$

    C. $\dfrac{dy}{dx} = x + y^2$ D. $\dfrac{dy}{dx} = x^2 y^2$

6. Integrate: $\displaystyle\int (4 - x^2)^{-3/2}\, dx$

7. A swimming pool has the shape of an ellipse with the equation $\frac{x^2}{64} + \frac{y^2}{16} = 1$. Every vertical cross section of the pool perpendicular to the ground and parallel to the y-axis is a square. Find the volume of the pool.

8. Evaluate: $\displaystyle\lim_{x \to 0^+} (e^x - 1)^{2x}$

9. Let $x = t - t^2$ and $y = \sqrt{2t + 5}$. Approximate $\dfrac{dy}{dx}$ at $t = 8$.

10. Determine whether the sequence $a_n = \left(\dfrac{n + 2}{n}\right)^n$ converges or diverges. If it converges, state its limit.

11. A particle moves along the x-axis so that its velocity at time t $(0 < t < 4)$ is given by $v(t) = \dfrac{1}{\sqrt{16 - t^2}}$.
    (a) At what time t is the particle at rest?
    (b) Approximate the acceleration of the particle at time $t = 1$.

12. A curve is given parametrically by the equations $x = 3t - t^3$ and $y = 3t^2$. Find the length of the curve from $t = 0$ to $t = 5$.

1. The graph of $r = 2 - 2\sin\theta$ is a
   A. Circle
   B. Rose curve
   C. Cardioid
   D. Dimpled limaçon

2. Integrate: $\int \log_5 (2x)\, dx$

   A. $\dfrac{1}{2x \ln 5} + C$
   B. $\dfrac{1}{4x \ln 5} + C$
   C. $\dfrac{1}{4x} + C$
   D. None of these

3. Which of the following series converge(s)?

   I. $\displaystyle\sum_{n=1}^{\infty} \dfrac{3}{3^n}$
   II. $\displaystyle\sum_{n=1}^{\infty} \dfrac{4^n}{3^n}$
   III. $\displaystyle\sum_{n=1}^{\infty} \dfrac{1}{2^{n+1}}$

   A. I only
   B. III only
   C. I and III only
   D. I, II, and III

4. If $x = 2t^2$ and $y = t^3$, then $\dfrac{d^2 y}{dx^2}$ equals what at $t = 3$?

   A. $\dfrac{1}{16}$
   B. $\dfrac{9}{2}$
   C. $\dfrac{3}{4}$
   D. $\dfrac{9}{4}$

5. Evaluate: $\displaystyle\sum_{n=1}^{\infty} \dfrac{3^{n+1}}{4^n}$

6. Integrate: $\displaystyle\int \dfrac{1}{x^2 (x+1)}\, dx$

7. Use differentials to approximate the cube root of 65. Remember $(64)^{1/3} = 4$.

8. Find the equation of the line tangent to the curve defined by $x = t^2 + t$ and $y = 2t + 3$ when $t = 1$.

9. Find a unit vector normal to $y = 3x^2 - 4x + 12$ at $x = 1$.

10. Simplify: $\dfrac{d}{dx} \displaystyle\int_1^x \cos (t^3)\, dt$

11. A ball is dropped from a height of 12 feet. Each time it hits the floor, it rebounds to a height of $\frac{4}{7}$ of its previous height. Find the total distance the ball will travel.

12. Find the length of $y = \dfrac{1}{3}(x^2 + 2)^{3/2}$ from $x = 0$ to $x = 1$.

1. The graph of $r = 2 + 2 \sin \theta$ is a

    A. Circle   B. Rose curve   C. Cardioid   D. Dimpled limaçon

2. Integrate: $\int \log_7 (2x)\, dx$

    A. $\dfrac{1}{2x \ln 7} + C$ B. $\dfrac{1}{4x \ln 7} + C$ C. $\dfrac{1}{4x} + C$ D. None of these

3. Which of the following series converge(s)?

    I. $\displaystyle\sum_{n=1}^{\infty} \dfrac{3}{3^n}$ II. $\displaystyle\sum_{n=1}^{\infty} \dfrac{\pi^n}{3^n}$ III. $\displaystyle\sum_{n=1}^{\infty} \dfrac{1}{2^{n+1}}$

    A. I only   B. III only   C. I and III only   D. I, II, and III

4. If $x = 2t^2$ and $y = t^3$, then $\dfrac{d^2 y}{dx^2}$ equals what at $t = 1$?

    A. $\dfrac{3}{16}$ B. $\dfrac{9}{2}$ C. $\dfrac{3}{4}$ D. $\dfrac{9}{4}$

5. Evaluate: $\displaystyle\sum_{n=2}^{\infty} \dfrac{3^{n+1}}{4^n}$

6. Integrate: $\displaystyle\int \dfrac{2}{x^2(x + 1)}\, dx$

7. Use differentials to approximate the cube root of 66. Remember $(64)^{1/3} = 4$.

8. Find the equation of the line tangent to the curve defined by $x = t^2 + t$ and $y = 2t + 3$ when $t = 4$.

9. Find a unit vector normal to $y = 8x^2 - 14x + 13$ at $x = 1$.

10. Simplify: $\dfrac{d}{dx} \displaystyle\int_1^x \ln (t^3)\, dt$

11. A ball is dropped from a height of 10 feet. Each time it hits the floor, it rebounds to a height of $\frac{4}{7}$ of its previous height. Find the total distance the ball will travel.

12. Approximate the length of $y = \dfrac{1}{3}(x^2 + 2)^{3/2}$ from $x = 0$ to $x = 4$.

Calculus, Second Edition

1. Which of the following series converge(s)?

   A. $\displaystyle\sum_{n=1}^{\infty} \left(\frac{2}{3}\right)^n$ B. $\displaystyle\sum_{n=1}^{\infty} \frac{2n}{3}$ C. $\displaystyle\sum_{n=1}^{\infty} \frac{1+n}{n}$ D. All of these.

2. Suppose k is a positive real number such that $\displaystyle\int_{1}^{k} \frac{\sin x}{x}\, dx = 1$. Then the value of $\displaystyle\int_{-k}^{-1} \frac{\sin x}{x}\, dx$ is

   A. 1   B. 0   C. −1   D. Indeterminate

3. Which of the following is true for the parametric curve determined by $x = t^3$ and $y = te^t$ at the point where $t = 2$?

   A. The tangent line is horizontal.   B. The first derivative $\dfrac{dy}{dx}$ is positive.

   C. The tangent line is vertical.   D. None of these is true.

4. Let $x^2 + y^2 = 25$. Evaluate $\dfrac{d^2 y}{dx^2}$ at the point $(0, 5)$.

5. Integrate: $\displaystyle\int \frac{1}{x(x+3)}\, dx$

6. Evaluate: $\displaystyle\sum_{n=3}^{\infty} \frac{1}{n(n+2)}$

7. Find the derivative of the vector function $\vec{f}(t) = \ln(t)\,\hat{i} - \sqrt{t+2}\,\hat{j}$.

8. Write the equation of the ellipse $x^2 + 4y^2 = 9$ in polar form.

9. Find the area of the region in the first quadrant bounded by $y = \sqrt{4 - x^2}$ and the coordinate axes.

10. Use a three-term Maclaurin series for $\sin x$ to approximate $\sin 0.5$.

11. Determine whether the series $\displaystyle\sum_{n=2}^{\infty} \frac{n}{n+1}$ converges or diverges. Explain your answer.

12. Integrate: $\displaystyle\int x^2 \cos x\, dx$

1. Which of the following series converges?

   A. $\displaystyle\sum_{n=1}^{\infty}\left(\frac{4}{3}\right)^n$

   B. $\displaystyle\sum_{n=1}^{\infty}\frac{2n}{3}$

   C. $\displaystyle\sum_{n=1}^{\infty}\frac{1+n}{n}$

   D. None of these.

2. Suppose k is a positive real number such that $\displaystyle\int_{1}^{k}\frac{\cos x}{x}\,dx = 0.1$. Then the value of $\displaystyle\int_{-k}^{-1}\frac{\cos x}{x}\,dx$ is

   A. 0.1   B. 0   C. −0.1   D. Indeterminate

3. Which of the following is true for the parametric curve $x = t^3$ and $y = te^t$ at the point where $t = 1$?

   A. The tangent line is horizontal.

   B. The first derivative $\dfrac{dy}{dx}$ is positive.

   C. The tangent line is vertical.

   D. None of these is true.

4. Let $x^2 - y^2 + 25 = 0$. Evaluate $\dfrac{d^2y}{dx^2}$ at the point $(0, 5)$.

5. Integrate: $\displaystyle\int \frac{4}{x(x-3)}\,dx$

6. Evaluate: $\displaystyle\sum_{n=2}^{\infty}\frac{1}{n(n+2)}$

7. Find the derivative of the vector function $\vec{f}(t) = (\cos t)\hat{i} - \sqrt{t+2}\,\hat{j}$.

8. Write the equation of the ellipse $4x^2 + y^2 = 9$ in polar form.

9. Find the area of the region in the first and second quadrants bounded by $y = \sqrt{4 - x^2}$ and the x-axis.

10. Use the first four terms of the Maclaurin series for $\sin x$ to estimate $\sin 0.5$.

11. Determine whether the series $\displaystyle\sum_{n=2}^{\infty}\frac{3n}{4n+1}$ converges or diverges. Explain your answer.

12. Integrate: $\displaystyle\int x^2 \sin x\,dx$

1. Which of the following series diverges?

    A. $\displaystyle\sum_{n=1}^{\infty} \frac{2n}{n^2}$ B. $\displaystyle\sum_{n=1}^{\infty} \frac{1}{n^2+1}$ C. $\displaystyle\sum_{n=1}^{\infty} \frac{3n}{n^3}$ D. None of these.

2. What is $\displaystyle\lim_{x\to\infty} \frac{x^2 + x \ln x}{1 + x^2}$?

    A. 0   B. 1

    C. ∞ D. The limit does not exist.

3. The graph of $r = 3 + 4\cos\theta$ is a

    A. Circle   B. Lemniscate   C. Limaçon   D. Cardioid

4. The trigonometric substitution that should be employed for the integral $\displaystyle\int \frac{4}{\sqrt{9 - x^2}}\, dx$ is

    A. $x = 3\sin\theta$ B. $x = 3\sec\theta$ C. $x = 2\sec\theta$ D. $x = 2\tan\theta$

5. Let $f(x) = x^x$. Find $f'(2)$.

6. Use the integral test to determine whether the series $\displaystyle\sum_{n=2}^{\infty} \frac{1}{n \ln n}$ converges or diverges.

7. Integrate: $\displaystyle\int \frac{x+1}{(x^2+1)(x-1)}\, dx$

8. Determine whether the series $\displaystyle\sum_{n=1}^{\infty} \frac{18}{\sqrt[6]{n^{13}}}$ converges or diverges.

9. Determine the concavity of the parametric curve determined by $y = 5t - 4$ and $x = 2t^2 + 5$ at the point where $t = 1$.

10. The slope of the line tangent to the graph of a particular equation at any point (x, y) is $\frac{y}{x}$. Find the equation of the curve given that its graph passes through the point $(1, 4)$.

11. Let R be the region between $y = \dfrac{1}{x^2}$ and the x-axis on the interval $[5, \infty)$.

    (a) Determine whether the area of R is finite. If so, find the area of R.

    (b) Find the volume of the solid formed when R is revolved around the y-axis.

12. A particle is moving on the x-axis with velocity $v(t) = t^2 - 7t + 6$. Find the average velocity of the particle on the interval of time $[0, 7]$.

Calculus, Second Edition

1. Which of the following series converge(s)?

   A. $\displaystyle\sum_{n=1}^{\infty} \frac{1}{n^2 + 1}$ B. $\displaystyle\sum_{n=1}^{\infty} \frac{2}{n^2}$ C. $\displaystyle\sum_{n=1}^{\infty} \frac{3n}{n^4}$ D. All of these.

2. What is $\displaystyle\lim_{x\to\infty} \frac{x^2 + x^2 \ln x}{1 + x^2}$?

   A. 0   B. 1

   C. ∞ D. The limit does not exist.

3. Which of the following is the graph of $r = 3 + 4\cos\theta$?

   A.   B.   C.   D.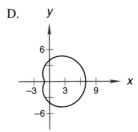

4. The trigonometric substitution that should be employed for the integral $\displaystyle\int \frac{4}{\sqrt{x^2 - 9}}\, dx$ is

   A. $x = 3\sin\theta$ B. $x = 3\sec\theta$ C. $x = 2\sin\theta$ D. $x = 2\tan\theta$

5. Let $f(x) = x^x$. Find $f'(3)$.

6. Use the integral test to determine whether the series $\displaystyle\sum_{n=2}^{\infty} \frac{\ln n}{n}$ converges or diverges.

7. Integrate: $\displaystyle\int \frac{2x + 2}{(x^2 + 1)(x - 1)}\, dx$

8. Determine whether the series $\displaystyle\sum_{n=1}^{\infty} \frac{18}{\sqrt[6]{n^5}}$ converges or diverges.

9. Determine the concavity of the parametric curve determined by $x = 5t - 4$ and $y = 2t^2 + 5$ at the point where $t = 1$.

10. The slope of the line tangent to the graph of a particular equation at any point (x, y) is $\frac{y}{x}$. Find the equation of the curve given that the graph passes through the point $(1, 6)$.

11. Let R be the region between $y = \dfrac{1}{x^3}$ and the x-axis on the interval $[5, \infty)$.

    (a) Determine whether the area of R is finite. If so, find the area of R.

    (b) Find the volume of the solid formed when R is revolved around the y-axis.

12. A particle is moving on the x-axis with velocity $v(t) = t^2 - 7t + 6$. Find the average velocity of the particle on the interval of time $[0, 10]$.

Calculus, Second Edition

1. The area of one loop of the graph of the polar equation $r = 2 \sin(3\theta)$ can be represented as

   A. $4 \int_0^{\pi/3} \sin^2(3\theta) \, d\theta$ B. $2 \int_0^{\pi/3} \sin(3\theta) \, d\theta$ C. $2 \int_0^{\pi/3} \sin^2(3\theta) \, d\theta$ D. $2 \int_0^{2\pi/3} \sin^2(3\theta) \, d\theta$

2. Which of the following series diverges?

   A. $\sum_{n=1}^{\infty} \dfrac{n}{n^n}$ B. $\sum_{n=1}^{\infty} \dfrac{n^2}{n!}$ C. $\sum_{n=1}^{\infty} \dfrac{2^n}{n^2}$ D. None of these.

3. Integrate: $\displaystyle\int_{-\infty}^{\infty} e^{-|x|} \, dx$

4. Integrate: $\displaystyle\int_{-e}^{e} \dfrac{1}{x} \, dx$

5. Find the length of the parametric curve $x = \dfrac{1}{2}(t-1)^2$, $y = \dfrac{4}{3} t^{3/2}$ from $t = 0$ to $t = 1$.

6. Integrate: $\displaystyle\int \dfrac{x^2 + x + 1}{x^2 + 1} \, dx$

7. Evaluate: $\displaystyle\lim_{x \to 1} [x + \sin(\pi x)]^{\csc(x-1)}$

8. Find $\dfrac{dy}{dx}$ at the point $(1, 0)$ given that $x = \cos y - y$.

9. Find the third partial sum of $\displaystyle\sum_{n=1}^{\infty} \dfrac{5 + 2n}{n^2}$.

10. Find the derivative of the vector function $\vec{f}(t) = \arctan(e^{2t})\,\hat{i} + e^{-(t+2)}\hat{j}$.

11. (a) Use the ratio test to determine whether the series $\displaystyle\sum_{n=1}^{\infty} \dfrac{n+1}{n+4}$ converges or diverges.

    (b) Use another method to determine whether the series $\displaystyle\sum_{n=1}^{\infty} \dfrac{n+1}{n+4}$ converges or diverges.

12. Find the area of the region bounded by the graph of $r = 4 \cos(3\theta)$.

Calculus, Second Edition

1. The area of one loop of the graph of the polar equation $r = 2 \cos (3\theta)$ can be represented as

   A. $4 \int_0^{\pi/3} \cos^2 (3\theta) \, d\theta$ B. $\int_0^{\pi/3} \cos (3\theta) \, d\theta$ C. $2 \int_{\pi/6}^{\pi/2} \cos^2 (3\theta) \, d\theta$ D. $2 \int_{\pi/2}^{2\pi/3} \cos^2 (3\theta) \, d\theta$

2. Which of the following series diverges?

   A. $\sum_{n=1}^{\infty} \dfrac{n^3}{n^n}$ B. $\sum_{n=1}^{\infty} \dfrac{2^n}{n^2}$ C. $\sum_{n=1}^{\infty} \dfrac{n^2}{n!}$ D. None of these.

3. Integrate: $\displaystyle\int_{-\infty}^{\infty} e^{-|2x|} \, dx$

4. Integrate: $\displaystyle\int_{-\pi}^{\pi} \dfrac{1}{x} \, dx$

5. Find the length of the parametric curve $x = \dfrac{1}{2}(t-1)^2$, $y = \dfrac{4}{3}t^{3/2}$ from $t = 0$ to $t = 4$.

6. Integrate: $\displaystyle\int \dfrac{4x^2 + x + 1}{1 + 4x^2} \, dx$

7. Evaluate: $\displaystyle\lim_{x \to 0} \left[x + \cos (\pi x) \right]^{\sec (x - \pi/2)}$

8. Find $\dfrac{dy}{dx}$ at the point $(1, 0)$ given $y^2 = \cos x - y$.

9. Find the third partial sum of $\displaystyle\sum_{n=3}^{\infty} \dfrac{4 + n}{n^3}$.

10. Find the derivative of the vector function $\vec{f}(t) = \operatorname{arccot} (e^{2t}) \hat{i} + e^{-(t+2)} \hat{j}$.

11. (a) Use the ratio test to determine whether the series $\displaystyle\sum_{n=1}^{\infty} \dfrac{1}{n^2}$ converges or diverges.

    (b) Use another test to determine whether the series $\displaystyle\sum_{n=1}^{\infty} \dfrac{1}{n^2}$ converges or diverges.

12. Find the area of the region bounded by the graph of $r = 4 \sin (3\theta)$.

Calculus, Second Edition

1. Which of the following equations is a particular solution found in the given slope field?

   A. $x^2 + y = 1$ B. $\sqrt{xy} = 2$

   C. $y = e^{x+2}$ D. $\sqrt{x} + y = 2$

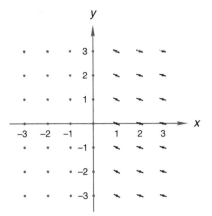

2. Let $F(x) = \int_0^x \sqrt{\tan t}\ dt$. Then $F'\left(\dfrac{\pi}{6}\right)$ equals

   A. $3^{-1/4}$ B. $\dfrac{1}{2}(3^{1/4})$

   C. $\dfrac{3}{8}(3^{1/4})$ D. $\dfrac{1}{2}(3^{1/4})$

3. Integrate: $\displaystyle\int_{-1}^{2} \dfrac{|x|}{x}\ dx$

   A. 3   B. 2
   C. 1   D. The integral does not exist.

4. The absolute maximum value of the function $f(x) = x^2 e^{-x}$ on the interval $[0, 10]$ is

   A. $4e^{-2}$ B. 2   C. $100e^{-10}$ D. e^{-1}

5. Evaluate: $\displaystyle\sum_{n=2}^{\infty} \dfrac{4^n + 1}{7^n}$

   A. $\dfrac{11}{14}$ B. $\dfrac{16}{3}$ C. $\dfrac{16}{11}$ D. The sum is infinite.

6. Use Euler's method with one iteration to approximate the value of y when $x = 2.3$ given the differential equation $\dfrac{dy}{dx} = x^3$ and the initial condition $y = 1$ when $x = 2$.

7. Find the slope of the line that can be drawn tangent to the polar curve $r = 2\cos\theta$ at $\theta = \dfrac{\pi}{12}$.

8. Set up an integral that represents the area inside the graph of $r = 3 + 3\sin\theta$.

9. A particle moves along the x-axis so that its velocity is given by the equation $v(t) = \sin t + \cos t$. Find the maximum velocity of the particle.

10. Evaluate: $\displaystyle\int_0^1 \dfrac{x + 2}{4 + x^2}\ dx$

11. Determine whether each of the following series converges or diverges.

    (a) $\displaystyle\sum_{n=1}^{\infty} \dfrac{4n}{n^2 + 1}$ (b) $\displaystyle\sum_{n=1}^{\infty} \dfrac{1}{2n}$ (c) $\displaystyle\sum_{n=1}^{\infty} \left(\dfrac{4n}{n^2 + 1}\right)\left(\dfrac{1}{2n}\right)$

12. Does the series $\displaystyle\sum_{n=1}^{\infty} \dfrac{\sin n}{n^3}$ converge or diverge?

Calculus, Second Edition

1. Which of the following equations is a particular solution found in the given slope field?

   A. $x^2 + y^2 = 9$ B. $y = \ln |x| + 1$

   C. $y = \sqrt{x} + 2$ D. $y = e^{x+1} + 1$

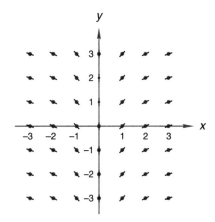

2. Let $F(x) = \int_0^x \sqrt{\tan t}\ dt$. Then $F'\left(\dfrac{\pi}{4}\right)$ equals

   A. 0   B. 1

   C. 0.7071   D. 0.8660

3. Integrate: $\displaystyle\int_{-2}^{2} \dfrac{|x|}{x}\ dx$

   A. 3   B. 2

   C. 1   D. The integral does not exist.

4. The absolute maximum value of the function $f(x) = x^2 e^{-x}$ on the interval $[-10, 10]$ is

   A. 0.005   B. 0.368   C. 0.541   D. 2

5. Evaluate: $\displaystyle\sum_{n=2}^{\infty} \dfrac{4^n + 1}{3^n}$

   A. $\dfrac{64}{21}$ B. $\dfrac{16}{3}$ C. $\dfrac{16}{11}$ D. The sum is infinite.

6. Use Euler's method with three iterations to approximate the value of y when $x = 2.3$ given the differential equation $\dfrac{dy}{dx} = x^3$ and the initial condition $y = 1$ when $x = 2$.

7. Determine the slope of the line that can be drawn tangent to the polar curve $r = 2 \sin \theta$ at $\theta = \dfrac{\pi}{3}$.

8. Set up an integral that represents the area inside the graph of $r = 3 + 3 \cos \theta$.

9. A particle moves along the x-axis so that its velocity is given by the equation $v(t) = 5 \sin t + 3 \cos t$. Find the maximum velocity of the particle.

10. Evaluate: $\displaystyle\int_0^1 \dfrac{x + 2}{4 + x^2}\ dx$

11. Determine whether each of the following series converges or diverges.

    (a) $\displaystyle\sum_{n=1}^{\infty} \dfrac{4n^3}{n^4 + 1}$ (b) $\displaystyle\sum_{n=1}^{\infty} \dfrac{1}{2n}$ (c) $\displaystyle\sum_{n=1}^{\infty} \left(\dfrac{9n^2}{n^2 + 4}\right)\left(\dfrac{8}{3n^2}\right)$

12. Does the series $\displaystyle\sum_{n=1}^{\infty} \dfrac{\cos n}{n^3}$ converge or diverge?

      Calculus, Second Edition

Test 35, Form A   **SHOW YOUR WORK**   Name: _____

1. Let $f(x) = \int_{2}^{x^3} \sin(t^4)\, dt$. Then $f'(x)$ equals

   A. $\sin(x^4)$ B. $4\cos(x^3)$ C. $3x^2 \sin(x^{12})$ D. $12x^5 \cos(x^{12})$

2. Let $f(x) = \begin{cases} x & \text{when } x \leq 0 \\ x^3 & \text{when } x > 0. \end{cases}$ Then $\int_{-1}^{1} f(x)\, dx$ equals

   A. $-\dfrac{1}{4}$ B. $\dfrac{1}{4}$ C. $\dfrac{3}{4}$ D. -1

3. In an epsilon-delta proof of $\lim_{x \to 5} 2x - 1 = 9$, which of the following choices of δ is the largest that could be used successfully with any arbitrary value of ε?

   A. $\delta = 2\varepsilon$ B. $\delta = \varepsilon$ C. $\delta = \dfrac{\varepsilon}{2}$ D. $\delta = \dfrac{\varepsilon}{3}$

4. Let $f(x) = x^3 + 5x + 4$ and let h be the inverse function of f. Find $h'(10)$.

5. The graph of a curve is defined by the parametric equations $x = t^3 - 2$ and $y = t^2 - 4$. Determine the slope of the line tangent to the curve at the point where $t = 5$.

6. A cannon has a muzzle velocity of 1000 feet per second. Determine the angle at which the barrel of the cannon should be placed in order for the ball to strike a target 8000 feet downrange.

7. Integrate: $\displaystyle\int \dfrac{x^2}{x^2 + 4}\, dx$

8. Set up the integral needed to find the length of $y = x^3$ from $x = 1$ to $x = 2$.

9. Graph the polar equation $r = 3 - 3\sin\theta$ and identify the resulting figure.

10. Find the values of a and b such that the function $f(x) = \begin{cases} ax^3 + b & \text{when } x \leq 1 \\ \sin(\pi x) & \text{when } x > 1 \end{cases}$ is everywhere differentiable.

11. Use a two-term Maclaurin polynomial for $\cos x$ to approximate $\cos 0.3$.

12. Determine whether the series $\displaystyle\sum_{n=1}^{\infty} (-1)^{n+1} \dfrac{n}{n^2 + 1}$ converges absolutely, converges conditionally, or diverges.

Calculus, Second Edition

Test 35, Form B   **SHOW YOUR WORK**   Name: _____

1. In an epsilon-delta proof of $\lim_{x \to 5} x - 1 = 4$, which of the following choices of δ is the largest that could be used successfully with any arbitrary value of ε?

   A. $\delta = 2\varepsilon$ B. $\delta = \varepsilon$ C. $\delta = \dfrac{\varepsilon}{2}$ D. $\delta = \dfrac{\varepsilon}{3}$

2. Let $f(x) = \displaystyle\int_{2}^{x^4} \cos(t^4)\, dt$. Then $f'(x)$ equals

   A. $\sin(x^4)$ B. $4 \cos(x^3)$ C. $3x^2 \sin(x^{12})$ D. $4x^3 \cos(x^{16})$

3. Let $f(x) = x^3 + 5x + 4$ and let h be the inverse function of f. Find $h'(4)$.

4. Let $f(x) = \begin{cases} x^2 & \text{when } x \le 0 \\ x^3 & \text{when } x > 0. \end{cases}$ Find the value of $\displaystyle\int_{-1}^{1} f(x)\, dx$.

5. The graph of a curve is defined by the parametric equations $x = t^3 - 2$ and $y = t^2 - 4$. Determine the slope of the line tangent to the curve at the point where $t = 3$.

6. A cannon has a muzzle velocity of 1000 feet per second. Determine the angle at which the barrel of the cannon should be placed in order for the ball to strike a target 7000 feet downrange.

7. Integrate: $\displaystyle\int \frac{x^2}{x^2 + 9}\, dx$

8. Approximate the length of $y = x^3$ from $x = 1$ to $x = 2$.

9. Graph the polar equation $r = 3 - 3 \cos \theta$ and identify the resulting figure.

10. Find the values of a and b such that the function $f(x) = \begin{cases} ax^3 + b & \text{when } x \le 1 \\ \cos\left(\dfrac{\pi}{2}x\right) & \text{when } x > 1 \end{cases}$ is everywhere differentiable.

11. Use a four-term Maclaurin polynomial for $\cos x$ to approximate $\cos 0.3$.

12. Determine whether the series $\displaystyle\sum_{n=1}^{\infty} (-1)^n \frac{n}{n^2 + 1}$ converges absolutely, converges conditionally, or diverges.

Calculus, Second Edition

1. The Maclaurin series for e^x is

    A. $1 + x + \dfrac{x^2}{2} + \dfrac{x^3}{3} + \cdots$ B. $1 + x + \dfrac{x^2}{2!} + \dfrac{x^3}{3!} + \cdots$

    C. $1 - x + \dfrac{x^2}{2!} - \dfrac{x^3}{3!} + \cdots$ D. $1 + \dfrac{x^2}{2!} + \dfrac{x^4}{4!} + \cdots$

2. Which of the following series diverge(s)?

    I. $\displaystyle\sum_{n=1}^{\infty} \dfrac{(-1)^n}{3n + 2}$ II. $\displaystyle\sum_{n=1}^{\infty} \dfrac{(-1)^n n}{3n^2 + 2}$ III. $\displaystyle\sum_{n=1}^{\infty} \dfrac{(-1)^n n^2}{3n^2 + 2}$

    A. I only   B. III only   C. I and II only   D. II and III only

3. For which of the following functions is $\displaystyle\sum_{n=0}^{\infty} \dfrac{(-1)^n x^n}{n!}$ the Taylor series?

    A. $\sin x$ B. e^x C. e^{-x} D. $\ln(1 + x)$

4. Evaluate: $\displaystyle\sum_{n=1}^{\infty} \dfrac{2^n - 4^n}{3^n}$

    A. 2   B. 5   C. 6   D. The sum diverges.

5. Let $xy + y = 6x$. What is $\dfrac{dy}{dx}$ when $x = 2$ and $y = 4$?

6. Use Euler's method with two iterations to approximate the value of y when $x = 1.4$ given $y = 2$ when $x = 1$ and the differential equation $\frac{dy}{dx} = x - 4y$.

7. A cannon has a muzzle velocity of 500 feet per second. If a cannonball is to strike a target 20,000 feet downrange, at what angle from horizontal should the barrel of the cannon be placed?

8. Let R be the region between $y = \sec x$ and the x-axis from $x = 0$ to $x = \frac{\pi}{4}$. Find the volume of the solid formed when R is revolved about the x-axis.

9. Find a unit vector parallel to the tangent of $y = x^3 + x - 2$ at the point $(1, 0)$.

10. Find the area of the region that is inside $r = 2 + 2\cos\theta$ and outside $r = 3$.

11. Determine the third-degree Taylor polynomial for $f(x) = \cos x$ about $a = \dfrac{\pi}{6}$.

12. Let $\vec{p}(t) = 3\cos\left(\dfrac{t}{3}\right)\hat{i} + 2\sin\left(\dfrac{t}{3}\right)\hat{j}$ be the position function of a particle moving in the xy-plane.

    (a) Find the velocity of the particle when $t = \pi$.

    (b) Find the speed of the particle when $t = \pi$.

    (c) Find the acceleration of the particle when $t = \pi$.

         Calculus, Second Edition

1. The Maclaurin series for e^{-x} is

   A. $1 + x + \dfrac{x^2}{2} + \dfrac{x^3}{3} + \cdots$

   B. $1 + x + \dfrac{x^2}{2!} + \dfrac{x^3}{3!} + \cdots$

   C. $1 - x + \dfrac{x^2}{2!} - \dfrac{x^3}{3!} + \cdots$

   D. $1 + \dfrac{x^2}{2!} + \dfrac{x^4}{4!} + \cdots$

2. Which of the following series diverge(s)?

   I. $\displaystyle\sum_{n=1}^{\infty} \dfrac{(-1)^n n}{3n + 2}$

   II. $\displaystyle\sum_{n=1}^{\infty} \dfrac{(-1)^n n}{3n^2 + 2}$

   III. $\displaystyle\sum_{n=1}^{\infty} \dfrac{(-1)^n n^2}{3n^2 + 2}$

   A. I and III only   B. III only   C. I and II only   D. II and III only

3. For which of the following functions is $\displaystyle\sum_{n=0}^{\infty} \dfrac{(-1)^n x^{2n}}{(2n)!}$ the Taylor series?

   A. $\cos x$ B. e^x C. e^{-x} D. $\ln(1 + x)$

4. Evaluate: $\displaystyle\sum_{n=1}^{\infty} \dfrac{5^n - 2^n}{3^n}$

   A. 2   B. 5   C. 6   D. The sum diverges.

5. Let $xy + y = 6x$. What is $\dfrac{dy}{dx}$ when $x = 1$ and $y = 3$?

6. Use Euler's method with three iterations to approximate the value of y when $x = 1.6$ given $y = 2$ when $x = 1$ and the differential equation $\frac{dy}{dx} = x - 4y$.

7. A cannon has a muzzle velocity of 700 feet per second. If a cannonball is to strike a target 21,000 feet downrange, at what angle from horizontal should the barrel of the cannon be placed?

8. Let R be the region between $y = \csc x$ and the x-axis from $x = \frac{\pi}{4}$ to $x = \frac{\pi}{2}$. Find the volume of the solid formed when R is revolved about the x-axis.

9. Find a unit vector parallel to the tangent of $y = x^3 + x - 2$ at the point (2, 8).

10. Find the area of the region that is inside $r = 2 + 2\cos\theta$ and outside $r = 3$.

11. Determine the third-degree Taylor polynomial for $f(x) = \sin x$ about $a = \dfrac{\pi}{6}$.

12. Let $\vec{p}(t) = 3\sin\left(\dfrac{t}{3}\right)\hat{i} + 2\cos\left(\dfrac{t}{3}\right)\hat{j}$ be the position function of a particle moving in the xy-plane.

    (a) Find the velocity of the particle when $t = \pi$.
    (b) Find the speed of the particle when $t = \pi$.
    (c) Find the acceleration of the particle when $t = \pi$.

Calculus, Second Edition

Test 37, Form A   **SHOW YOUR WORK**   Name: _____

1. Which of the following is the Maclaurin series for $\cos x$?

   A. $1 + \dfrac{x^2}{2!} + \dfrac{x^4}{4!} + \dfrac{x^6}{6!} + \cdots$

   B. $1 - \dfrac{x^3}{3!} + \dfrac{x^5}{5!} + \dfrac{x^7}{7!} + \cdots$

   C. $1 - x + \dfrac{x^2}{2!} - \dfrac{x^3}{3!} + \cdots$

   D. $1 - \dfrac{x^2}{2!} + \dfrac{x^4}{4!} - \dfrac{x^6}{6!} + \cdots$

2. A series expansion of $\dfrac{\sin t}{t}$ is

   A. $1 - \dfrac{t^2}{3!} + \dfrac{t^4}{5!} - \dfrac{t^6}{7!} + \cdots$

   B. $1 + \dfrac{t^2}{3!} + \dfrac{t^4}{5!} + \dfrac{t^6}{7!} + \cdots$

   C. $\dfrac{1}{t} + \dfrac{t}{2!} + \dfrac{t^3}{4!} + \dfrac{t^5}{6!} + \cdots$

   D. $\dfrac{1}{t} - \dfrac{t}{2!} + \dfrac{t^3}{4!} - \dfrac{t^5}{6!} + \cdots$

3. A vector of magnitude 5 that has the same direction as the vector $2\hat{i} + 7\hat{j}$ is

   A. $\dfrac{10}{\sqrt{53}}\hat{i} + \dfrac{35}{\sqrt{53}}\hat{j}$

   B. $\dfrac{35}{\sqrt{53}}\hat{i} - \dfrac{10}{\sqrt{53}}\hat{j}$

   C. $\dfrac{2}{\sqrt{53}}\hat{i} + \dfrac{7}{\sqrt{53}}\hat{j}$

   D. $5\hat{i}$

4. What is $\lim\limits_{x \to 0} 6x \csc(7x)$?

   A. $\dfrac{7}{6}$

   B. $\dfrac{6}{7}$

   C. 6

   D. 7

5. Determine the area of the region bounded by the graphs of $y = x^5$ and $y = x^2$.

6. Find the interval of convergence for the series $\displaystyle\sum_{n=1}^{\infty} \dfrac{(x-1)^n}{n^2}$.

7. Determine whether the series $\displaystyle\sum_{n=1}^{\infty} \dfrac{3^n}{n^n}$ converges or diverges.

8. Determine the integral that represents the length of the parametric curve given by $x = 2t$ and $y = t^2$ on the interval from $t = 0$ to $t = 5$.

9. Set up the integral necessary to find the volume of the solid formed when the region bounded by $y = \sin x$, $x = 2$, and the x-axis is revolved around the line $x = 3$.

10. Integrate: $\displaystyle\int_0^2 \dfrac{1}{x^2 - 1}\, dx$

11. Use the first three terms of the Maclaurin series for e^x to approximate $\displaystyle\int_0^1 e^{t^3}\, dt$.

12. Given the Maclaurin series for $\frac{1}{1+x}$ is $1 - x + x^2 - x^3 + x^4 - \cdots$, determine the Maclaurin series for the following:

    (a) $\dfrac{1}{1 + x^3}$

    (b) $\ln(1 + x)$

Calculus, Second Edition

Test 37, Form B   **SHOW YOUR WORK**   Name: _____

1. Which of the following is the Maclaurin series for $\cos(-x)$?

   A. $1 + \dfrac{x^2}{2!} + \dfrac{x^4}{4!} + \dfrac{x^6}{6!} + \cdots$

   B. $1 - \dfrac{x^3}{3!} + \dfrac{x^5}{5!} - \dfrac{x^7}{7!} + \cdots$

   C. $1 - x + \dfrac{x^2}{2!} - \dfrac{x^3}{3!} + \cdots$

   D. $1 - \dfrac{x^2}{2!} + \dfrac{x^4}{4!} - \dfrac{x^6}{6!} + \cdots$

2. A series expansion of $\dfrac{\cos t}{t}$ is

   A. $1 - \dfrac{t^2}{3!} + \dfrac{t^4}{5!} - \dfrac{t^6}{7!} + \cdots$

   B. $1 + \dfrac{t^2}{3!} + \dfrac{t^4}{5!} + \dfrac{t^6}{7!} + \cdots$

   C. $\dfrac{1}{t} + \dfrac{t}{2!} + \dfrac{t^3}{4!} + \dfrac{t^5}{6!} + \cdots$

   D. $\dfrac{1}{t} - \dfrac{t}{2!} + \dfrac{t^3}{4!} - \dfrac{t^5}{6!} + \cdots$

3. A vector of magnitude 1 that has the same direction as the vector $2\hat{i} + 7\hat{j}$ is

   A. $\dfrac{1}{\sqrt{53}}\hat{i} + \dfrac{7}{\sqrt{53}}\hat{j}$
   B. $\dfrac{2}{\sqrt{53}}\hat{i} - \dfrac{7}{\sqrt{53}}\hat{j}$
   C. $\dfrac{2}{\sqrt{53}}\hat{i} + \dfrac{7}{\sqrt{53}}\hat{j}$
   D. $1\hat{i}$

4. What is $\lim\limits_{x \to 0} 9x \csc(8x)$?

   A. $\dfrac{8}{9}$
   B. $\dfrac{9}{8}$
   C. 8
   D. 9

5. Approximate the area of the region bounded by the graphs of $y = x^7$ and $y = x^2$.

6. Find the interval of convergence for the series $\sum\limits_{n=1}^{\infty} \dfrac{(x-1)^n}{n}$.

7. Determine whether the series $\sum\limits_{n=1}^{\infty} \dfrac{n^n}{3^n}$ converges or diverges.

8. Approximate the length of the parametric curve given by $x = 2t$ and $y = t^2$ on the interval from $t = 0$ to $t = 5$.

9. Approximate the volume of the solid formed when the region bounded by $y = \sin x$, $x = 2$, and the x-axis is revolved around the line $x = 3$.

10. Approximate the coordinates of the point of intersection of the functions $y = x^2 + 1$ and $y = -x^3$ accurate to five decimal places.

11. Use the first four terms of the Maclaurin series for e^x to approximate $\int_0^1 e^{t^3}\, dt$.

12. Given the Maclaurin series for $\frac{1}{1+x}$ is $1 - x + x^2 - x^3 + x^4 - \cdots$, determine the Maclaurin series for the following:

    (a) $\dfrac{1}{1+x^2}$

    (b) $\ln(1+x)$

Calculus, Second Edition

Show **all** work on this paper. Do not write on the test.

1.

2.

3.

4.

5.

6.

7.

8.

9.

10.

11.

12.